DATE DUE

DE 2 0 00			
JE 1 1 01			

DEMCO 38-296

KOREAN ELDERLY WOMEN IN AMERICA:

EVERYDAY LIFE, HEALTH, AND ILLNESS

IMMIGRANT COMMUNITIES & ETHNIC MINORITIES IN THE UNITED STATES & CANADA: No. 69

Series Editor: Robert J. Theodoratus
Department of Anthropology, Colorado State University

Continued at back of book

KOREAN ELDERLY WOMEN IN AMERICA:

EVERYDAY LIFE, HEALTH, AND ILLNESS

Keum Young Chung Pang

AMS Press, Inc.
New York

Library of Congress Cataloging-in-Publication Data

Pang, Keum-Young Chung.
  Korean Elderly Women in America, Everyday Life, Health and Illness / by
Keum-Young Chung Pang.
     — (Immigrant communities & ethnic minorities in the United States &
Canada ; no. 69)
  Includes bibliographical references.
  ISBN 0-404-19479-6
  1. Korean American women—Health and hygiene. 2. Women immi-
grants—Health and hygiene—United States. 3. Aged women—Health and
hygiene—United States. 4. Mind and body—Korea. 5. Health behavior—
Korea. 6. Social medicine—Korea. 7. Cultural psychiatry—Korea. I. Title.
II. Series: Immigrant communities & ethnic minorities in the United States
& Canada ; 69.
RA448.5.K65P36   1991
306.4′61′095190973—dc20
                                                                    89-48311
                                                                        CIP

All AMS books are printed on acid-free paper that meets the guidelines for performance and durability of the Committee on Production
Guidelines for Book Longevity of the Council on Library Resources.

AMS PRESS
56 East 13th Street
New York, N.Y. 10003, U.S.A.

MANUFACTURED IN THE UNITED STATES OF AMERICA

ACKNOWLEDGEMENTS

I am most grateful to the elderly Korean women who so generously shared their valuable life experiences with me. I thank the United States Public Health Service for including me in the 1980 National Research Service Award. This award enabled me to study medical anthropology at the Catholic University of America providing me with a precious academic opportunity of the greatest importance to my development as an anthropologist.

I should like to express my sincere gratitude to my major professor, Dr. Lucy M. Cohen for her thoughtfulness, courtesy, support, advice, and genuine concern for true scholarship during my studies at the university. She contributed generously of her invaluable time and resources throughout all phases of this research and during my entire course of study at the Catholic University of America tolerating my weaknesses while focusing on my strengths. I am indebted to my readers, Dr. Timothy R. Ready and Dr. Patricia S. Maloof, for their priceless suggestions. A special thanks to Mrs. Anna Buc for her painstaking care and generous help in editing and correcting the manuscript.

I am especially appreciative of the high measure of understanding, encouragement, and support given by my family; particularly my parents-in-law, my parents, and my husband. I am very thankful to my son for assisting me in my fieldwork with true eagerness and an untiring spirit of cooperation. Words cannot adequately express what they have been and done for me during this time.

TABLE OF CONTENTS

LIST OF TABLES

LIST OF CHARTS

FIGURE

CHAPTER I

INTRODUCTION

NATURE OF THE RESEARCH PROBLEM

This study focuses on health and illness beliefs and
practices, and an analysis of the health care system of elderly
Korean immigrant women. Descriptions of the daily life experience of elderly Korean women are needed in order to understand
their sociocultural context and illness as a cultural construction. Health and illness behavior and patient-practitioner transactions are directly influenced by the value systems expressed
in the daily life experiences of a group.

This research evolved from a pilot study about the sociocultural aspects of health and illness among selected Koreans
in the Greater Washington Metropolitan Area. A review of the
literature showed that there is limited knowledge about the
culture, health, and illness of Korean immigrants, even though
there is a growing number of Koreans in the United States.

A study of population trends shows that with the passage
of the Immigration and Nationality Act of 1965,[1] the restric-

_____

[1]Public Law 89-236, October 3, 1965. This Act abolish-
the long standing inequitable quota system which discriminated
against Asian immigration to the United States.

tive national origin quota system was no longer in effect,
and consequently, the number of immigrants from East and Southeast Asian countries increased. The number of Korean immigrants
increased by 1,300 percent between 1965 and 1974, ranking numer-
ically second only to the Filipino immigrants, whose larger original American population increased by 1,050 percent over the
same period.[2] According to the 1981 statistical report of the
Foreign Ministry of the Republic of Korea, there are 638,310
Korean residents in the United States.[3] Seven percent of the
Korean residents in the United States are composed of Korean
elderly persons sixty and over, so that it is estimated that
there are 45,000 elderly Korean residents in the United States.[4]
Korean elderly leaders in local Korean churches and the Elderly
Korean Association estimate that there are 800 to 2,000 Korean
men and women over the age of 61 in the Greater Washington
Metropolitan Area.

Monteiro points out that immigrants represent a rather
unique epidemiological subgroup, whose health status can be
expected to differ from that of nonimmigrants and of the host
population. Environmental changes, altered social relations,

---

[2]This percentage is derived from the statistics in Table 6 of the 1965 and 1974 Annual Report, Immigration and Naturalization Service, U.S. Department of Justice, Washington, D.C.

[3]Dong-A Il Bo (newspaper, Seoul). December 30, 1981.

[4]Personal interview with Joon Young Chung, a Korean-
American statistician, May 7, 1982.

cultural values, and psychological demands are some of the specific variations which may be reflected in physical and psychosomatic illness among immigrants (1980: 185-194). However, the research literature on elderly Korean immigrants in the United States offers limited data on their lives, their health, and their illnesses.

In the summer of 1981, during a pilot study which focused on cultural beliefs and practices of health and illness among Koreans, I became aware of the need for investigating the health and illness behavior of elderly Korean immigrants. Several areas merited attention. First, there was need for information on the pattern of elderly Koreans' daily life. What is it really like to live as elderly Korean immigrant women in the United States? Second, research was needed regarding their health and illness beliefs and practices in their sociocultural context as these related to health promotion and to illness behavior. I was told by health practitioners and researchers that the unavailability of research evidence about the health behavior among Korean immigrants made it difficult to do health planning and give proper health care to this population. I expected that elderly Korean women, because they are assumed to be more culturally conservative, would demonstrate the most traditional beliefs and practices related to the maintenance of health and the treatment of illness. Therefore, as a third area of interrest, I wanted to gain knowledge about the patterns of pluralistic medical practices and health promotion of a group of elderly Koreans. Fourth, the cultural construction of illness of elderly Korean immigrant women needed an examination. "Culture

affects the way we perceive, label, and manage illness"
(Kleinman 1980: 178).

With these interests and trends as background, my
specific research aims were: (1) to describe and interpret
sociocultural changes in the lives of elderly Korean immigrant
women in relation to their traditional values, beliefs, the
influences of immigration life, and advanced age, (2) to study
their health and illness beliefs and practices, (3) to discuss
the pattern of cultural construction of a Korean popular illness called Hwabyung, and (4) to describe the characteristics
of clinical interactions between patients and practitioners in
traditional Korean medical practice and in biomedical practice.

Kleinman believes that a cross-cultural study of medicine needs to be studied "in a holistic manner as socially
organized responses to disease that constitute a special cultural system: the health care system." The health care system
"integrates patterns of belief about the causes of illness;
norms governing choice and evaluation of treatment; socially-
legitimated statuses, roles, power relationships, interaction
settings, and institutions." Thus, the study of health and illness beliefs and practices requires examination within the context of a health care system as a cultural system (Kleinman
1980: 24-25).

The configuration of the health care system is shaped
by the internal structure of the system and the external structure. The external structure includes political, economic, social structural, historical, and environmental determinants.
The external factors often function as important determinants

of change (Kleinman 1980: 45).

This study is primarily concerned with the inner workings of health care systems. According to Kleinman, the internal
structure of a health care system is composed of "three overlapping parts: the popular, professional, and folk sectors."
The popular sector of health care is the largest part of any
system; however, it is "the least studied and most poorly understood." It is manifested at several levels: individual, family,
social network, and community beliefs and activities. "It is the
lay, non-professional, non-specialist, popular culture arena" in
which illness is first defined and treatment is initiated
(Kleinman 1980:50). According to M. Lock, popular health care
is practiced among family members or individuals in close networks without the influence of professional medical services
(1980:15).

The professional sector comprises "the organized healing professions." In most societies, the professional sector of
health care refers to "simply modern scientific medicine."
Kleinman states that there are "professionalized indigenous
medical systems" (Kleinman 1980:53-54). The examples of the professionalized indigenous medical systems are traditional Chinese
medicine and traditional Korean medicine (Leslie 1976:1-12).
For the professional sector of health care, M. Lock (1980:14)
used the term cosmopolitan medical system as Dunn (1976:133)
did. M. Lock termed also cosmopolitan medicine "Western,"
"modern" or "scientific" (1980:14).

The folk sector is "non-professional" and "non-bureaucratic." However, this folk sector employs a specialist. Folk

health care is composed of different components: "Some are
closely related to the professional sector, but most are related to the popular sector." Folk medicine is often divided
into "sacred and secular" realms, but this classification is
frequently not clear in reality, and the two are integrated
(Kleinman 1980:59). The Korean Mudang, a female shaman, combines sacred ritual such as a healing ceremony and practical
healing by means of counseling (Harvey 1976:191-198).

The structural components of health care systems interact primarily because patients alternate between them. A patient
encounters different systems of meanings, norms, and power as he
moves   between the sectors of a health care system. Thus, each
sector can be viewed as a separate culture (Kleinman 1980:59-60).

Kleinman states that each health care system holds five
core functions which are universal aspects of medicine: (1) "The
cultural construction of illness as psychosocial experience,"
(2) "The establishment of general criteria to guide the health
care seeking process and to evaluate treatment approaches,"
(3) "The management of particular illness episodes through
communicative operations such as labeling and explaining,"
(4) "Healing activities" which "include all types of therapeutic
interventions, from drugs and surgery to psychotherapy, suppor-
tive care, and healing rituals," and (5) the management of
therapeutic outcomes, including cure, treatment failure, recurrence, and chronic illness (Kleinman 1980:71-72).

The first function, "the cultural construction of the
illness as psychological experience" is that sickness as a
"natural phenomenon" is shaped into a particular cultural con-

figuration through the categories that are used "to perceive, express, and valuate symptoms." The cultural construction of illness is often "a personally and socially adaptive response" (Kleinman 1980:72). A label one applies to "subjective symptoms" or "objective signs," is a cultural category (Kleinman 1980:76). An illness in a cultural form is rich with specific meaning and cast as a particular configuration of human action. No matter what the nature of the disease and its cause, the disease involves "a psychological, social, and cultural reaction" which constructs illness (Kleinman 1980:78).

The second core clinical function refers to "the establishment of general strategies and criteria for choosing and evaluating health care alternatives." The selection of a particular treatment by individuals or groups is determined by values embedded in illness labels. This core function is concerned with "the health ideology and values that guide the health seeking process...." In a health care system, certain categories of illness call for particular types of health care. Schutz's term "structure of relevance" (1968:111-122 and 312-322) is interpreted in the treatment decision process by Kleinman: "which health problems are most important, most feared, and require most immediate action" (1980:80). The health seeking activities differ between sectors. According to Kleinman, "the same structure of relevance is used to decide how long to continue one type of care and when to change to another." "Value structures play a crucial role in evaluations of practitioners and patients. Such conflicts often lead to major problems in clinical care (Kleinman 1980:80-81). Structures of relevance are used interchangeably with what Schwartz (1969:201-202) calls "hierarchies of resort."

The second and third functions, the management of particular illness episodes through communicative operations such as labeling and explaining, are combined and called "cognitive and communicative features of health care" (Kleinman 1980:83). "Individuals are in contact with different beliefs and normative systems as they move from sector to sector." As they move between distinct sectors of a health care system, "they carry with them their own cognitive and value frameworks" (Kleinman 1980:99). Here the important question is how to compare the systems of medical knowledge and practices constituted by and expressed by patients and practitioners in the different sectors of health care systems. In order to solve this problem, a tool is required to compare various cognitive and communicative systems to one another. For this purpose Kleinman developed the explanatory framework model. "Explanatory models are the notions about an episode of sickness and its treatment that are employed by all those engaged in the clinical process." "Explanatory models are held by patients and practitioners in all health care systems. They offer explanations of sickness and treatment to guide choices among available therapies and therapists and to cast personal and social meaning on the experience of sickness" (Kleinman 1980:104-105). The explanatory model describes the dynamics of cognitive and communicative interactions in the health care process and it offers "a mean of comparing these transactions in traditional and modern medical settings, and of evaluating their efficacy" (Kleinman 1980:118).

The fourth function, healing activities, refers to two related but distinct clinical practices: the curing of disease and the healing of illness. The curing of disease is "the establishment of effective control of disordered biological and psychological processes." Healing of illness refers to "the provision of personal and social meaning for the life problems created by sickness" (Kleinman 1980:82). Kleinman states that different sectors of a health care system could result in an unsuccessful and a disappointing cure and healing (Kleinman 1980:82).

The fifth function, the management of therapeutic outcomes, includes "cure, treatment failure, recurrent sickness, chronic illness, impairment, and dying." This function is considered important through the sectors in a health care system. This function deals with medical as well as social concerns. Conflicting interpretations of therapeutic outcomes are often faced by members of the different sectors of a health care system (Kleinman 1980:83).

Kleinman emphasizes that health care systems are "socially and culturally constructed." This cultural and social system is concerned with "the world of human interactions" existing among individuals. These systems include a "transactional world in which everyday life is enacted, in which social roles are defined and performed, and in which people negotiate with each other in established status relationships under a system of cultural rules." An individual's behavior is affected by symbolic meanings, norms of society, his perception of the world, his communication with others, and his understanding of his own internal and interpersonal environment. Socialization takes place in the family and society through "education, occupation, ritual, play, and the general process of internalizing norms from the world he lives in" (Kleinman 1980:35-36). These social influences are called "social reality" by Kleinman and this social reality which is reflected in health and illness practices is named "clinical reality." Clinical realities differ between different health care systems and sectors (Kleinman 1980:44-45).

STUDY POPULATION

The target population was elderly Korean immigrant women in the Greater Washington Metropolitan Area who were sixty years old or older as measured by the luni-solar calendar.[5] The Hwangap is a significant point in life among Koreans. According to Adams, when one reaches age sixty he celebrates the Hwangap, the most important event of his entire life. The attainment of this birthday is a very happy occasion, calling for special celebrations. Usually a big family reunion is held and the honored person is beautifully attired (Adams 1980:278). Upon reaching the sixtieth birthday, Koreans consider that a person has reached a unique age, because they used to believe that people did not live beyond sixty. They wish the elderly a long life. They celebrate the birthday joyously with all their family, relatives, and neighbors. Socially, after Koreans

---

[5]In the luni-solar calendar every year is designated by a combination of one twelve year animal cycle (rat, cow, tiger, rabbit, dragon, snake, horse, sheep, monkey, chicken, dog, and

reach the age of sixty, they begin to retire from active work
in the family and society.

There were three reasons why I decided to choose elderly women as my informants. First, as a women researcher it was
culturally acceptable to interview and observe other women.
According to Korean norms, men and women should not be alone
together except in a legitimate joint relationship such as husband and wife. According to a Confucian classic, male and female
should not sit together after they reach the age of seven. Second,
women in households are considered consultants as well as practitioners of family health problems (Kim and Sick 1977:76). Third,
they are believed to be conservative enough to retain traditional health and illness beliefs and practices. It was my hope,
therefore, that research among these women would offer insights
of both the traditional and changing aspects of Korean immigrants.

The population was a convenience sample of twenty elderly Korean immigrant women. Ten of them were from my neighborhood and the other ten of them were from a 5 to 10 minute drive
from the above neighborhood, in different senior citizen's
apartments, and at a nearby a Korean church which has a clinic
for elderly people. The population could be divided roughly into three groups: those who were in my neighborhood, those in
the vicinity of the Korean church, and those who lived in the
senior citizen's apartments. Incidentally, three of the twenty
informants lived in senior citizen's apartment and near the

---

pig) and one ten year "stem" cycle. The combination rotates
every sixty years.

Korean church. The contacts in my neighborhood were first made
by my son who informed me about an elderly Korean reading a
Korean newspaper under a tree. I was able to make initial contacts with other elderly Koreans through this person. I learned that seven elderly women who later became my informants,
lived in my neighborhood. Later, another three informants
moved into the neighborhood. The elderly Koreans had seen my
son in the neighborhood, so that it helped my entry into their
group. I had also contacted a minister who is a son of one of
my informants. There were two reasons for this action. The son
is a respected Korean community leader and his house had informally become a meeting place for the elderly people in my neighborhood. He gave me permission to visit his mother. After this
contact, it was possible to reach the rest of the elderly women
in my neighborhood. The informants I had already known, introduced me to their acquaintances through their networks of friends
and relatives.

Out of my population, I selected two key informants
(Mrs. Yun and Mrs. Ahn) who lived with their children near my
neighborhood and another two key informants (Mrs. Yik and Mrs.
Rhim) who live independently in senior apartments.[6] I also inter-
viewed several officials of the Korean Elderly Association and
Korean community leaders as my key informants.

The data on age showed that the age range of the informants was from 64 years to 80 years. With regard to marital
status, fifteen of the informants (75%) were widows and five

---

[6]Pseudonyms are used to protect the informants.

of the informants (25%) were married. The average number of
children the informants had was four. There were no childless
women. The children of eight of the informants lived in Korea
and other countries as well as in the United States. All of the
children of the remaining twelve of the informants lived in the
United States. All of the informants except one had grandchildren. Three informants had great grandchildren. Of the total
number of informants , ten informants (50 %) went to primary
school and three informants (15%) did not attend school at all
while four informants (20 %) completed high school, and the
remaining three informants (15%) had university education.
One informant (5%) was illiterate.

The mean period of residence in the United States was
eight years. The informants had been living in this country
from six months to twenty-one years. Those informants who lived
in the senior citizen's apartments depended mainly on Social Security pensions. Those who lived with their children depended
mainly on their children for support, but six of them received
a Social Security pension or some kind of financial aid from
the county, or state. The other seven informants did not receive
financial aid because they were too young or had not resided
in the United States long enough to qualify. Some of them were
not aware of the availability of financial aid or they had not
applied for it due to their children's busy schedule. Some
would not apply out of shame.

The majority of the informants were housewives
in Korea. In this United States, approximately 50 percent,
nine informants, held honorary or voluntary positions within

the Korean community. Occasionally, two of the informants helped in their children's business such as grocery store. But,
they were not paid for their labor because they considered it
their duty as a family member to help the family. They did not
expect to be paid. But, they were given pocket money and her
other financial needs were usually looked after by their children without mentioning direct reciprocity. Three of the informants cared for infants and toddlers in their apartments. Occasionally, Mrs. Hwang and Mrs. Yun who were in their sixties,
worked as housekeepers. Another informant, Mrs. Lee had a housekeeping job, but she had to give it up because she developed
"arthritis." Most of the informants who lived with their children cared for grandchildren and did some cooking and housekeeping for the family.

As for the informants' religious beliefs, seventeen of
them (85%) attended Korean Christian churches. Two of them
(10%) worshipped their ancestors, one of them (5%) was Buddhist.
Among the Christians there were thirteen Baptists, two Methodists, one Presbyterian, and one Catholic. The majority of these
informants appear to be similar to the relatively recently
arrived elderly Korean immigrant women elsewhere in the United
States in relation to age, marital status, relationship with
children, education, economic status, employment status, and
religious background(Choy 1979:239-274 and Yu 1980:75-98).

METHODOLOGY

The methods used for data collection were participant observation (Spradley 1975:355-369 and 1980), semi-structured interviews (Liebow 1967:232-256 and Spradley 1979), and examination of documentary sources. Participant observation was used to gather data about daily life to enrich sociocultural aspects which an interview guide cannot yield. Pelto and Pelto's statement illustrates the central role of participant observation in conducting effective field work:

> The relatively unsystematized scanning of information through participant observation is basic to all the other, more refined, research techniques. Preliminary data from participant observation provide the fieldworker with insights and clues necessary for developing interview questions, psychological tests, or other more specialized research tools. Participant observation also provides the further checking and monitoring of field information that is necessary for evaluating data gathered by the specialized techniques. The chronicle of a field project usually consists of the interplay between participant observation and the other modes of data collection (Pelto and Pelto 1979:69).

In this study, participant observation focused on sociocultural influences on aging particularly in relation to sociocultural change, adaptation patterns in family and society, health and illness beliefs and practices, and alternative health practices of elderly Korean immigrant women.

The activities of elderly Korean immigrant groups were observed in settings of private homes, in senior citizen's apartments, in church, at the Elderly Korean Association meetings, at elderly picnics, in small social groups, and in the elderly university. Other activities included birthday parties, wedding

ceremonies, and a one hundred day celebration party.[7] Observations of the elderly were conducted in places other than
home settings where the informants visited most often. They
included a clinic run by a physician in a church, homes or
office of Korean traditional healers. In the clinic, therapeutic relationships between the women in the present and
practitioners were observed according to Kleinman's practi-
tioner-patient interaction guidelines which is composed of
an institutional setting, characteristics of the interpersonal interaction, communication pattern, clinical reality,
and therapeutic stages and mechanisms (Kleinman 1980:207-208).

I had permission to observe an acupuncturist who is a
member of the elderly center in a Korean church. In addition,
I met five Korean traditional medical physicians. With one
exception they were part-time practitioners. I was allowed to
observe one of these practitioners in clinical practice. I went
to his clinic with informants a few times. The practitioner was
concerned that his secrets about his treatment and business
might be publicized. One acupuncturist demonstrated his clinical
examination technique. He simulated his diagnostic art on me
with a machine which substitutes traditional diagnostic
methods such as pulse taking. One of the practitioners declined

---

[7]When a child becomes one hundred day old, Korean people
celebrate this occasion with family members, relatives, and neighbors. One informant volunteered to explain about the possible origin of this celebration. In olden days, it was rare for infants to
survive beyond 100 days, so that they started to celebrate this
event. Others offered animistic and shamanistic interpretations
that this custom was followed to appease a child's guardian spirits and to drive away evil spirits for securing a long life for
a child(see Chapter IV, Section, Living with Children, Friendship, and Reciprocity).

my request to observe her clinical sessions because she wanted
to give her full attention to her clients. Most of the practitioners see their clients in their homes.

Twenty sixty year old or older Korean immigrant women
lived with their children or lived independently in senior
citizen's apartments in an area of high concentration of Korean
immigrant population.

The semi-structured interview guide had six parts:
(1) demographic and background information, (2) meaning of old
age, (3) significance of children, (4) daily life patterns,
(5) health beliefs and practices, and (6) illness beliefs and
practices.

The first part on demographic data and background
included information such as residence, composition of household members, occupation, source of income, religion, education,
age, marital status, and length of residence in the United
States.

The second part follwed Keith's framework who suggested
that anthropologists should attempt "to understand the meaning
of old age from the point of view of the old, or to observe the
old among themselves" (Keith 1980:343). The informants' meaning
of old age, thoughts and feelings of old age, concerns and joys
of old age, wishes in old age, some possible changes in thinking
and actions of the old age, and meaning of living in the modern
age were elicited.

The third part of the guide focused on the significance
of children to the elderly Korean women in this study. This part
of the interview guide elicited information regarding the mean-

ing of their children, joys, concerns, and wishes in regard to their children, some of their sources of conflicts
in their relationship with their children, matters of
independency and dependency on their children, and the
pattern of conflict resolution.

The fourth part elicited material about the life
patterns of the elderly Korean immigrant women. The purpose of this section was to elicit information about their
everyday life patterns, their perceptions of change in
their lives, and social activities. I also elicited
material on their joys, concerns, thoughts, and feelings
about their everyday life experiences. The informants
described leisure activities and factors which encouraged
or discouraged these activities.

The fifth and sixth parts of the interview guide
addressed health beliefs and practices of the elderly
Korean immigrant women. The main purpose of this part of
the interview guide was to learn about their concepts of
health, health measures, and perceptions of their health
status. Furthermore, to elicit their understanding of illness behavior, Kleinman's openended questions about patient's
explanatory models were used (Kleinman 1980:106).

Parts I, V, and VI of the semi-structured interview
guide were pretested in the summer of 1981. Revisions were
made and then the rest of the interview guide was constructed. Parts on the meaning of old age, children, and
patterns of everyday life of the elderly Korean immigrant
women were added. The whole interview guide was pretested.

The semi-structured interview guide was constructed
first in Korean, and then I translated the Korean version into
English. There was no essential difference between the original
and the final Korean version. The final Korean text was translated from the English version by an English-Korean bilingual
humanities student.

All interviews were conducted in Korean. I did not bring
the interview guide along with me, but memorized the questions
and posed questions appropriately according to each informant's
educational and sociocultural background without distortion of
the original meaning of the interview guide.

Interviews usually took place from about ten in the
morning to twelve noon and from one o'clock to three o'clock
in the afternoon so that mealtimes and family hours were avoided.
Most of the interviews were done at informants' homes or at an
elderly center of a church. The informant was interviewed alone
or sometimes in the presence of friends or family members. When
people were present other than the informant, no effort was made
to avoid the other people in order to interview the informant
in a natural setting so that interaction with friends and family
members could be observed. This also helped to avoid any suspi-
cion or insecurity on the part of the informant. Most of the questions were answered during casual everyday conversation, probably because the questions covered the informants' concerns
and interests in everyday life.

If the informants were in the middle of work at home
such as making Kimch'i (a traditional Korean pickled vegetable)
doing the laundry, or baby sitting with grandchildren, I helped

them until they finished their work or settled down. Sometimes
I was not able to conduct an interview at all, but by being a
participant I gained insight into a different dimension of their
lives. Sometimes I listened to their problems and tried to do
something for them. For example, I provided some mental health
service information to an old couple who live with a mentally
ill son. Sometimes I filled out welfare request forms all morning and spent all afternoon in a county welfare office with an
informant. These were good opportunities to understand their
problems. One time, Mrs. Yik, one of the informants and her
friend engaged in a heated political, social, and religious
debate. It was helpful to me in understanding some of their
views about the world.

The informants in the neighborhood were interviewed
and observed formally and informally at different times with
each session lasting from 1 to 2 hours. The longest amount
of time was spent with Mrs. Ahn and Mrs. Yun who were seen
more than forty times for a total of 50-60 hours. The shortest
amount of time was spent with two informants in the senior
citizen's apartments, Mrs. Myong and Mrs. Sunu, who were interviewed once for three hours. The active field work took place
from April 1982 to January 1983.

The documentary materials used were as follows: publish-
ed and unpublished Chinese and Korean traditional medical materials, reports, newsletters, newspapers, journals about elderly
Korean immigrant life, Korean ethnographic materials, information
about remedies and treatment instructions from clients and prac-

Entry of the Field

In order to have a trusting relationship with the informants, it was essential for me to be introduced to them by a respected authority figure who had a long term close relationship with them such as a son or minister. In this way, we could interact as neighbors and get to know each other. We shared a great deal and supported each other. We had meals together and shared food items such as seasonal dishes, traditional Korean foods, and vegetables. We collected money and could buy cucumbers and chestnuts much cheaper than if an individual bought these alone. We exchanged information about buying groceries, sales, medical treatment, employment, benefits for the elderly, and other useful information such as availability of an overnight oven cleaner. We also consulted and talked about health, illness, and death as well as family problems. We comforted each other when we were discouraged but we also gossiped and joked about life. We visited one another when one of us was not feeling well.

The women selected for this study appreciated my help with English, giving them rides, shopping, providing medical or health information and going to clinics together. They, in turn, were concerned enough to give me advice about how I could help my husband to improve his health after they described him as "lean and pale." They were kind to my son when he played in the neighborhood and never failed to stop him and ask him about what I was doing. They were also concerned about his Korean because he does not speak it readily. I was allowed to visit some of the

informants in my neighborhood any time without an appointment.
They were kind to invite me to birthdays, weddings, trips to
vegetable farms, neighborhood visits, and grandchild's 100 day
old celebrations.

The situation was different when I visited the informants
in the senior citizen's apartment who were not my neighbors.
Since, I had not been introduced to the informants by one of
their trusted leader, it was not easy for them to accept me,
a middle aged Korean women, as a student. They were disappointed when they learned that I was not a volunteer who could give
them a ride, be an interpreter, and teach them English. One
point was that they appeared, at times, to have perceived me
as someone who investigates about eligibility for Social
Security and housing benefits. One of the influential children
of the informants made the same observation.

The majority of the Korean elderly tenants in five
senior citizen's apartment complex, only one elderly Korean
woman out of 15, Mrs. Rhim, accepted my invitation to participate in this study. In another apartment complex, two out
of seven participated (Mrs. Yik and Mrs. Uh). Still in another
two apartment buildings no elderly people collaborated. These
three informants who participated had higher education and had
held responsible positions in Korea. The average elderly
Korean women depends on male authority or children in their
family for major decisions for their family and for themselves
so they are not used to spontaneous and independent decision
making. This situation appears to be further accentuated when
they come to the United States because they are repeatedly told

by their children and friends that they do not know anything
about America and do not speak English so that they should not
do anything without consulting with family members or a trusted
person in their group. I was told by one of the informants'
daughters that her mother and her mother's friends did not
know anything but that they were like children.

Four church elders participated in my research although
they live in senior citizen's apartments. One of them, Mrs. Myong,
knew my father-in-law, a minister, because her husband, also a
minister, and my father-in-law were friends in Korea. The other
three informants, Mrs. Choi, Mrs. Sunu, and Mrs. Kang, were
told about me by a minister who was a friend of my father-in-law.
Also, Mrs. Choi's son is a minister of a church which has a
clinic for elderly persons. This minister is also a friend of
my husband · This was one of the reasons why entry to the church
clinic was smooth.

The recognition of me as one of their kind and not just a
student appeared to be important in establishing rapport with my
informants. They accepted my invitation to participate in this
research after they knew that I shared a similar sociocultural
background with them and I spoke Korean. Particularly, the informants in my neighborhood were able to trust me after they
were acquainted with my son and husband as well. My role as a
mother and a neighbor helped me to mingle with informants because these roles are similar to those which they themselves
have been assuming in their families and community. A similar
religious background was also helpful for the informants to
accept me in the field. The important factor in my being

allowed to study my informants in a Korean church clinic was
my association with a reknown Christian Korean minister through
marriage. By the way, when I asked   permission to interview
Koreans in a Buddhist temple, the request was not granted
after they were told that I was not a Buddhist.

For my fieldwork I used different means of transportation: walking, bus, metro, and automobile. In my neighborhood,
I could walk because it is a large apartment complex. There
are no high rise buildings so that it sometimes reminded me
of a Korean hamlet. All along I thought that it was ideal for
the nature of my study. One round trip to visit the informants
in the senior citizen's apartment or church by car took me
about 45 minutes to one hour. Going to other places such as
a vegetable farm, a Korean traditional clinic, a picnic, some
of the informants' houses or a wedding took me 2-3 hours round
trip travel time.

Confidentiality

The nature and the objective of this study and the
informants' right to anonymity and confidentiality were fully
explained. Their verbal consent for participation in this
research was obtained before data collection was started. All
the data were kept in locked files and were accessible only
to me.

Data Recording, Coding, and Analysis

The data collected by interview and participant observation were recorded on 5"x8" unisort cards and coded. These

data were analyzed according to content analysis and inferential interpretation. Demographic data and material on health
and illness beliefs and practices were also analyzed quantitatively to show frequency and distribution of certain factors
and possible relationships among them.

Reliability and Validity:
Cross-Cultural Aspects of Interviewing among Koreans

Among Koreans the importance of interpersonal relationships is emphasized and shame is viewed as a positive
energizer for moral and social conduct. In an article "Some
Ways of Looking at Village Value," in Studies in the Developmental Aspects of Korea edited by Andrew Nahm, Vincent Brandt
discussed shame in Korea. He noted that "Koreans have resistance to authoritarian leadership outside the family and respect for individual face." He continued:

> Face is another tricky word. What I mean by it is the
> potential for shame and esteem vis à vis one's fellowmen
> that is involved in any particular social situation. A
> moment's reflection shows that there are areas of both
> reinforcement and conflict between the two ethical do-
> mains. Actually, I see this dimension as a continuum ra-
> ther than a clearcut bi-polar division, with both tradi-
> tions usually discernible, (although to different extent)
> in any specific interpersonal situation (Brandt 1969:87).

A sense of shame is reflected directly and indirectly
in Korean life as indicated in another writing:

> The tremendous influence of face is obvious in the
> everyday manner of the Koreans. The excessive polite-
> ness, to avoid the slightest hint of offense....
> (Materi 1949:69-70).

Korean background on honor and shame is all cast in
a framework regarding the behavioral expectations for men

and women. There are virtues reinforced by Confucian teaching:
filial piety, harmony among men, loyalty, faithfulness, ceremonial appropriatemess, justice, and purity (Hsu 1971:147).
The elderly Korean informants appeared to feel shame when
they realized that they were not following behavioral norms
based on Confucian value and belief systems in their everyday life. Generally, informants were sensitive to certain
questions, so that they often were ashamed of or had feelings
of loss of face about their situation. Consequently, they at
times avoided answering or they gave different responses
from reality when their information was compared with others
or judged with observation data. For these reasons, I approached them unobtrusively with observation techniques,
culturally acceptable indirect interviews, and/or key informant
methods. A non-judgmental, unbiased, and empathic attitude was
very beneficial.

At the time of this study, some of the women were
suffering from uneasy feelings about receiving aid from the
government such as living in a senior citizen's apartments,
receiving an old age assistance check or Social Security benefits. Consequently, they had low self-esteem. Under such circumstances, when they met other Koreans, such as myself, they
felt shame and were sensitive talking about themselves. Visits
in natural settings such as occasional neighborly visits were
useful in getting the above mentioned information during casual
conversation. Key informant interviewing was also helpful.

Several informants said that they had been comforting

themselves about being government aid recipients with the knowledge that their children paid respectable amounts of taxes. Although, some of the informants receive state assistance of Social Security pensions, their ultimate source of support is attributed to their children. They have been socialized in a society where dependency on their children is customary in old age.

The informants who lived in senior citizen's apartment showed some hesitancy about revealing their reasons for living there instead of living with their children. Some informants felt that they should live by themselves to create a mutually satisfying and free atmosphere between their children and themselves. Other informants stated that their children expected them to live alone. Whether the decision was made by the parent or by their children, it was against their traditional family value system. Also, it was suggested that there was potential or actual family interpersonal disharmony which they and their children were reluctant to admit. In the traditional society, it was unthinkable to change the family structure in order to pursue individual freedom and independence. It brought shame and loss of face for the entire family particularly for those who are traditionally oriented.

The informants believed in filial piety and harmonious family atmosphere. Thus, a question such as "How are you getting along with your son or daughter-in-law? How do they treat you?" would not have been acceptable. Although, unfair treatment of a family member could take place, it would not

be disclosed easily, but kept from others, because Koreans
are socialized to tolerate any family condition or problem.
Therefore, such questions were not asked directly, but were
inferred by observing and asking about other matters, e.g.
"What changes have you made?" Thus, questions regarding interpersonal relationships were explored by discussing other related subjects.

In a similar vein, some of the informants hesitated
or avoided revealing causes of illnesses such as Hwabyung
when these were related to strains in the family or other
human relationships because of their moral value of loyalty
for their group.

Employment appeared to have a complex meaning for an
informant so that a person would not readily respond when
faced with a question about work. Work means to these women
that they were allowed to work by their children instead of
being supported by them. Furthermore, leisure among the old
has been the behavioral norm in Korean society. Other reasons
in hesitancy in answering questions about work were that the
kinds of work some elderly persons were known to do were not
considered respectable. There was also a possibility that
Social Security benefits might be affected by the income
derived from the informant's work.

A straightforward response was not obtained when
an inquiry about leisure activities was posed, but self-
reproaching remarks were made about what they do. For example,
they did not seem to put a high value on social meeting where

"only spending time" for themselves took place. They felt that they should be engaged in activities which contributed to the well-being of family members or others. For example, if a lady is educated, she is likely to be expected to teach grandchildren traditional Korean ways or hobbies for esthetic pursuit such as calligraphy, gardening, and reading.

Some informants were evasive when they were asked whether or not they had taken restorative medicinals. One informant said "Why should old people take those to live longer? I prefer to live just the life span which was given to me. It is shameful, greedy, and ugly to live a long time. When the time comes, we have to die natually." To try to live longer with added means such as medicine was viewed negatively by some informants. Also, for their children's sake some believed that they should not extend life unless it were a full and meaningful life.

Some of the non-Christians who were familiar with shamanism and/or ancestor worship hesitated to reveal their beliefs until the researcher's non-judgmental and empathic attitude was conveyed. They did not want to be ridiculed by people who did not understand their views.

Some informants severely criticized one of their neighbors because they perceived that her mothering was not adequate according to their standard. When one's parenting behavior is believed to be out of a certain norm, it is bitterly criticized. A high priority of obligation and duty is placed on parenting. An informant, who used some English words with

her grandchildren such as "Yes," "No," and "Come here," was
ridiculed by her friends when she was not present. The issue
they were concerned with was that the informant was not ful-
filling her responsibility of teaching her grandchildren
Korean according to them. Americanization is perceived as a
shame sometimes. Among the informants there exists an un-
written rule that the preservation of the traditional value
system is encouraged. The informants, who had children who
had married interethnically, did not utter a word about the
fact themselves, but I was told about this by their friends
and key informants.

When a Korean's situation is perceived as outside of
a particular group's norms, she seems to suffer from shame or
loss of face, and they are subject to criticism by the group.

OVERVIEW

The Korean health care system as a cultural system in
terms of professional, popular, and folk sectors in relation
to Kleinman's health care system's model, construction of illness, and explanatory models will be discussed in Chapter II.
Chapter III will present the sociocultural background and the
immigration experience of the study population. Chapter IV will
examine the changing lives of the elderly Korean immigrant women studied comparing and contrasting their traditional values
and beliefs with their everyday life pattern. Chapter V will
include their concepts of health and illnesses, with particular

emphasis on <u>Hwabyung</u>, the cultural construction of illness
and the meaning of illness in old age. In Chapter VI, the
pluralistic health and illness behaviors in relation to curing,
healing, and prevention in their health care system will be
studied. Therapeutic transactions between patients and practitioners in traditional Korean medical and in biomedical fields
will be examined based on different explanatory models and
cultural construction of illness. In Chapter VII the summary
and conclusions will be presented.

CHAPTER II

THE KOREAN HEALTH CARE SYSTEM AS A CULTURAL SYSTEM

HEALTH CARE SYSTEM AS A CULTURAL SYSTEM

Health and illness are universal. However, health
and illness beliefs and practices can vary among different
cultures. A health care system is viewed as a cultural sys-
tem(Dunn 1976:133-158, Glick 1977:58-70, Kleinman 1978:251-
258 and 1980:24-25, and Kunstadter 1975:351-384, and 1978:
393-398). Kleinman elaborates on this concept:

> In the same sense in which we speak of religion or
> language or kinship as cultural systems, we can view
> medicine as a cultural system, a system of symbolic
> meanings anchored in particular arrangements of social
> institutions and patterns of interpersonal interactions.
> In every culture, illness, the responses to it, individ-
> uals experiencing it and treating it, and the social
> institutions relating to it are all systematically inter-
> connected. The totality of these interrelationships is
> the health care system. Put somewhat differently, the
> health care system, like other cultural systems, integ-
> rates the health-related components of society. These
> include patterns of belief about the cause of illness;
> norms governing choice and evaluation of treatment;
> socially legitimated statuses, roles, power relation-
> ships, interaction settings, and institutions.
>   Patients and healers are basic components of such
> systems and thus are embedded in specific configurations
> of cultural meanings and social relationships. They can-
> not be understood apart from this context. Illness and
> healing also are part of the system of health care. With-
> in that system, they are articulated as culturally con-

stituted experiences and activities, respectively. In the
context of culture, the study of patients and healers,
and illness and healing, must, therefore, start with an
analysis of health care systems (Kleinman 1980:24-25).

The health care system is a concept and a conceptual

model to study a particular health care situation and how

people in that setting "think about health care." It refers

to the illness beliefs, treatment choices, and outcomes of

care of a group of people (Kleinman 1980:25-26). The health

care system includes people's beliefs and behaviors that

constitute "instrumental and symbolic activities" which are

influenced by and interacted among the following particular

variables:

> ...social institutions (e.g., clinics, hospitals,
> professional associations, health bureaucracies), social
> roles (e.g., sick role, healing role), interpersonal
> relationships (e.g., doctor-patient relationship, pa-
> tient-family relationship, social network relationships),
> interaction settings (e.g., home, doctor's office), eco-
> nomic and political constraints, and many other factors,
> including, most notably, available treatment interventions
> and type of health problems (Kleinman 1980:26).

The health care system is organized through the inter-

action of these variables. It represents the adaptive response

to problems of illness (Kleinman 1980:26-27).

Health care systems are social and cultural construc-

tions. Kleinman refers to them as forms of "social reality"

as follows:

> Social reality signifies the world of human interac-
> tions existing outside the individual and between indi-
> viduals. It is the transactional world in which everyday
> life is enacted, in which social roles are defined and
> performed, and in which people negotiate with each other
> in established status relationships under a system of
> cultural rules. Social reality is constituted from and
> in turn constitutes meanings, institutions, and relation-

ships sanctioned by society. Social reality is constructed or created in the sense that certain meanings, social
structural configurations, and behaviors are sanctioned
(or legitimated) while others are not. The individual
absorbs (internalizes) social reality---as a system of
symbolic meanings and norms governing his behavior, his
perception of the world, his communication with others,
and his understanding of both the external, interpersonal
environment he is situated in and his own internal, intra-
psychic space--during the process of socialization
(or enculturation). Socialization takes place in the
family, but also in other social groupings via education,
occupation, rituals, play, and the general process of
internalizing norms from the world we live in (Kleinman
1980:35-36).

Changes from old to new social forms influence a

health care system as it does other cultural systems. In such

situations, social reality holds a special combination of

modern and traditional beliefs, values, and institutions, held

together in varying patterns of "complementarity, conflict, and

contradiction." Social reality may be different as one

moves from one sociocultural domain to another due to variables

such as family, socioeconomic condition, education, occupation,

religion, and ethnicity (Kleinman 1980:37).

Kleinman states that the social reality of health

and illness beliefs and practices is what he calls "clinical

reality." Each clinical practice represents a unique social

milieu, for example, a traditional Korean clinic and a biomed-

ical clinic. Without considering the sociocultural aspects it

is almost impossible to understand illness beliefs and prac-

tices. The health care system is a collective view and shared

patterns of usage operating in the system. "Social factors

such as class, education, religious affiliation, ethnicity,

occupation, and social networks all influence the perception

and use of health resources in the same locality and thereby
influence the construction of distinctive clinical realities
within the same health care system." Systems of health care
may differ with respect to cultural, historical, socioeconomic, and political variables (Kleinman 38-40).

"Symbolic reality" plays an important role in the
health care systems model. The clinical reality of a health
care system is "mediated by symbolic reality," by inter-
preting symbolic meanings, norms, and power in relation to
illness and treatment. For example, recognition of sources
of power such as supernatural, social, political, religious,
technological natures (Glick 1977:58-61) becomes effective
in health care by avenues of social reality which is "formed
by the individual's acquisition of language and systems of
meaning" (Kleinman 1980:41-44).

Culture is not the only variable to form patterns
of health care systems, but also there are other variables
which are divided into external and internal structures of
health care systems. The external variables are "political,
economic, social structural, historical, and environmental
factors (Kleinman 1980:45). According to Kleinman, the environmental determinants include:

> ...geography; climate; demography; environmental
> problems, such as famine, flood, population excess,
> pollution; agricultural and industrial development;
> and so forth. In addition, there are local epidemi-
> ological patterns of disease (prevalence, attack rates,
> and virulence of specific disorders) that combine with
> genetic endowment and susceptibility of the population
> and specific stressors to influence not only health,
> but also health beliefs and healing practice (Kleinman
> 1980:45-46).

Health care systems are also affected by ecological
determinants and "the level of technological and social development, including the status of therapeutic institutions, biomedical technologies, treatment interventions, and professional personnel (Kleinman 1980:49).

The internal structure of health care systems has
three overlapping segments: the "popular, professional, and
folk sectors." The popular sector is "the lay, non-professional, non-specialist, popular culture arena in which illness is
first defined and health care activities initiated." According to Kleinman, the popular part of health care is the largest
part of any system. However, it is not recognized as much as
it should be. The popular sector of care is practiced at different levels such as individual, family, social networks,
and community beliefs and activities. The popular sector is
the point of departure and arrival from the professional sector or folk sector. People may leave or return to the popular
sector as they see the need. "Self-treatment by the individual
and family is the first therapeutic intervention resorted to
by most people across a wide range of cultures. This is only
one of the essential activities taking place in the popular
sector" (Kleinman 1980:50-51).

Kleinman describes an individual's illness behavior
as it takes place in the popular sector:

> In the popular sector, individuals first encounter
> disease in the family. We can think of the following
> steps occurring, at least initially: perceiving and
> experiencing symptoms; labeling and valuating the
> disease; sanctioning a particular kind of sick role

(acute, chronic, impaired, medical, or psychiatric, etc.);
deciding what to do and engaging in specific health care-
seeking behavior; applying treatment; and evaluating the
effect of self-treatment and therapy obtained from other
sectors of the health care system. The sick person and
his family utilize beliefs and values about illness that
are part of the cognitive structure of the popular culture.
The decisions they make cover a range of possible alternatives. The family can disregard signs of illness by
considering them to be ordinary or 'natural,' or they can
validate the sick person's sick role. They can institute
therapy with treatment modalities known to them or they
can consult with friends, neighbors, relatives, and lay
experts about what to do (Kleinman 1980:51-52).

These illness behavioral processes--recognizing,

diagnosing, taking an appropriate sick role, treating, evalu-

ating outcomes, replanning with alternatives and/or disregard-

ing signs of condition--are carried out based on one's popular

sector beliefs and values. Kleinman remarks that the popular

sector is not only concerned with illness, but also "health

maintenance" and prevention of illness (Kleinman 1980:53). For

example, some Koreans are familiar with a popular illness,

called Hwabyung. They believe that this illness is caused

by different worries in life. A characteristic of this ill-

ness is complaining of physical sickness, but not mental ill-

ness. For treatment of this condition, Koreans usually inte-

grate both popular and professional care.

The professional sector in a local health care system

includes "the organized healing professions," which is "modern

scientific medicine" in most societies. Kleinman states that

classical indigenous medical traditions such as Chinese med-

icine are professional medicine (Kleinman 1980:53-54). Tradi-

tional Korean medicine is viewed as   professional medicine

because it has been influenced by Chinese medicine (Leslie

1976a:1-12 and Spector 1979:211).

In the professional sector, Kleinman also included
the processes of indigenization and popularization (Kleinman
1980:56). Indigenization is viewed as changes that modern professional medicine undergoes after it is in contact with
contrasting indigenous societies. These changes involve the
system of knowledge, health care institutions, and clinical
reality. Indigenization is a process of transformation of professional care into a care pattern which is appropriate to an
indigenous group's use. Popularization means that "certain
aspects of professional care" are changed and diffused after
they enter the popular sector (Kleinman 1980:56).

Kleinman states that the folk sector of health care
is provided by a "non-professional, non-bureaucratic specialist." According to Kleinman, folk medicine is said to be "a
mixture of many different components; some are closely related
to the professional sector, but most are related to the popular
sector." Folk medicine is usually a mixture of "sacred and
secular nature." However, the demarcation line is not clear
in practice because the two commonly overlap. Kleinman points
out that "the mundane secular forms of healing: herbalism,
traditional surgical and manipulative treatments, special
systems of exercise, and symbolic non-sacred healing," have
been neglected in anthropological research fields because the
early anthropologist's study interests originated from
folk religion (Kleinman 1980:59).

The structural components of health care systems, the
popular sector professional sector, and folk sector, interact

because patients move among the three sectors (Kleinman 1980:
59-60). The aims of the concept of the health care system for
a cross-cultural comparative study are to interpret similarities and differences of health care systems. The clinical
workings of the different sectors vary from one another.
Kleinman states: "Popular, professional, and folk cultures
and their subcultural components shape the illness and therapeutic experiences in distinct ways." If one leaves a sector
and enters a different sector, he encounters "different sets
of beliefs and values in the cognitive structures of the sector
(Kleinman 1980:52).

HEALTH CARE SYSTEM IN KOREAN SOCIETY

Health and illness beliefs and practices can be explained in a sociocultural context. Caudill states: "Culture and social structure are interrelated with the occurrence of disease
and its treatment. This is true for both major and minor illnesses, and for the attitudes, beliefs and behaviors that make
up the everyday care of the body" (Caudill 1976:159). Hessler
et al.(1978:362) have a similar view as that of Caudill that
the social structure of ethnic groups is related in a complex
fashion to individual medical responses. The value orientation
of a cultural group helps to determine how health and illness
are defined and what beliefs the group holds concerning health
and illness, and what health actions they pursue.

Korean health and illness behavior has been influenced

by Confucianism, Taoism, Buddhism, and shamanism. Chinese
medicine has strongly affected medical institutions in Korea
(Leslie 1976a: 1-12 and Spector 1979:211). Chinese traditional
medicine teaches that health is a state of spiritual and physical harmony with nature. This concept is rooted in Confucianism
(Creel 1953:142-143). Porkert (1976:63-68) attributes differences between Chinese and modern scientific medicine to a conceptual system concerned with the functional attributes of an
organic whole. Thus, classical Chinese medicine regards most
diseases to be caused by disharmony in the system of correspondences that extends from the cosmos to man, while Western
medicine regards most diseases in terms of the organ-specific
lesions they produce. Chinese medicine is based on principles
of imbalance in the body's Ŭm and Yang in the systemic correspondences of the Five Evolutive Phases or Five Elements--Wood,
Fire, Earth, Metal, Water, and blockage of the balanced circulation of Ki (Ch'i),[8] vital energy (Kleinman 1980:264-265).

The characteristic of Chinese medical practice is
almost totally aimed at reestablishing balances that are lost
within the body when illness occurs. Disrupted harmonies are
regarded as the sole cause of diseases (Spector 1979:216).
The human body was considered to be a reproduction of the
cosmos. A state of health was simply the reflection of a state
of general harmony obtained from separate virtues while illness
was the sign of a disturbance of this harmony (Gernet 1962:168).

---

[8]The romanized form of vital energy is Ki in Korean and
Ch'i in Chinese.

Illness also had its origin in an excess of the seven senti-
ments--joy, anger, sadness, fear, love, hate, and desire
(Gernet 1962:168). The typical treatments in Chinese medicine
are medicaments, acupuncture, and moxa burn which are also
practiced in Korea.

Next to Confucianism, the important stream in Chinese
thought is Taoism, which was also influential in Korea. "The
one who knows does not speak, and the one who speaks does not
know. Do nothing and nothing will be not done," --that is,
everything will be spontaneously achieved. If left to itself,
the universe proceeds smoothly according to its own harnomies.
Man's efforts to change or improve nature, only destroys
these harmonies and produces chaos (Reischauer and Fairbank
1960:74).

The Taoist search for elixirs probably led to the
experimental eating of all kinds of organic and inorganic
substances. Among the Taoistic beliefs was the one that eating
food out of "a bowl made of gold which was transformed from
mercury," would promote longevity (Cha 1978:76). Gradually
these Taoistic practices evolved into the general hygiene
system that is still popular in China. Many Chinese still believe that through carefully regulated breathing and quiet
concentration they can prevent disease and delay aging
(Schafer 1967). In Korea, some people do abdominal breathing
exercise, putting a magnet on a body part to promote health
and ultimately longevity (Kim 1983). These practices originated
from Taoism.

Buddhism introduced to China another conception of
man and nature different from the cosmic theory just discussed. These theories are part of the traditional medical belief
system in Korea. According to Buddhism, man is part of natural
order governed by law. If he complies with this law, he works
out his fate in this life and dies a fulfilled individual. But,
if he acts unnaturally, he activates principles inherent in the
law of nature which cause him to be reborn. The Buddhist theory
of rebirth affects ideas about health and sickness. Some souls
are antipathetic to their mothers or fathers because of some
bad relationship in a former life (Topley 1976:250-252).

Shamanism is another religion in Korea which is embedded in Korean people's lives. Shamanism is the oldest indigenous system of religion in Korea. Yet, according to some
sources, it continues to be the strongest in Korea today
(Rader 1977:45-47). This indigenous culture of the Korean
people was part of the prevailing one in Siberia and Northeast
Asia. The root of this culture was shamanism, the earliest
known religion in Korea. Shamanism was characterized by the
animistic form of worship common to all tribes of the region.
Korean shamanism includes "the worship of thousands of spirits
and demons. They may be spirits of the earth, spirits of the
air, spirits of the water, spirits of the hills, spirits of
the living and of the dead, spirits of the rocks, trees,
mountains and streams." All these play an important part in the
Korean's animistic orientation (Rader 1977:49). Man's misfortunes are considered to result from an improper relationship

with the spirits. Some spirits, especially those of a person
who died away from home or violently, were accorded the ability
to cause serious illness.

Traditional Professional Sector

Korean medicine in the prehistoric period is explained
with a myth. According to Samguk-Yusa, one of the oldest Korean
classics, Hwan-ung Chonwang, the Heavenly King, descended from
atop Taibaik Mountain, opened the Sacred City by the Sacred
Tree accompanied by the Wind-maker, Rain-maker, and Cloud-
maker, and governed 360 affairs of the human world of which 5
major affairs, including life and disease, were the most important. Thus, Hwan-ung Chonwang is called the father of Korean
medicine. About 4300 years ago, the legend of Tan-gun, the
mythical ancestor of the Koreans describes a story in which
his mother was incarnated from a bear. After praying to the
Heavenly King, the bear received a bunch of mugwort and garlic
from him. The bear was transformed into a woman and conceived
Tan-gun (Cha 1978:75, Kim n.d.:6, and Rogers 1962:145). Mugwort and garlic have thus been used as medicinal herbs since
ancient times.

Huang-ti Su-wen, The Yellow Emperor's Plain Questions
(ca. 50 B.C.) writes "stone needle was originated from the
East." The East in the old Chinese writings refers to Korea.
The stone needles were used as surgical tools and acupuncture
needles. In the old Chosun Period B.C. 2333 for 2000 years),
Koreans believed in the existence of soul and body. The soul

was believed immortal. Causes of disease were dirty poisons and spirit invasions. Koreans cleaned themselves well to prevent disease and boiled the water for the same reason (Kim n.d.:7).

Three kingdoms were established: in the southeast of the Korean peninsula, Silla (57 B.C. to 935 A.D.), Koguryo (37 B.C. to 668 A.D.) in the north including Southern Manchuria, and Paekche (18 .B.C. to 660 A.D.) in the southwest. During this three kingdom period, Korean medicine was gradually influenced by Chinese medicine of the Han dynasty (204 B.C. to 260 A.D.). Korean medicine influenced by Chinese medicine is called Hanyak (Han refers to Han Dynasty and Yak means medicine in Korean.) (Cha 1978:76).

The origins of Chinese medicine go back to the legendary culture heroes of antiquity in a mythical age who are believed to have given to the inhabitants of the Yellow River basin the fundamentals of Chinese civilization. Medicine was among their gifts, for to Shen-nung is attributed the first pharmacopoeia (traditional dates 3737-2697 B.C.). As the founder of agriculture, he tasted hundreds of herbs to find which were beneficial for the people's illnesses and recorded his findings in the Pen-ts'ao, or Herbal. His successor, Huang-ti, the "Yellow Emperor," contributed a complete treatise on the principles of health and medicine, the Huang-ti Nei-ching, The Yellow Emperor's Classic of Internal Medicine, which became the main text of Chinese medicine (Croizier 1968:13-14).

In the beginning, Chinese medicine was related to magic and supernatural beliefs. As late as Confucius' time

(600 B.C.) doctors and shamans were classified together as healers. The etymology of the chracter for medicine, or doctor 醫 , shows the shamanistic origins of the healing profession. Later, the character for shaman or priest Wu 巫 , was replaced by the character for wine, Chiu 酉 , as the application of drugs and medicine came to predominate over charms and incantations in the treatment of illness. By the late Chou dynasty (700-200 B.C.) secular scientific medicine was separated from the sacred, supernatural tradition and a class of secular physicians emerged clearly distinct from priests or sorcerers. During the Han dynasty (204 B.C. to 260 A.D.) a distinct secular medical tradition and profession emerged (Croizier 1968:14-15).

The signs of illness and symptoms of disease in Korean medicine are interpreted and practiced on the basis of the Chinese metaphysical cosmological philosophy--Ŭm-Yang and the Five Elements (Cha 1978:76, Kang 1981:12-29, Kim n.d.:7, Kim and Sich 1977:100, Lyu 1975:2-4, and Sunu 1982:465 and 1983: 435).

Korean traditional doctors work with "concepts and healing techniques that are rooted in the great tradition of Chinese medicine and that are acquired by scientific learning ...." (Kim and Sich 1977:84). However, Chinese medical principles cannot be translated into Western medical concepts and Western medical principles cannot be translated into Chinese medical concepts because of the difference in medical philosophy between the two medical traditions (Croizier 1976:341-355).

The Yellow Emperor's Nei-ching, Classic of Internal
Medicine, takes the form of a dialogue between the Emperor
and his chief minister, Ch'i po. It is comprised of two sec-
tions: the Su-wen, "Plain Questions," and the Ling-shu,
"Mystical Gate." The dialogue addresses the general principles
of health and the human body. It includes also, specific
therapeutics reflecting the natural world, the universe, and
man's place in it. It lays a firmly rational theoretical basis
for the empirical knowledge of Chinese medicine. Early Han
cosmological logic is considered to be naturalistic and ration-
alistic (Croizier 1968:16 and Palos 1971:5). The Yellow Emper-
or's Nei-ching became the fundamental textbook for traditional
Korean physicians and medical students.

The central concept of Chinese cosmology has been the
dual forces of Ŭm and Yang, whose continuous interaction lies
behind all natural phenomena, including the functioning of the
human body (Croizier 1968:17). Man cannot therefore be divorced
from Nature; he forms an organic part of it and is closely linked to the universe (Croizier 1968:18-19). Thus, nature, as a
macrocosm, and man, as a microcosm are both ruled by Ŭm and Yang
forces (Creel 1954:142-143 and Palos 1971:24). Microcosm-macro-
cosm relationships and balance or harmony appear to be the
most central concept of Chinese medicine (Agren 1975 and Bennett
1978). Yang signifies not only the apparent, "active, excited,
external, upward, forward, aggressive, volatile, hard, bright,
hot, but also the abstract and functional. "In contrast, Ŭm
signifies not only the "passive, inhibited, unclear, inward,

downward, retrogressive, cold, dark, soft, unaggressive, but also the material and concrete" (Lin 1980:97). The theory of Ŭm and Yang describes anatomico-physiological relations (Lin 1980:97).

Chinese medicine divides the internal organs into two large groups: the storage (passive) and working (active). In terms of the Ŭm and Yang principle, Ochang, the five storage organs are called Ŭm organs and Yukbu, the six organs are Yang organs. Ŭm organs are the lungs, the spleen, the heart, the kidneys, and the liver. The Yang organs are the stomach, the small intestine, gall bladder, triple warmer, large intestine, and urinary bladder. The Ŭm organ called controller of the heart is a functional cycle of the peripheral part of the blood circulation. The Yang organ called triple warmer is the functional cycle which controls the chemical environment of the organism, comprised of the interaction of respiration, digestion, and the urogenital system (Palos 1971:42-43).

Huang-ti Nei-ching (The Yellow Emperor's Classic of Internal Medicine) explains how maintenance of the proper balance of Ŭm and Yang within the body is essential for good health. The range of the ways of obtaining this harmony is from proper conduct and peace of mind to dietary rules and acupuncture. This principle of harmony, which views illness as essentially due to its interference through external, internal, physical, emotional causes, has remained central to all of Chinese medicine (Croizier 1968:17 and Gallin 1978:174). according to Croizier (1968:17), "Behind it all lies a stress on main-

taining balance or harmony, a concept central to the social
and natural philosophy of the emerging bureaucratic-gentry
society."

In addition to the concept of Ŭm and Yang, Five Elements about the composition and dynamic function are called
Ohang. The concept originated from astronomical observation
and from the composition of the inorganic world, i.e., Metal,
Wood, Water, Fire, and Earth. Thus, its macrocosm-microcosm
correspondence is evident when it is applied to human beings
and to medicine. The simple rules of sequential facilitation
and inhibition result in an intricate system of interdependence and mutual regulation. The doctrine of the Five Elements
provided deep roots from which sprang basic Chinese medical
concepts and terminology used in relation to diagnosis and
treatment of disease (Lin 1980:97-100, Palos 1971:31-33, and
Quinn 1973:68).

These elements can exist in a helpful relationship to
each other or they can work against one another. The interplay of these five forces is illustrated in the chart of a
pentagonal cycle as shown in Figure 1 with the elements succeeding each other in a clockwise rotation as represented
by the outer lines. This is the "creative cycle for each
element succeeding it, as the mother engenders her son." The
inner dotted lines in the form of a star represent the de-
structive cycle. These relationships may be explained by the
fact that "wood burns to create a fire; the ashes left behind from the burned wood create earth; from which would

nourish and create wood." Likewise, the structure of the de-
structive cycle is developed from similar reasoning. Thus,
"Wood destroys earth by covering it; earth destroys water by
damming it; water destroys fire by extinguishing it; metal
destroys wood by cutting it" (Quinn 1973:67).

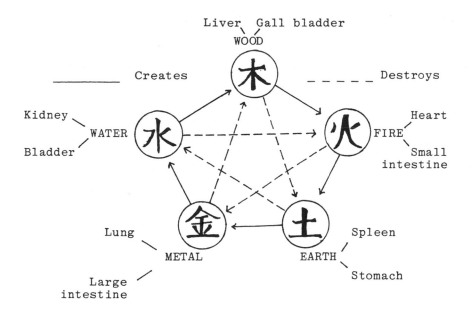

Fig. 1. Five Element Pentagonal Cycle

(Quinn 1973:68)

The relationships among <u>Um-Yang</u> force, Five Evolutive
phases, and internal organs are as follow:

Fire element: Ŭm--heart   <u>Yang</u>--small intestine
Earth element: Ūm--spleen   <u>Yang</u>--stomach
Metal element: Ūm--lungs   <u>Yang</u>--large intestine

```
Water element:    Ŭm--Kidneys    Yang--bladder
Wood element:     Ŭm--liver      Yang--gall bladder
```

D. Choi states that each of these Five Elements corresponds to a season. To remain true to the number five, an extra
season, late summer, was added: wood belongs to spring, fire
belongs to summer; earth belongs to late summer; metal belongs
to autumn; and water belongs to winter. These concordances are
expanded to include points of the compass, flavours, odors,
climates, planets, musical notes, grains, animals and behavior,
as well as the physical organs. According to D. Choi, once a
therapist becomes familiar with the system and the linked
expansion of the concordances, they play a vital part in the
theory of both diagnosis and treatment. For example, in the
concordances of wood, "wood equals the east, which equals the
emotion anger, which equals the action of shouting, which
equals the organ the liver, which equals its pair-organ the
gall-bladder." D. Choi states that "one of the first signs
of liver or gall bladder trouble is a choleric disposition
and a slightly greenish tinge to the complexion"(Choi, n.d.:
3-4).

It was observed that Ŭm-Yang pairs belonging to the
same element were often interrelated. If the one organ was in
a condition of hyperfunction, it could mean a functional weakness on the part of the corresponding organ. In order for
harmony to be achieved it would be necessary to stimulate the
Lo or passage point which exercises an equalizing function
between the two organs. If, for example, the activity of the
gall bladder is weak while the function of the liver is too

strong, then the Lo point of the liver has to be stimulated
in order to establish balance. If the opposite were the case,
then the passage point of the gall bladder would have to be
treated (Palos 1971:48).

Another important aspect of the system of macro-micro-
cosm correspondences is the Ching-lo (meridian) system and the
circulation of Ki (vital energy) and its myriad variants. Ki
is the vital energy for all parts of the body. It has its main
origin from the stomach which grinds food and transforms them
into an energy. When this energy is combined with the air from
the lungs, Ki is formed. Ki is circulated sequentially via all
the meridian tracts to provide nourishment and vitality for all
parts of the body. Blood is viewed as mainly containing "con-
structive energy" while Ki is viewed as containing more "de-
fensive energy." Since Ki is so important in the maintenance
of all vital functions, it is also is virtually irreplaceable.
Any loss of Ki, or obstruction of its circulation is considered
to have grave consequences. The manifested symptoms of dysfunctions of Ki are recognized according to the energy circulation system (Lin 1980:100-101).

D. Choi explains the interrelationship among Ŭm and
Yang, Ki, vital energy, and meridians in the body:

> The meridians act as channels for universal or divine
> energy. They are the interconnections or Ŭm and Yang, the
> interaction of which produces vital or life energy. They
> are like eletrical conductors, channeling the universal
> energy received, throughout the body. When this energy is
> travelling freely along the meridians, maintaining the
> correct balance between Ŭm and Yang, the body will be
> strong and healthy and in harmony with the greater uni-
> verse. When the energy flow is blocked by an imbalance
> of Ŭm and Yang, and becomes weak or erratic, the body

will experience pain, illness and disease. And, as all
organs within the body are connected, illness in one area
causes corresponding imbalance and sickness throughout
the whole system. In fact, the principle of the flow of
energy along the meridians can be likened to a stream
bed: if the water in the stream can flow without obstruction, it will remain clear and pure and be capable of
supporting life. If, however, it is blocked, or banked,
the water will become sluggish and stagnant (Choi, n.d.:
4).

Confucianism brought the concept of balance. The Ŭm, female

nature, and Yang, male nature, are contained within the Ki,

the energy of life and the basic principle of the entire uni-

verse. They create all matter and its changes. The Ki is the

beginning and the end, and death (Creel 1954:142-143).

The following are some examples of how these princi-

ples are applied in the treatment process of common illnesses.

Below are excerpts from a comprehensive manual of Chinese med-

cine issued by the New Medical College of Kiangsu in 1972.

These excerpts were quoted from Chinese Civilization and So-

ciety: A Sourcebook edited by P. Ebrey in 1981. Here, all

diseases are analyzed according to the theory of Ŭm (Yin)[9]

and Yang, and Ki (Ch'i), vital energy (Ebrey 1981:404-406).

These are followed by a discussion from the traditional Korean

medical tradition. The etiology and pathophysiology of hyper-

tension is as follows:

> The underlying cause of this disease is the over-abun-
> dance of Yang or the over-depletion of Yin. The factors
> leading to the occurrence of the diseases are extended
> periods of tension and strong emotional stimuli such as
> worry and anger, for these can lead to the imbalance of
> Yin and Yang of the liver and the kidneys' Yin weakens.

---

[9]Ŭm and Yin have the same meaning but they are romanized differently: Ŭm in Korean and Yin in Chinese.

This is reflected in the symptoms showing repletion in
the external and exhaustion in the internal. The excess
of the Yang in the body, when accompanied by emotional
stimuli, strengthens the Ch'i in the heart and the liver,
which in turn causes the over-exuberance of the Yang. As
a result, fire and wind are disturbed and the symptoms of
'wind Yang attacking upward' appear. If the fire turns
saliva into phlegm, then symptoms of 'phlegm fire burning
inward' will appear. When the over-exuberance of Yang continues for a long time, the Yin fluid will be depleted.
Old patients and ones with weak liver and kidneys will
easily have the rising of exhausted Yang or even exhaustion of both Yin and Yang.
  If the disease is allowed to last for a long time, or
if there is a sudden development for the worse so that
the wind Yang carries phlegm through the meridians and
even attacks the brain, then dangerous consequences such
as paralysis and unconsciousness may result. It is also
possible to have the complication of heart failure resulting from the total exhaustion of the heart and kidneys,
which causes the circulation of Ch'i and blood to fail
(Ebrey 1981:404-405).

Diagnosis and cure of high blood pressure in traditional

Chinese medical principles are as follows:

  To cure this disease, it is necessary to differentiate
between the symptoms of repletion and depletion. The former usually results from wind Yang and phlegm fire, and
dissolving the phlegm. The latter should be further dif-
ferentiated into Yin and Yang symptoms. One should nourish
the liver and the kidneys when their Yin is depleted. If
the case is complicated by the exhaustion of the Yin of the
heart, then one should nurture the heart. If the exhaustion of Yin is extended to Yang, Yang should also be
remedied. It often happens that the symptoms of repletion
and depletion occur at the same time, so one has to take
both into consideration when treating the patient. For
example, in a case of depleted Yin and repleted Yang,
the symptoms are headache, dizziness, blurred vision,
flushing easily when engaged in physical activity or
when excited emotionally, thirst, loss of weight, backache, weak legs, involuntary ejaculation, reddened tongue,
and thin and rapid pulse (Ebrey 1981:404-405).

  Ebrey states that another common disease, diabetes

was   reported   in China earlier than any other country in

the world. It was treated in the Yellow Emperor's Classic of

Internal Medicine, and there are detailed records of continuous

discussions about its symptoms and complications in later
periods. In Chinese medicine diabetes belongs to the category
of draining diseases (Ebrey 1981:405). Etiology and pathophysiology of diabetes in Chinese medicine are as follows:

> This disease is closely connected with weakness of the
> kidneys and insufficiency of Yin. The immediate causes for
> its occurrence include intemperance in eating and drinking
> and excessive intake of fried, greasy food; blockage in
> the middle heater; malfunction of the spleen and the stom-
> ach; heat and unrest, injuring the Yin fluid; failure to
> nourish the lungs and kidneys. There are two major courses
> of development of this disease, the exhaustion of Yin and
> heat-unrest, and one can arise from the other. When heat
> burns the lungs, there is excessive intake of fluid; when
> heat fills the spleen and the stomach, there is excessive
> eating of food; when there is depleted fire in the kidneys,
> urine becomes voluminous.
> If the disease is allowed to become prolonged, the
> exhaustion of Yin often leads to the exhaustion of Yang
> and of Ch'i. In late stages there may even appear symp-
> toms of injured Yang in the kidneys. In other cases
> even the early stages show of weakened Ch'i.
> A patient who remains uncured for a long time may
> develop complications such as tuberculosis, ulcers, and
> blindness as a result of extreme Yin exhaustion and heat-
> unrest. When the Yin fluid is reduced excessively and the
> Yang becomes unrestrained, there may appear symptoms of
> ketone acidosis, irritability, thirst, sunken eyes, red-
> dened lips, dried tongue, headache, and hyperventilation.
> In the end the patient may, because of total exhaustion
> of both Yin and Yang, lapse into a coma, his limbs turn-
> ing cold and his blood pressure dropping (Ebrey 1981:406).

The treatment approach is cultivating the Ŭm fluid,
quenching the heat, and tempering unrest. For prolonged cases
in which the injury of Ŭm extends to Yang, one should mend the
Yang of the kidneys by warm medications (Ebrey 1981:406).

In Asian medicine, etiology is often related to an im-
balanced state of social conduct and the effort to keep oneself in harmony internally and externally. The Chinese understanding of human physiology and anatomy is set up in a holistic
framework. It emphasizes the functional interrelationships

among major working and storaging organs of the body. The
concept of holism in East Asian medicine is that of considering all the parts of the body to be interrelated and influencing one another in the environmental, social, and physiological domain (Lock 1980:29, 34, and 217).

The principles of Ŭm-Yang and Five Evolutive Phases--
Fire, Earth, Metal, Water, and Wood--are essentials of traditional Korean professional medicine as they are in Chinese
medicine (Kim n.d.; 7-8). Sunu, a traditional Korean professional physician, presents etiology and pathophysiology of
hypertension and diabetes in terms of Ŭm-Yang and the Five
Elements in his article "Modern Diseases are also Cured by
Hanbang" (Sunu 1982:452-461). The immutable course of nature
is believed to act through two opposing and unifying forces;
Ŭm and Yang. In a normal person, the two opposing forces are
in balance and assist the vital energy. A deficiency or excess of vital energy in the circulation causes an imbalance
of the two forces and thus results in disease. Pathologic
symptoms are regarded as manifestations of the absence of
inner vital life (Bonica 1974: 1544).

The causes of illness in traditional Korean medicine
are similar to those in Chinese medicine (Kim n.d.:10 and
Lyu 1975:2-4). During the Unified Silla Period (668 A.D. to
935 A.D.) in Korea, causes of illness were dichotomized: endo-
genic pathogenesis and exogenous pathogenesis. The intrinsic
causes of illness are food, dwelling, inharmonious state of Ŭm
and Yang, joy and anger, congenital predispositions and con-

stitional predispositions. The extrinsic causes are environmental conditions such as wind, rain, hot, and cold weather
which are related to seasons and terrain (Kim n.d.:16).

"Wind" refers to any pathogenic force acting swiftly
and therefore potentially more damaging. Symbolically, wind
is implied in many diseases with acute onset or with an unpredictable nature. In combination with cold, hot, dampness,
and dry conditions, wind provides the qualities of their being
actively invading and rapid, and hence makes them even more
dangerous (Lin 1980:96). Heat in the summer is associated with
headaches, fits of sweating, and circulatory disorders. Damp
may cause boils, jaundice, and arthritis. Illnesses caused by
dryness, whether dry heat or dry cold occur mainly in fall
and the associated symptoms are headaches, coughing, vomiting,
sore throat, or pains in the chest. Fire causes inflammation,
redness, and tumors.[10]

Wind, cold, and dampness are believed to cause arthritis:

> When the Ch'i in the body is low, and the resistance
> is weak, then the evil elements of wind, cold, and damp-
> ness will invade the body. They pass through the merid-
> ians, block the joints, and affect the circulation of
> Ch'i and blood; the blockage results in pain and paral-
> ysis (Ebrey 1981:405).

According to the above passage, arthritis belongs to the
paralysis disease category, and is caused directly by seasonal extrinsic factors, wind, cold, and damp, through passages of Ch'i (vital energy). These causes of illnesses are

---

[10]Huang-ti Nei-ching Su-wen. 1959, chapter 42 and
Huang-ti Nei-ching Ling-shu. 1957, chapter 20.

applied in present day medicine according to Sunu (1982:457 and 464-466).

Physicians trained in the traditional school of Chinese medicine diagnose by means of eight principles and the four methods of physical examination. The eight principles are concerned with whether the illness is Ŭm or Yang in character, whether it has external or internal symptoms, whether it is of a cold or warm nature and whether it is due to an increased or reduced function (Palos 1971:93). Parish and Parish state that in traditional Korean medicine, there are three areas in which disease can be found: the hollow organs, the surface of the body, and the areas between the two (1971:163).

The Nei-ching lists four diagnostic methods: visual observation, a history of the illness, auditory symptoms, and taking the pulse. Taking the pulse is the major characteristic diagnostic method (Veith 1973:97-99). Physicians are often able to make a diagnosis from the pulse alone (Bonica 1974:1544 and Croizier 1968:21-22). A disease is diagnosed according to the conditions and symptoms of patient's pulse. According to a Korean medical historian, D. Kim, conditions of the pulse are classified into 24 varieties such as "floating, sunk, smooth, accelerated, vacant, real, diminished, thin, soft, weak, and slow" (Kim n.d.:16).

Traditional Korean medical treatment is based upon the supposition that disease needs to be moved from its location. If a Hanui, a traditional Korean physician, cannot force the disease to the surface, he may try to drive it into a hollow organ, from which it can then expelled (Parish and Parish 1971:164).

Acupuncture called Ch'im in Korean is a unique medical treatment method in Chinese medicine. It is one of the most important methods available. Acupuncture is based upon the supposition that stagnant blood will not flow properly through its normal channels (Parish and Parish 1971:164). K. Sunu, a traditional Korean physician, explains that the stagnant blood results because the Ki is weakened and it is not able to transport blood normally (Sunu 1983:434-435). The acupuncture method involves piercing the skin with sharp silver needles, ranging in length from 3 to 6 inches. After entering the skin, the needles are turned to the left or right to strengthen or weaken Ŭm or Yang (Parish and Parish 1971:164). The purpose of these treatments is to stimulate acupuncture points so that the functioning of internal organs restores balance or harmony. These treatment include what Westerners consider psychological functioning (Veith 1963:139-158).

Moxa is known as D'ŭm in Korea. Moxa uses heat. Several types of D'ŭm are recognized depending upon the way the heat is applied to the body. The most common D'ŭm in Korea is the mugwort fire ball method which is made by crushing a stalk and rolling it into a small ball. Before being placed on the afflicted area, it is set on fire. D'ŭm is designed to cause sweating, which will bring "the disease to the surface, where it will be exposed" (Parish and Parish 1971:164). According to Borman(1966:111), acupuncture and D'ŭm are usually done together: acupuncture is done first followed by D'ŭm.

Breathing exercises were known in ancient China. It was Taoism which, by and large, first used this discipline as a type of therapy. Respiratory exercises were used in this connection in order to attain inner immortality. Respiratory therapy is concerned with internal exercises in contrast to external gymnastic ones. Respiratory therapy includes both movement and rest, both components being essential for the achievement of a state of harmony. Constant relaxation is as bad for the health as constant vigorous exercise (Palos 1971: 126-151). In Korea, a breathing exercise of the lower abdomen called Danchŏn is popular for health promotion and longevity among people (Kim 1983).

The Chinese believed that man's original medical tool was his hand, which he has always used instinctively in order to alleviate pain. Whenever he is struck or injured, he puts his hand to the painful spot in order to protect and heal it. A remedial massage has the advantage of not requiring either medicines or tools other than hands. Massage produces its effect both by movement of the fatty tissue and by mechanical stimulation of the skin receptors. In this way the circulation of the blood can be encouraged in the harmony of Ŭm and Yang. Remedial massage can stimulate muscular metabolism, strengthen weak muscles, and relieve cramps (Palos 1971:152-153). Different forms of massage for adults are thrusting, grasping, pressing, rubbing, rolling, pinching, and tapping (Palos 1971:153-157).

Sugi, finger pressure, is "the Korean refinement of a method" of healing based on natural techniques and philosophic thought which began in China. According to Choi, Sugi is incorporated in the systems of universal balance and harmony as explained by the theory of Ŭm and Yang. Choi defines:

> Sugi is the combination of two words: Su, meaning hand, and Gi [sic], meaning life force or universal energy.... It is the energy which is the universe, or cosmos, and from which all things emanate, including ourselves, our planet and all the things we can find within it, without it, and upon it. Sugi, therefore, means the transference of this universal energy, which is also the basis of the spiritual experience we call love. Without energy there is no love. Without love, there is no harmony. Without harmony there is no health (Choi n.d.:1).

There is a healing method called cupping in Korea. This process has a long tradition in China. The methods of cupping are used in the treatment of colds, rheumatic ailments, abdominal pains, diarrhea, and headaches. The cupping process is as follows: cotton wool, medicinal herbs, or paper are soaked in oil or alcohol and then burned in the cupping glass so as to warm the air inside it. When the adequate degree of temperature is obtained, the burning material is removed from the glass. Then, the cupping glass is placed, upside down, on the part of the body to be treated. It is left there some 10 to 15 minutes and is then tipped over on one side and removed. Because air contracts on cooling, this cupping process exerts a strong suction force on the skin. Sometimes, a small blister is produced which fills with blood. In the past an animal horn was used and it was later replaced by a cupping glass. Bamboo tubes were also used. Nowadays a glass cup is commonly used (Palos 1971:171-173).

The _Hanyak_ treatment, traditional Korean medicaments, is well over four thousand years old. It was modified by some Korean innovations (Borman 1966:103). The Chinese have used medical herbs from the earliest times in Chinese history. Shennung(traditional dates 3737 B.C. to 2697 B.C.), who is believed to be the father of Chinese medicine, taught men the use of the plough and of the herbs. The earliest surviving pharmacopoeia, attributed to Shen-nung contains 365 names and descriptions of medicines (The number corresponds to the days of a year. This is part of the Han system of numerical concordances). This was compiled about the first century B.C (Croizier 1968:19-20). About two thirds of these medicines are of vegetable origin. Li Shih-chen, the noted Chinese pharmacologist who lived towards the end of the 16th century listed medicaments in his pharmacopoeia, which included material from earlier periods together with his own. Many of the drugs have proved to be highly effective today, because the medicaments in his pharmacopoeia were developed through centuries of empirical research (Croizier 1968:20).

Hume noted "almost universal acceptance of the idea that medicaments are potent not only because they produce measurable pharmacological effects, but because they correspond, in some mysterious way...." (1940:124). An example is the famous medicinal root, ginseng, which was thought efficacious because it had the shape of human figure (Croizier 1968: 20-21). The Chinese apparently obtained and learned about medicinal materials indigenous to Korea. Ginseng was used to promote longevity (Cha 1978:76). Ginseng is believed to have

tonic and antifatigue effects, a possible cancer prevention

function, and efficacy of quieting the spirit, improving men-

tal efficiency and working capacity, regulating blood pressure,

controlling cholesterol, and atherosclerosis, an antidiabetic

effect, improvement or cure for indigestion, and a remarkable

hematinic effect (Hou 1978:171-192).

Since the Chinese believed that elderly people tend

to become physically unfit, mentally impaired and that they

are prone to more diseases than the young, the efficiency of

the individual organs and the body as a whole lessens with

age. Ginseng is believed to be and excellent remedy of tonifi-

cation for the aging and the aged (Hou 1978:209).

Traditional Chinese medicine divides medicaments into

three main groups: those of vegetable, of animal, and of miner-

al origins. The first of these groups is by far the largest.

The roots, blossoms, leaves, seeds, and fruits of herbs are

used. The drying of medicinal herbs is common (Palos 1971:181

-182).The main characteristic method of preparing medicine is

in a boiled broth made from natural herbal ingredients. When

this Chinese herbal medicine is prescribed all the principles

of Ŭm-Yang, Ki, and Hot and Cold are applied (Croizier 1968:21).

Surgical techniques were not developed as medical

treatment in traditional Chinese medicine. This neglect of

practical anatomy has often been attributed to the Confucian

"abhorrence of dissection as a gross violation of filial piety."

The Classic of Filial Piety states "The body, hair, and skin

are all received by the parents; not to resume to injure
them is the beginning of filial piety." [11] Dissection has
apparently also been forbidden in traditional Korean medicine
(Parish and Parish 1971:163). Traditional Chinese medicine
has consistently relied upon an "inductive and synthetic"
method; consequently, it did not develop any known anatomy,
and no histology, or biochemistry has evolved (Porkert 1976:
76). The main goal in Confucianism is not to change society
radically in order to improve it, but to continue to follow
the way of life practiced by one's ancestors. All emphasis
is laid on imitating the past, not on constructing the future.
Above all, a man's actions must exemplify filial piety
(Brandt 1971:173). Due to this emphasis, veneration of ancestors, became an integral part of the religion. A body cannot
be touched after death except by the family, and a postmortem
examination is out of the question. Also, proper burial rites
must be observed. Even today in Korea, many patients are removed from the hospital shortly before death so that they can
die at home and their spirits remain there. The ancestor's
spirits are believed to help the descendants (Maloney 1956:
383-384).

The traditional Korean medical system influenced
Japan during the three kingdom periods (Silla, Koguryo, and
Paekche from 57 B.C. to 935 A.D.). The cultural exchange between Korea and Japan is documented in the oldest Japanese
history book called Nihonshoki (Cha 1978:76). In 414 A.D. a

---

[11]Hyo-kyung (Classic of Filial Piety). Chapter 1.

Japanese king requested that Silla send him a physician. Kim Mu became the pioneer physician of Japanese medicine. Many Korean Buddhist priests went to Japan and served as physicians. Korean medicine had a strong influence upon Japanese medicine (Parish and Parish 1971:165).

During the Koryo Dynasty (918-1392), different medicinal materials reached Koryo from all over the world. Since this was a Buddhist Kingdom, Indian medical influence was strong. Chinese translations of Indian medical books of the Ayurveda school were brought into Korea (Cha 1978:77).

In the medieval period (918-1392), signs of independence and the originality of Korean medicine began to emerge. Korean medical books included some prescriptions based on the experiences of Koreans, in addition to quotations from various Chinese books of the Sung Dynasty (960-1279). In 1226, Jongjun Choi wrote two volume of medical books called Shinjip Oeui Chwalyo Bang. In the mean time, King Kojong's Library Office compiled a three volume treatise called Hyangyak Kukupang on domestic drug prescriptions. This is the oldest medical book written by Koreans and remaining today. In the book the emphasis was on the use of local Korean medicinal resources rather than those imported from China or other places (Cha 1978:78).

In 1610 after 13 years of intensive work, J. Ho wrote a medical book called Dong-eui Bogam, Treasury Book of Eastern Medicine. This book consists of five parts: (1) Internal, (2) External (trauma, eye, nose, ear, skin, and genitourinary diseases), (3) Miscellaneous (pathology, diagnosis, palliative

treatment, emergency treatment, epidemic diseases, obstetrics
and gynecology, and pediatrics), (4) Materia Medica (Clinical
Pharmacology), and (5) Acupuncture-Moxa. In this work, metic-
ulous references were made to one of more than eighty-six medical classics of China and Korea. Although the text was written in the classical Chinese style, Hangul (Korean alphabet)
was added to the name of many local Korean herbs. Dong-eui
Bogam has been printed eighteen times in Korea, China, and
Japan. Since its publication in 1610, it has replaced almost
all the previously existing books on medicine throughout
Korea, China, and Japan (Cha 1978:79-81 and Griffis 1883:46).

With regard to medicine was not introduced into Korea until
1884 due to Korea's "closed door policy" toward foreign influences. Western medicine was accepted in the late nineteenth
century when a medical missionary, Horace B. Allen saved the
life of prime minister Min who had been stabbed and wounded
critically (Cha 1978:82-83 and Parish and Parish 1971:166).

With regard to medicine in the present period in
Korea, according to Maloney, in the 1950s the majority of
the people were not cared for by professional physicians.
This author believed that they were treated mostly by practitioners of traditional Korean medicine. In 1951, the Ministry
of Education approved the establishment of the College of
Oriental Medicine. That same year the National Assembly re-
established the licensure of such practitioners previously
removed by the United States military government (Maloney
1956:383). Kyong Hui University in Seoul has programs to

prepare practitioners of traditional medicine for a national

qualifying examination. A doctoral study program of tradition-

al Korean medicine was also approved in 1975. Two more univer-

sities established a traditional Korean medical program: one

in 1973 and the other in 1978 (Yun and Kim 1980:36).

There are two kinds of traditional professional med-

ical college graduates and those who acquired their knowledge

and skill by studying the medical classics and by an apprentice-

ship of 2-5 years. According to Kim and Sich, many of the tra-

ditional Korean doctors are highly educated (1973:101).

According to Kim and Sich, traditional Korean physi-

cians are not only well established in traditional Korean

culture, but also have participated to a considerable degree

in the medical modernization process. Kim and Sich put it:

> Great efforts are invested by this profession to make
> it comparable to Western medicine as the establishment
> of university faculties for Eastern medicine shows. A
> whole gamut [Sic] of research is invested into the meth-
> od of function of traditional healing techniques and
> their effectiveness as well as into the development of
> technology for pulse and meridian point measuring, etc.
> In addition, the practicing traditional doctors are using
> many Western drugs and techniques. Many young people be-
> come interested in studying traditional medicine, in do-
> ing comparative research and in establishing the role of
> traditional medicine as a dignified profession (1973:100).

In 1975, there were 2,379 Hanyak clinics, about 30% of

whole medical and health facilities, and in 1978, 2,821 Hanui,

traditional Korean medical physicians (Yoo 1979:197).

Hanbang, traditional Korean medicine, is part of a sub-

sector of the professional sector of Korean health care systems.

In their study of health and illness behavior Kim and Sich

showed that this behavior is positively related to the Korean

way of life, world view, customs and beliefs.[12] Their respondents had used healing techniques of the traditional Korean
physician for musculo-skeletal pain, gastrointestinal trouble,
common cold and related conditions, general weaknesses, strains,
obstetric and gynecological conditions, cardiovascular conditions, snake bites, tuberculosis, and meningitis. They believe
that traditional healing was more effective than biomedical
treatments. Kim and Sich stated that these results show the
importance of traditional Korean medicine as a health care
resource. Kim and Sich added that the traditional Korean
physicians have "elements in their practice that the clients
cherish and which they miss" in biomedical service. The
major element is their concern for the ill individual "as
an integrated human being in his self understanding and social
environment" (Kim and Sich 1973:107).

Folk Sector: Therapy by a _Mudang_

D. Kim, a Korean medical historian, states that an
understanding of Korean indigenous medical practice begins
with folk medicine (Kim n.d.: 4). Shamanism has strongly
influenced Korean medical treatment. Shamanism originated
among the Tungus, a Ural-Altaic or Mongolian tribe in Siberia.
The people believe that the _Mudang_ is the intermediary between
them and the spirits who bring about illness and cure (Kim

---

[12]Kim and Sich obtained a stratified random sample
251 households out of 1,275 households in a Korean island
village near Seoul in 1973 for their study about traditional

1967:193).

Disease was believed to be due to the act of a spirit or its invasion into the human body and hence the sick were cured by the exorcism of the spirit through a ritual perform- ed by the Mudang (Kim n.d.: 4). The Mudang, a mediator between the world of man and the spirits, believes in a universe where the inanimate as well as the animate objects are endowed with spirits (Chang 1973:667). Thus, to relieve man's distress or cure illness, a Mudang is called in to perform a ritual called Gut or to have Chŏm, divination and fortune-telling, through which the relationships are harmonized between man and spirit.

Mudangs in Korea are almost exclusively consulted by women. In general, Korean men are not as psychologically re- pressed as Korean women. They have more socially acceptable outlets to express their feelings and thoughts such as going to a Sulchip (a place where men drink and meet informally with intimate friends after work). The Mudang is trusted and told the details of the family and related matters by Korean women. She often suggests that clients make changes or do cer- tain rituals to bring harmony in the household (Harvey 1976: 190). Most of the time, a husband does not approve of a wife's visit to a Mudang. Most Korean men, who adhere to Confucian principles, do not consider Mudang practice as serious. The wife tends to conceal this visit to avoid conflict with her

---

Korean medicine and illness behavior. Local housewives as re- search assistants, interviewed and observed respondents of each household. The respondents were the wives in households since housewives are usually the ones who care for the sick (Kim and Sich 1973).

husband (Harvey 1976:190). Clients come from all levels of
society, and sometimes with their friends and/or relatives
who accompany them. Clients do not go to see a Mudang in their
own neighborhood; they suspect that such a Mudang may use
personal knowledge of clients in treatment (Harvey 1976:191).
While waiting for their turn, clients behave as though they
were at an informal social gathering, participating in the
Chŏm in progress with comments. The group reaction helps to
support the client in counseling as a form of awareness
(Harvey 1976:191).

A Mudang's main ceremony for healing is called Gut.
When she wants to ask a spirit to diagnose a disease, a
Mudang lets a client hold a stick 3 to 4 feet long decorated
with straw ropes and paper strips. The Mudang prays to the
spirit before the stick. According to Kim the prayer might go
like this:

> Oh, my North Mountain Spirit! Please come to Miss
> Kim, 29 years old, born on the 7th of September, in the
> year of the horse. Please help her understand what is the
> cause of the disease, how to treat the disease and how
> she can get well again soon. We are humble, miserable,
> worthless; come and help us. We do not know how to treat
> the disease (Kim 1967:194).

While she is praying, the Mudang sings and dances with a big
fan in her right hand and a bundle of small bells in her left
hand. She has helpers to beat drums. When she is dancing she
wears specially made colorful Mudang's garments (Kim 1967:194).

When the spirit comes to the stick holder, the stick
and the holder vibrate softly at first, and vigorously after-
ward. If the Mudang recognizes that the spirit has come to the

stick holder, she tries to welcome the spirit heartily, expressing her gratitude in more singing and dancing . The coming
of the spirit to the stick holder means that the holder is in
a trance. When the spirit comes, the stick holder will know
and act like a spirit. The Mudang then asks about the cause,
treatment, and prognosis of the disease. The answers are indicated through movement of the stick. For example, with regard
to the prognosis, if the enchanted stick points up, the patient
will get well soon; if the stick points in the direction of
the horizen, the patient will suffer for a long time; and if
the stick points downward, the patient will die soon (Kim 1967:
195).

The last thing the Mudang must do is to find a therapeutic method by asking the spirit what has to be done to effect
a cure. She might ask "What shall I do to treat the patient?
Shall she serve the spirits with some rice?" If the stick has
no answer, the Mudang asks again, "What shall the patient do?
Shall she worship thee as you tell her to?" Usually in this
case quite a large amount of rice and money will be demanded.
The stick finally answers and tells the Mudang what to do for
the patient to recover (Kim 1967:195).

Kim interprets the Mudang's curing art as a form of
hypnosis. The Mudang uses the form of prayer to her spirit,
but actually she gives suggestions to the stick holder. Her
singing, dancing and praying work as suggestions and cause the
stick holder to go into a trance. Thus, the Mudang acts as a
"hypnotist" (Kim 1967:196).

Mudangs are, on the whole, keenly intuitive and per-
ceptive people who make good use of their knowledge of people
and human problems in helping their clients make the best of
their situations (Harvey 1976:196). In Korea, unlike the majority of psychiatrists or psychologists, a Mudang is usually
socially inferior, but her therapeutic role is recognized.
Therapy is possible without unnecessary restraints and inhibi-
tions. According to Harvey, the Mudang is suitable as a therapist for Korean women who have a communication gap between
different sexes and between different generations, with no
way of ventilation of feelings, and limited opportunities for
diversion. Mudangs are easily accessible to clients. They are
able to meet client's emotional and social needs through empathic approaches of support, reassurance, understanding, providing a comfortable and acceptable atmosphere, assistance to
clients to gain insight into problems, direction, redirection,
confrontation, advice and follow up if necessary, based on
similar value and belief systems.

In general, Koreans have regarded "the recruitment of
a person into the shaman role as an unfortunate act of predestination over which human beings have no control. "As evidence for predestination by supernatural ordination, they
point out the afflictions which defy natural explanations or
conventional remedies." It is believed that spirits possess
those human beings whose soul or heart is already in a weakened state (Harvey 1979:250-251). This state of mind and body of
a woman is called "Shin Byung." Shin Byung, "a culture-bound

depersonalization syndrome, often occurs in the course of a
prolonged psychosomatic illness, psychosis. or psychoneurosis.
The possessed person has a "revelation" through a dream in
which she is persuaded to become "cured" of her ailment. It
is believed that Shin Byung can be cured only through a shamanistic rite and that the called person is obliged to become
a Mudang herself (Rhi 1970:35-46).

The initiation rite marks the transition from that of
afflicted victim to that of a Mudang. "Through the rite, the
possessing spirits are officially invited to descend and enter
into the woman. Thereafter, the relationship between the Mudang
and the possessing spirits is transactional; the Mudang provides the spirits with access to human beings and their affairs
and is in turn relieved of the afflictions which had tortured her
before becoming a   Mudang and which can again trouble her if
she resists her role" (Harvey 1979:251).

Mudangs are not only intimately concerned with the
nursing of the sick in families but also in the raising of
young children. They are mothers and grandmothers. Many of
them are close to or at the age where they, as "mother in law,"
become most respected by young women and the young family. In
other words, they have a profound influence on the socialization of children. This is an indication of the fact that the
shamanistic tradition in rural Korea is far from dying out and
ill probably continue to influence behavior for a long time to
come (Kim and Sich 1977:90). According to Y. Harvey (1979:190
and Rader 1977:45-46), the Mudang practice of divination and

fortune-telling is common in urban areas also.

The following example of spiritual involvement as
etiology and its treatment regimen as prescribed by a Mudang
is presented by Harvey (1976:92-93).

> Although an ardent Christian convert who had forsaken
> ancestor worship, the mother-in-law was now despondent.
> Not only was she ill again but her only son was becoming
> withdrawn, depressed and without appetite. She wanted to
> know if her daughter-in-law as a newcomer was disagree-
> able to the spirits of the household and thus the locus
> of their problem.
> The Mudang's analysis was that the illness was caused
> by an angry and unappeased female ancestral ghost, sup-
> ported by other ancestral ghosts who resented their ne-
> glect. She advised the mother-in-law either to give up
> Christianity, resume the duties to the ancestors and have
> an exorbitant Kut [Sic] to purify the house, or let the
> son and his wife start a separate household and assume the
> duties of ancestral rites which are his responsibility.

This case shows that Mudang as a therapist gives spiritual as
well as practical advice to clients.

Kim and Sich found through their study about traditional healing techniques and illness behavior of rural Korean
people, that 90% of the interviewed housewives believe in the
Mudang's therapeutic ability, and 50% of them had visited a
Mudang. Most of the visits were to cure illnesses and 42% were
satisfied with their services (Kim and Sich 1977:107).

Popular Sector

Kleinman states that popular medical practice in a
health care system is carried out among individuals, family
members, or friends without a specialists' advice (1980:50).
M. Lock says that popular beliefs and practices are passed on
informally from person to person in a close human group (1980:

15). Kleinman also mentioned that popularization may occur when different sectors of health care have contact with the popular health sector (Kleinman 1980:56).

The concept of illness prevention has been important among Koreans. Koreans believed that the causes of illness are related to interferences of evil spirits. In order to remove evil spirits they burn hair and bamboo trees because it is believed that the burning hair odor and bamboo noise will drive away evil spirits (Kim 1981:43). This health notion appears to be adopted from the folk sector as shown in Table 1.

From a supernatural dimension yet directly related to social, moral, and ethical conduct, i.e. filial piety, Koreans believe that happiness and good health will be attained, if they drink the wine which was served at the ancestor worship ceremony. In order to secure health supernaturally and socially, this ritual custom is observed.

A hot spring bath and steam bath are indigenous popular health practices and remedies in Korea. Parish and Parish (1971:166) state "... of all the Yi rulers, King Sejong (1397-1450) showed the most concern for public health. He visited thirty hot springs and requested that his scholars study ways of utilizing the salubrious water." A hot spring bath is well known for skin disease prevention and/or other treatments as shown Table 1. People say that the content of sulphur helps the skin. Some people would say: "It is just good for your body." A warm sand bath is known to bring good health without colds in winter (Kim 1981).

TABLE 1

POPULAR KOREAN HEALTH CARE

Related Sector	Belief or Problem	Practice
I. Popularized folk sector	A. Interference of evil spirits	A. Burn hair and bamboo trees
II. Popularized traditional professional sector	A. Good health is related to ancestors.	A. Share the wine offered in ancestor worship ceremony.
	B. Care, control, regulation, optimum environment	B. Practice good hygiene, adequate sleep, regular quality food intake
	C. Maintenance and promotion of vital energy	C. Ginseng, deer horn or deer blood
	D. Prevention of ascaris	D. High green onion content in daily food intake
III. Indigenous popular sector	A. Sweating is good for health maintenance and promotion	A. Sweat in sudatorium
	B. Hot spring water is good for disease prevention	B. Take hot spring bath
	C. Sweating in warm moist atmosphere provides defensive energy	C. Take warm sand bath in summer

A hot steam sweat bath is an integral part of the Korean popular health care system. For this bath, people stay in a large hot steamy clay oven covering themselves with heavy cotton or straw blankets. Korean people believe that this hot moist bath is good for health maintenance and promotion as shown Table 1. It is especially good for all internal ailments such as hypertension, arthritis, neuralgia. People without particular health problems take this bath for the promotion of internal harmony and better circulation. Near the sudatorium, other treatment measures such as acupuncture, cupping, massage, and moxa are provided. Some people receive one or more treatments after the bath. Koreans value highly hot wet or moist health measures. Some of them take these baths for relief of fatigue, relaxation, or plain joy. Hot spring resorts are very popular for honeymooners.

There are popularized traditional Korean professional medical treatments. When persons feel weak from lack of "vital energy" they cook soup with ginseng and sweet rice in young chicken and drink the broth only, or, eat the rest as well. This way they can restore their essential energy (Kim 1981:57). The common cure-all is ginseng root. It is regarded as the first tonic of the universe. Some people believe that it ought to relieve the ills of man because its shape closely resembles the human body (Hou 1978).

Deer horn is also one of their treasured remedies. This horn is taken in different ways; powder, stew, and wine which is preserved with sliced deer horn. The powder is consummed mixed with ginseng and honey. Fresh warm deer blood is valued as a tonic. A century ago, Griffis (1883:45) quoted what one of the Korean Christian missionaries said about the efficacy

of the horn: "When one has a drink of it, the steepest mountains seem to be a plain, and one can make the tour of the
kingdom without fatigue." Together with ginseng, deer horn is
one of the important medicinals in traditional Korean professional institutions at the present time. The same medicines,
moreover, are used in different sectors, for different purposes and with different reasons. For example, ginseng is used
as a tonic in the popular sector usually, but in traditional
Korean professional sector, it is used to cure specific sicknesses. Another example of a popularized form of treatment is
acupuncture which is performed by a lay person without consultation with a specialist. This healing process takes place
casually as part of everyday living. The participants in the
healing are family members and friends. They themselves diagnose, refer, and treat themselves according to their medical
beliefs (Rutt 1964:74) as shown in Table 2.

Osgood presents some examples of popular medical
practices in Korea. In addition to the biomedical cures, the
people also resort to lay practitioners with special repu-
tations for curative powers. Table 2 shows popular medical
practices generally known to most persons. Castor oil is used
as a laxative procured from the homegrown garden. The flower
and top stem of opium poppies may be boiled and taken for
diarrhea. A live lizard is swallowed for venereal disease.
C. Osgood's explanation for this remedy is that the people
believed a lizard accumulates penicillin from the soil (Osgood
1962:43-44).

In 1972-1973, C. Lee collected data about popular medical practices in the East coast of Kyungbuk province located in the South East coast of Korea. He interviewed and observed informants who were men and women age fifty or older. The most popular medical practices found among them to treat major and minor illnesses and both acute and chronic diseases were as follow: (1) Remedies for common cold are such as bean sprout soup, garlic broth, and hot honey water. These remedies are believed to stimulate perspiration. People believe that perspiration is a necessary process to go through in order to recover from a cold. Soft rice cooked in turnip stew juice is believed to melt away irritable secretions in the respiratory tract; (2) Egg yolk is given daily with a few drops of sesame oil to a person with tuberculosis of the lungs; (3) The urine of a man or a woman is given to a person who suffers from bleeding. Urine is believed to replace lost blood volume; and (4) Soy sauce is used to heal burns (Lee 1974:111-121).

According to Kwon who wrote Kachung Saenghwal Ch'ongram (Reference for Family Life), popular medicine aims to treat minor, major, acute, and chronic conditions. Mental disorders are treated as physical disorders with medical remedies. The most frequently cited examples of popular medicine found in Kwon's compilation (1965:295-338) as shown in Table 2 will be presented according to body systems.

In the gastrointestinal system, for symptoms of stomach spasm which becomes "hardened," pressure is added to the abdomen to relieve pain and warm compresses are applied. Among Koreans, this stomach condition is called Gasumari.

TABLE 2

POPULAR KOREAN MEDICAL PRACTICES

Sector	Condition	Practice
I. Indigenous popular sector	A. Gastrointestinal system	
	1. Stomach spasm (Gasumari)	1. Adding pressure and applying warm compress on abdomen
	2. In digestion from a. most food b. persimmon c. general food d. wine e. summer heat	2. a. castor oil b. soy bean paste c. malt juice d. ginseng broth e. night dewed mother juice
	3. Ascaris	3. Ground garlic every evening
	4. Constipation	4. Castor oil
	5. Diarrhea	5. Boiled juice of flowers and top stems of opium poppies
	B. Respiratory system	
	1. Colds	1. Bean sprout soup, garlic broth, hot honey water
	2. Irritable secretions in respiratory tract	2. Turnip stew juice
	3. Tuberculosis of lungs	3. Raw egg yolk
	C. Cardiovascular and excretory system	Ginseng
	1. High blood pressure	1. Sweating. A thumb size bundle of pine leaves daily

2. Stroke	2. Boiled root of mulberry juice
3. Nephritis	3. Boiled corn water
4. Diabetes	4. Aralia elata water
5. Anemia	5. Fruits, leaves of fig tree, and strawberries
6. Dizziness	6. Broth of cow brain or pancreas
7. Bleeding	7. Human urine

D. Neuromusculo-
skeletal system

1. Arthritis	1. Sweating in sudatorium. Crushed fruit of laurel tree on region
2. Neuralgia	2. Sweating sudatorium A mixture of grated taro and flour is applied on affected area
3. Fatigue	3. Sweating
4. Headache	4. Powder of peony root
5. Combined condition of insomnia, headaches, general malaise, loneliness, and fearfulness	5. Stewed juice of dates and licorice
6. Forgetfulness	6. Root of water lily
7. Insomnia	7. Raw or boiled green onions

E. Genitourinary and
dermatological
systems

1. Venereal disease	1. Eat live lizard
2. General skin diseases	2. Hot spring bath

3. Urticaria	3. Castor oil, trifoliate orange juice
4. Poison ivy	4. Burnt barley powder or raw egg yolk is applied
5. Burn	5. Apply sesame oil with salt

II. Popularized traditional professional medicine

A. General system

  1. Lack of vital energy   1. Ginseng, deer horn, deer blood

B. Digestive system

  1. Indigestion   1. Acupuncture

Kwon indicates that there are different kinds of indigestion. Remedies are different according to kinds of indigestion: malt juice is given for general food indigestion; ginseng broth is for indigestion from wine; night dewed mother wort juice is for indigestion due to summer heat; soy bean paste is for indigestion from persimmon; and castor oil can be taken for any kind of indigestion except for that from persimmon (Kwon 1965:298). Sickness from ascaris is treated by taking a clove of ground garlic every evening.

In the cardiovascular and excretory systems, for high blood pressure, a thumb size bundle of pine leaves is eaten daily and boiled root of mulberry tree juice is given for stroke patients. Nephritis is treated with boiled corn water. Diabetes is treated with boiled aralia elata water. For anemia, fruits and leaves of fig trees and strawberries are prescribed (Kwon 1965:328-329). Broth of cow brain or pancreas is taken for dizziness (Kwon 1965:328-329).

In the neuromusculoskeletal system, for arthritis the crushed fruit of a laurel tree is applied on the affected region. For neuralgia, a mixture of grated taro, ginger, and flour is applied on affected area. For headaches, powder of peony root is taken. Patients with complaints of insomnia, headaches, general malaise, loneliness, and fearfulness are given stewed juice of dates and licorice. For forgetfulness, root of water lily is recommended. Boiled or raw green onions are given for insomnia.

Several remedies are known for skin conditions. For urticaria, castor oil is taken two or three times and then boiled trifoliate orange (poncirus trifoliata) juice is drunk. Burnt barley powder or egg yolk is applied for skin conditions affected by poison ivy. Sesame oil with a pinch of salt is applied to a burned area (Kwon 1965:322-324).

Most of these remedies are prepared at home or shared with neighbors. These remedies are prescribed by family members or friends in the neighborhood. Kwon states that Korean people use popular medicine in the following cases: (1) when no physicians are available in poor farming areas; (2) it is too far to go to a physician's office; and (3) when people are too poor to use biomedical or traditional Korean practioners or facilities (Kwon 1965:290). According to Kwon, popular medicine is used because biomedical care is not affordable or available, although he believes that people generally value biomedical practice more than popular medicine.

Kwon also presents the popularized traditional professional medical view that illness can be prevented and suggests a clean enrironment and good personal health care. In his view, 7-8 hour sleep a day, moderation in smoking and drinking, adequate exercise, a balanced emotional state, a balanced diet, and ecological and environmental considerations of housing such as adequate ventilation, sunlight, and sewer system are important in health maintenance and promotion. He also recommends immunization and early diagnosis (Kwon 1965:291-294). His notion of health care also includes a popularized version of biomedical practice. This dimension of health care is contrasted with that of spiritual world.

Different illness beliefs and practices can compete with each other and create conflicts between generations. The following example shows how a family draws on popular and traditional medicine, professional, and folk practice. A young man who returned home after Western treatment for tuberculosis in a biomedical sanatorium run by Methodist medical missionaries was greeted in the following manner:

> The family assembled to greet him, but there was no warm welcome. They stood around him in a distant circle, eyeing him suspiciously. 'Did they give you snake soup or the blood from a live deer?' demanded Hyung's grandmother turned triumphantly to his father, 'You had better call the Mudang at once to give him needle puncture to let out the evil spirits he must now have inside him from being in that place....' (Hall 1978:402).

THE CULTURAL CONSTRUCTION OF ILLNESS: EXPLANATORY MODELS

Illness is always a cultural construction. In illness, there are the behavioral and social responses to the disease that provide it with meaning and symbols (Kleinman 1980:78). Illness as a physiological, psychosocial, and cultural construction requires interpretation (Clark 1980:3-6 and Kleinman 1980:72-73). According to Kleinman a sick person "makes use of the explanatory accounts available" to him in applying label "in a particular cultural, historical, and health care sector context." A label is applied according to "subjective feelings or objective signs" in a particular sociocultural context so that the label is a "cultural category." The illness label in a culture can be interpreted as "a non-medical label," such as a "moral, cosmological, religious, or economic problem" (Kleinman 1980:76). For example, Hwabyung among Koreans is an illness label which is related to the interrelationships of sociocultural, emotional, physiological, and cosmological domains (See Chapter V, Section Hwabyung.)

Kleinman describes how somatization as a constructed illness behavior can be understood in relation to how sociocultural context influences the emotional physiological process (Kleinman 1980:120-146). Prevalent life strains in certain cultures are related to emotional distress which can affect physiological harmony by interfering with the cosmological harmony in the body system.

In classical and contemporary Chinese thought, the

heart is viewed as "the seat of the emotions" and the liver
with anger. People frequently offer complaints of discomfort
of the chest and abdomen. The terms link emotional states,
physical symptoms with interpersonal relations, and other life
problems (Kleinman 1980:135-136 and Lin 1980:102). Lin emphasizes that "the most psychiatrically relevant aspect of traditional Chinese medicine is its unwillingness to differentiate
between psychological and physiological functions" (Lin 1980:
101). A holistic medical principle is pointed out in terms of the
interrelationship between psychic and somatic functions. As a
consequence, people do not learn to attend to the psychological aspect, so that they acquire little skill in communica-
ting emotional states (Kleinman 1980:174). In societies influenced by Chinese culture such as Korea, people rarely complain of anxiety, depression and other psychological problems.
People influenced by Chinese culture also view mental illness
as a stigmatizing and threatening experience so that psychotherapy is not sactioned (Kleinman 1980:139, Lin 1980:107,
and Kleinman and Lin 1980). Thus, people tend to present more
bodily complaints than psychological or mental illness complaints in expressing emotional distress, depression, or social
problems (Kleinman 1977a:3-10 and 1980:158-159, Kim 1981:58,
Lock 1980:220-221, and Tseng 1975:237-245). In the Korean
family, physical complaints are readily accepted. However,
psychological or mental complaints tend to be ignored or resisted (Kim and Rhi 1976:105).

For example, according to the report of the Clearview

Community Service Center in New York city, quite a number of
Korean clients complain of somatic symptoms such as palpitation, headache, insomnia, and numbness on upper and lower
extremities. These are due to "psychological pressure" from
the language barrier, loneliness, and interpersonal conflict
among Korean immigrants. The author of this report specified
that this phenomenon is unique among Korean immigrants. Both
sexes are affected equally.[13]

Internal organs are viewed as the center for combined
physiological and psychological functions. The heart, kidneys,
lungs, liver, and gall-bladder are important. The heart is
regarded as the organ related to the spirit or mind which is
the governing body or center of all psychological functioning
in Chinese society including the heart and kidneys (Lin 1980:
101-103).

The dysfunction of the stomach and lungs diminishes
vital energy. For this reason, the lungs are thought of as
susceptible to anxiety, worries, and sadness. The stomach
and spleen can be out of balance by anxiety or worries. The
liver and gall-bladder are related to anger. These ideas
have greatly affected Chinese concepts of psychological problems, When a patient suffers from emotional difficulties,
his attention is easily directed to physical condition (Lin
1980:102).

Similar concepts are found in Korea as in China. During

---

[13]Miju Dong-A (newspaper), December 15, 1981.

the United Silla Kingdom in Korea (668 A.D. to 935 A.D.) medical students learned the psychic as well as the physiological
functions of human organs as noted below. According to Kim
(n.d.:12) this knowledge is still essential for students of
traditional Korean medicine.

Physiologic functions of five viscera and six intestines are variously explained. Generally it was agreed that
five viscera store the spiritual action and the six intestines
absorb nutrition from "water and crops" (diet) which are
excreted out of the body. The specific functions of the five
viscera and the gall-bladder are:

> Lung: the primary organ of 'hemo-vascular movement,'
> besides psychic action.
> Heart: the center of sense (or reason) and closely re-
> lated with psychic action, as well as with 'hemovas-
> cular movement.'
> Liver: relates with 'hemovascular system' as well as
> psychic action.
> Spleen: besides psychic action, has digestive action
> along with the stomach.
> Kidney: stocks spirit and also the right kidney stocks
> the essence of reproduction while the left controls
> urination.
> Gallbladder: produces decisiveness and courage (Kim
> N.d.:14-15).

Social and emotional problems are manifested as illness by the interaction between mind and body. In Korea where
the large family system has traditionally existed, an individual learns to suppress disruptive feelings such as hos-
tility, especially toward superiors, in order to maintain
family harmony. As a result many of the repressed feelings
may turn into guilt feelings or depression (Hahn 1964:327).
E. Toupin points out that Korean culture conforms to North-
East Asian norms of patience, moderation, restraint, and

temperance. The suppression of verbal aggression and direct expression of one's feelings, and the avoidance of confrontation are personal qualities that are highly esteemed virtues in Asian societies (1980:82).

Kleinman has developed an explanatory model framework to understand the communication operations and interactions required to manage particular illness episodes. This model shows "the dynamics of cognitive and communicative transactions in health care" and it provides "a means of comparing these transactions in traditional and modern medical settings, and of evaluating their efficacy" (Kleinman 1980:118). The purpose of the explanatory model is to distinguish different or similar explanations of illness and beliefs and practices between individual patients and practitioners who usually belong to the separate sectors of a health care system (Kleinman 1980:104-105). Kleinman clearly states that:

> Explanatory models [hereafter called EMs] are the notions about an episode of sickness and its treatment that are employed by all those engaged in the clinical process. The interaction between the EMs of patients and practitioners is a central component of health care. The study of practitioner EMs tells us something about how practitioners understand and treat sickness. The study of patient and family EMs tells us how they make sense of given episodes of illness, and how they choose and evaluate particular treatments. The study of the interaction between practitioner EMs and patient EMs offers a more precise analysis of problems in clinical communication. Most importantly, investigating EMs in relation to the sectors and subsectors of health care systems discloses one of the chief mechanisms by which cultural and social structural context affects patient-practitioner and other health care relationships.
> Structually, we can distinguish five major questions that EMs seek to explain for illness episodes. These are: (1) etiology; (2) time and mode of onset of symptoms; (3) pathophysiology; (4) course of sickness (including

both degree of severity and type of sick role--acute,
chronic, impaired, etc.); and (5) treatment. EMs differ
in the extent to which they attempt to answer some or
all of these concerns (Kleinman 1980:105).

Thus, explanatory models describe and interpret personal and

sociocultural meaning in the experience of sickness.

Kleinman states that explanatory models represent

semantic sickness networks that weave a variety of "concepts

and experiences" of illness in a sociocultural context

(Kleinman 1980:106-107). An illness semantic network for a

patient may include "personal trauma, life stresses, fears

and expectation about illness, social reactions of friends

and authorities, and therapeutic experiences" in a particular

culture (Good and Good 1981:176).

Kleinman shows functions of semantic sickness networks

in clinical assessment in a health care system:

These semantic sickness networks draw upon beliefs
about causality and significance to make available particular treatment options; they enable instrumental and
symbolic therapies to be used together without concern
about mixing or confusing concepts from very different
sources. Within the semantic networks of the popular
health care sector, EMs interrelate illness beliefs,
norms, and experiences and function as the clinical
guides to decisions .... (Kleinman 1980:107).

Semantic sickness networks provide meaning to the concep-

tualization and experiences of a particular illness and indi-

cates the treatment direction based on sociocultural reality.

Meanwhile explanatory models show the interrelationship be-

ween illness beliefs and practices, and sociocultural context.

Kleinman states that by understanding the patient's

semantic sickness network and explanatory model, the "natural

history of illness," which is relevant to a particular health
care system, can be elicited for sociocultural relevance of
medical intervention (Kleinman 1980:107).

For example, according to Sunu, a Korean traditional
physician, in Hanbang (traditional Korean professional medical
clinic), the heart has psychological and physiological meanings: mind and organ. There are two common causes of heart
diseases: psychogenic and dietary. Psychogenic heart disease
occurs when seven emotions--happiness, anger, depression,
worry, sadness, fright, and fear--are demanded beyond the
threshold, and then the cardiac function becomes weakened.
Sunu states in a case study that his 40 year old patient with
cardiac valve disease caused by worries for her children was
cured by acupuncture and Hanyak (traditional Korean medicaments). Sunu added that in this case the biomedical physician
might have chosen to persorm an operation as treatment (1982:
457).

Explanatory model transactions reveal "the cognitive
basis of illness experiences" as the models disclose "the
cognitive operations" of clinical practice. Kleinman states
that cognitive structures demonstrate effectively the relationship between patient and healers (Kleinman 1980:120). The aim
of categories for comparing therapeutic relationships is to
compare different therapeutic relationships in different healing systems in order to determine their "universal and culture
specific aspects" (Kleinman 1980:208). A comparison of transactions between patients and healers in terms of explanatory

models and clinical realities is important because it is

directly related to the adaptation of the therapeutic process.

Kleinman employs the following categories for comparing thera-

peutic relationships to determine similarities and differences:

1. Institutional Settings (i.e., specific location in a
   given health care system's sectors and subsectors).
2. Characteristics of the interpersonal interaction
   a. Number of participants
   b. Time coordinates (i.e., whether it is episodic or
      continuous, the expected average length of treat-
      ment, the amount of time spent in each transaction,
      the time spent in communicating or explaining)
   c. Quality of the relationship (i.e., whether it is
      formal or informal with respect to etiquette, type
      of social role--primary, secondary, tertiary, emo-
      tional distance, restricted or elaborated communi-
      cative code, nature of transference and counter-
      transference; whether it is integrated into or di-
      vorced from everyday life experiences and ongoing
      daily activities)
   d. Attitude of the participants (i.e., how practi-
      tioners and patients view each other, particularly
      if they hold mutually ambivalent of the other)
3. Idiom of communication
   a. Model (i.e., psychological, mechanistic, somatic,
      psychosomatic, sociological, spiritual, moral,
      naturalistic, etc.)
   b. Explanatory models (i.e., shared, openly expressed,
      tacit, or conflicting; whether the EMs are drawn
      from single, unified belief systems or fragmented,
      pluralistic ones)
4. Clinical reality
   a. Sacred or secular (indigenous or Western)
   b. Disease-oriented or illness-oriented
   c. Symbolic or instrumental interventions
   d. Therapeutic expectations (i.e., concerning eti-
      quette, treatment style, therapeutic objectives,
      and whether these are shared or discrepant)
   e. Perceived locus of responsibility for care (the
      individual patient, family, community, or practi-
      tioner)
5. Therapeutic stages and mechanisms
   a. Tripartite organization or other structure
   b. Mechanisms of change (i.e., catharsis, insight,
      psychophysiological, social, etc.)
   c. Adherence, termination, evaluations of outcome
      (i.e., shared or discrepant assessments of satis-
      faction, efficacy, cost-effectiveness (Kleinman
      1980:207-208).

To my knowledge there is little information about the
transactions between patients and physicians in Korea, or among
Koreans in the United States. In research conducted by Kim and
Sich it has been learned that traditional Korean physicians have
concepts and healing techniques that originated in the great
tradition of Chinese medicine. A Hanui's explanatory models are
closely related to Korean cultural contexts. Kim and Sich thus
state: "...the behavior of the traditional doctor may correspond more closely to the behavior people desire a health practitioner to exhibit" (1977:85).

These same authors state that the Korean biomedical
physicians' explanatory models are often different from those
of their patients and this leads to ineffective therapeutic
relationship between practitioner and patient. They describe
their experiences in research on the subject, as follows:

> One of the authors is a German trained obstetrician
> and was often confronted in Korea with patients and re-
> latives who have been through an odissee [Sic] of visits
> to different kinds of health practitioners already. They
> are confused by bits of knowledge concerning their ill-
> ness that is derived from different explanatory models
> foreign to their own. They are unable to integrate these,
> and their expectation that the physician's explanation
> will help them to do this is necessarily frustrated. The
> physician is not able a) to identify the various under-
> lying beliefs and doubts concerning the illness and its
> cure as they exist in the client's mind and, even if he
> could do so, he is not able b) to translate his under-
> standing and therapeutical approach into the client's
> frame of reference. The client, therefore, remains dis-
> satisfied, and does not invest the necessary confidence
> to follow the suggested treatment regimen. Subsequently
> he may not improve, he may loose confidence entirely,
> and then he drifts to the next practitioner where the
> same course of events starts all over again. This is a
> description of patient behavior and physician-patient
> relationship as Korean physicians in general too, readi-
> ly admit, exists. It is interesting to find in this

study, that the tendency to consult various traditional
and modern health care resources simultaneously, pre-
exists in the population before any illness does indeed
occur (Kim and Sich 1977:86-87).

Kim and Sich explain that biomedical practitioners

in Korea do not have the understanding of Korean tradition

particularly in relation to "belief and religious practice,

as rural people do. They are rarely aware of how profoundly

rural peoples' health behavior is influenced by this back-

ground and by the availability of traditional health care

resources" (Kim and Sich 1977:101). These same authors state

that the Korean biomedical profession is not the only exist-

ing health care resources and has not integrated Korean

tradition with their discipline, "but tries to exist along-

side with it" (Kim and Sich 1977:107).

They further point out that the Mudang is important in

the Korean health care system because she "represent the most

traditional, most ancient resources for health care.... She

knows their hearts and minds and speaks their language." How-

ever, she is not highly esteemed although her services are

recognized.

With regard to patient-physician relations among

Koreans in the United States, the author could only locate

one newspaper report on the subject. In this source, Korean

professional physicians expressed concerns about the Korean

immigrant patients who are not familiar with biomedical beliefs

and practices. The biomedical physicians are aware that their

patients have explanations about illness different from theirs

and the Western biomedical point of view of illness. The
physicians were further alarmed about their patients' practice
such as self-diagnosis and cure, and felt that this was dangerous to their health. They also pointed out that their
Korean immigrant patients were not familiar with biomedically
oriented health settings, especially the appointment systems.
Finally, the physicians had a difficult time convincing their
Korean immigrant patients that injections were not always the
best form of therapy. Some Koreans valued the effect of injections and tended to expect this type of treatment.[14]

---

[14]Miju Hankuk (newspaper). February 12, 1983, Pp.11.

CHAPTER III

KOREAN SOCIOCULTURAL BACKGROUND

SOCIAL STRUCTURE, CULTURAL VALUES, AND ROLES OF

ELDERLY IN TRADITIONAL KOREAN SOCIETY

Confucianism which was introduced in Korea in A.D. 372,

exerted a strong influence on the Korean way of life. Osgood

describes the central principles of interpersonal relation-

ships in a family:

> Fundamental to the Confucian philosophy is the notion
> that a good life depends upon a knowledge and observance
> of the proper behavior between one individual and another.
> Five categories of interpersonal relations form the basis
> for instruction as to the duties and obligations involved.
> These relations are those (1) of parents and child, (2) of
> king and minister, (3) of husband and wife, (4) of elder
> brother and younger brother, and (5) of friend with friend
> (Osgood 1962:38).

Confucius asserted that men must play their assigned roles in

a society based on fixed principles of authority. "The ruler

should be a ruler and the subject a subject; father should be

a father and the son should be a son" (Reischauer and Fairbank

1960:70). Importance was placed on acceptance of a fixed posi-

tion in the family hierarchy and on observing the proper re-

lationships demanded by each specific tie of kinship. In effect,

this relationship pattern was applied to the whole of society,

providing a basis for authority and social order in political
as well as in domestic life (Reischauer and Fairbank 1960:30).

For Confucius, right living meant essentially the harmonizing by the man of virtue of his own personality into the
social order. His method was to look constantly and modestly
at the good examples of parents and elders, then at the ancient
wisdom of the past, and then to respect the ministers of state
and the prince (Soothill 1923:8).

Confucianism is the source of most of the distinctive
features of Chinese and Korean life which attract and puzzle
Westerners. The social organization and values of the people are
Confucian. Confucianism is a key to understanding the culture
of Korea (MacMahon 1977:62).

The concepts of dependence and authority are important
in Confucian society (Metzer 1980:7-27). Korean parents expect
obedience, cooperation, and dependence from their children and
in return parents depend on their children in their old age
(Brandt 1971:173). Solidarity, continuity of the group, and
collectivism of the group are valued among Koreans. Loyalty
to collectivity and interdependency especially family and kinship override individualism and independence in decision
making (Lee 1971:80-81).

During the Yi dynasty, the last kingdom in Korean history from 1392-1910, Korea was referred to by the Chinese as
"The Eastern Country of Courtesy" because of the people's rigid
adherence to Confucian ethical codes especially in the field

of ancestor worship and filial piety.[15] In the late nineteenth

century, C. Dallet, a French missionary, observed:

> Let us note only what it is like in Korea, for the
> mass of the people it consists in ancestor worship and
> in observation of the five great duties; duty towards
> the king, towards parents and relatives, towards husband
> or wife, towards old people, and towards friends.
> No virtue, in Korea, is esteemed and honored as much
> as filial piety, none is taught with more care, none is
> more magnificently recompensed by exemptions from taxes,
> by the erection of monumental columns or even temples,
> and by honors and public offices (Dallet 1954:137).

Filial piety was strong cultural tradition as seen in the

following quotations by this same author:

> A son who meets his father on the road must perform
> the great kneeling and prostrate himself in the dust and
> mud. In writing to him, he must use the most honorific
> formulars known to the Korean language. Mandarins fre-
> quently obtain leaves of greater or less duration in order
> to visit their relatives, and if they lose their father
> or mother, while on duty they must resign immediately in
> order that they may be occupied only with rendering the
> last duties to be deceased, and they may hold no office
> as long as the legal mourning lasts (Dallet 1874:129).

> A son must never play with his father, nor smoke
> before him nor assume too great a posture in his presence,
> and so in well-to-do families there is a special apart-
> ment where he can be at ease and play with his friends
> (Dallet 1954:128).

> Among government officials and the military, parents
> who have reached seventy years of age have one son ex-
> empted from the draft; those who have reached their
> eightieth year have two sons exempted; and all the
> children exempted of the parents who have reached
> ninety years of age.[16]

The father, also, avoids anything which might lower his dignity

in his son's eyes, and therefore does not joke or play with his

---

[15]Korea Its Land, People and Culture of All Ages.
Seoul, Rakwon Sa Ltd. 1963. p. 65.

[16]Materally d lia Opisaniia Korei (Data for a Descrip-
tion of Korea), no date.

son. In the traditional Korean family system, rights are exercised in order of hierarchy:

> Korean society being organized according to Confucian ideas we find the rights of parents over children, of elder over younger brothers.... (Rockhill 1891:180).

Filial piety can be fulfilled in two ways: negatively, one should not bring shame to parents by disgracing oneself and positively, a child should do his best to please his parents by bettering his character exalting his personality; and doing what they wish him to do. Filial piety in the moral philosophy of Confucius is so important that it is regarded as the root of perfect virtue (Sherley-price 1951:130-143). The important concepts of filial piety are submission, attendance, support, comfort of parents, realization of parents' wishes, the provision of funeral service for parents, and ancestor worship (Choi 1964). If children fail to fulfill filial piety toward elderly parents, it is considered most shameful and pitiful.

Among Koreans the sixtieth birthday is viewed as one of the greatest possible events in an individual's life cycle (Osgood 1962:43). It has been traditional that men who have passed their sixtieth birthday should retire and spend much of their time traveling about the countryside visiting friends or entertaining at home. In small poor villages, the activities of the elderly generally are confined to death anniversary ceremonies, weddings, funerals, and visits to kin. Except for these occasions most of the old men continue to work at home due to poverty (Brandt 1971:161).

Old age in traditional Korea is valued and respected. Elderly people belong to the highest rank in a family. They are respected and honored by their family members and other young people. They control economic, familial, moral, and social affairs with absolute authority. They inherit materials and lands. They teach moral issues, etiquette, social skills, and other knowledge. They choose schools for their children. They support their children materially and emotionally whenever necessary. The Korean elderly function as matchmakers. They advise, organize or perform at family ceremonies such as holiday, birthday celebrations, ancestor worship services, weddings, and funerals. The mother-in-law has the responsibility to educate her daughter-in-law to properly perform family affairs according to family tradition. The grandmother becomes a midwife for her daughter or daughter-in-law.[17]

Grandparents advise about nutrition, other health maintenance and preventive measures, and cures. The old advise and demonstrate good farming techniques. They contribute to promote interpersonal relationships in the family and community. The aged support and advise community affairs. Elderly people are privileged to eat finer foods and to wear finer clothes than the young. They are offered leisure while others work although they often decline this privilege and assist in work. They are given the best seats. They are addressed with honor-

---

[17]Personal conversation with Chin Yong Chung and Byung Ho Lee. July 27, 1981.

ifics. The young show respect by behaving with deference and honor to their elders.[18]

Korean elders are expected to retire gracefully from active life in thier later years. As they advance in years, fathers usually begin to relinquish control of sons and a mother-in-law gradually begins to delegate her responsibilities to her daughter-in-law (Janelli 1975 and Song 1976).

In Korea, ancestors are respected like living elders (Janelli and Janelli 1982:82). Koreans believe that their ancestral spirits are in close contact with them even after death. The ancestor worship ceremony is viewed as their duty and right. This ritual constitutes a refusal to accept the permanency of separation or death. The ancestor worship ceremony can be seen as a symbolic union between ancestral spirits and their offspring (Brandt 1971 and Lee 1973:40). Koreans also believe that their ancestors protect them and provide prosperity, high social position, many sons, health, happiness, and long life. Korean folklore is full of stories telling of how a son out of filial piety spent the whole of his patrimony on his family ritual (Hulbert 1902).

When a parent dies, filial piety requires that the eldest son assisted by his brothers and relatives, provide an elaborate funeral followed by ceremonial observances on the first and second anniversaries of the parent's death. These are all occasions when large numbers of people gather to eat

---

[18]Personal conversation with Chin Yong Chung and Byung Ho Lee. July 27, 1981.

and drink together. The emphasis is on lineage, and in fact
patrilineal kin have the most prominent roles at these affairs.
In addition, the bereaved son is provided with an opportunity
to demonstrate his filial devotion and to acquire respect and
good will through hospitality in a wider context. For the village as a whole, these are recurring festive occasions when
people put on their best clothes and eat and drink together
for several hours in an atmosphere of general good will
(Brandt 1971:120).

During the first year after death, everyday, three
meals are offered in front of the "spirit tablet." The spirit
tablet is kept in the ancestral tablet house or soul house
which is found connected with the residence of every well-to-do
gentleman (Hulbert 1902). A married daughter who visits her
natal home or persons who leave for or return after a long
journey greet the ancestors' spirit in the tablet house upon
arrival and departure. Also, they greet their ancestors in the
tablet house on the first day and fifteenth day of each luni-
solar calendar month. In addition, on the parent's death day,
an ancestor worship ceremony is annually held. On New Year's
day and Moon Festival day, Koreans also worship all their
ancestors for four generations back (Han 1974:254).

Life Cycle Events of Traditional Korean Women

The socialization principles of Korean women are based
on Confucian values (Rutt and Kim 1974). An individual must
correctly observe the rules of five basic relationships: ruler

and subject, parent and child, elder and younger, husband and
wife, and friend and friend. The right role behaviors should
be performed properly with right speech and action dependent
on the hierarchy of people. The father, as the family head
has authority in his household. Women suppress their needs.
According to tradition, "man honors himself by governing his
wife, and a women honors herself by surbordinating herself
to her husband" (Hall 1897:189).

In traditional Korean society the announcement of the
birth of a baby girl was often received with regret. Showing
affection to children, especially a girl, in front of parents-
in-law was discouraged. Segregation and seclusion from the
opposite sex were strictly practiced. In traditional Korean
society girls were taken away from ordinary social situations
at the age of seven and confined in the inner house. After
marriage, she was secluded in her husband's home (Hall 1897:
191).

With regard to socialization practices, Harvey states:
The resolution of situations of conflict between sisters and
brothers is usually made in favor of the brothers as a matter
of course regardless of their ages or issues involved (Harvey:
263). Obedience, suppression of wishes, and non-reciprocal
conformity are important socialization principles of Korean
women (Harvey 1979). However, the mother and daughter relationship is empathic and mutual (Osgood 1962:47).

Traditionally, marriage has been negotiated between
two parties based on socially recognized norms, but the woman's

opinion does not count in her own marriage decision. Her father
and her future husband's father make the marriage decision. The
woman belongs to three men in her life. Before marriage a woman
is to obey her father, after marriage, her husband, and in old
age, her son (Lee 1967:137). Her marriage is not always secure.
A woman could be sent to her natal home when she showed any one
of the following seven "evils": disobedience to parents-in-law,
adultery, jealousy, barrenness, an incurable disease, a quar-
relsome disposition, and theft (Lee 1967:137). In such cases
she would suffer from stigma throughout her lifetime and she
would bring shame to her father's home and to herself.

After marriage, any conflicts that existed between herself and other members of the household would be expected to be
resolved in the other party's favor. According to a popular
saying, Korean women who enter marriage are frequently advised
as follows: to become dumb for the first three years, deaf another three years, and blind still for three years to survive
particularly in their early marriage.

Becoming a daughter-in-law is known as a strenuous task.
She is expected to learn the different customs of her husband's
household. In the beginning, usually little understanding is
shown by her husband's relatives especially the mother-in-law
and sister-in-law. Furthermore, conflict between a mother-in-
law and daughter-in-law is heightened "by their rivalry over
the affections of the young husband." These two people see each
other as an obstacle in having harmonious relationship with
the young man (Janelli and Janelli 1982:40).

After she has given birth to her first child, especially a male child who becomes a direct male heir, a Korean woman establishes her place and identity in her husband's household. She keeps a delicate relationship with her mother-in-law, and gradually and unobtrusively she takes over family responsibilities from her mother-in-law. After she becomes a grandmother herself, she assumes the care of her daughter-in-law. Mother-in-law and daughter-in-law try to maintain a good relationship between themselves. This relationship is important for the two people. The daughter-in-law should not lead a harsh married life. Her security in old age is looked after by her daughter-in-law. According to Harvey, "This was the golden period of the traditional Korean women's life cycle, the one which made all the preceding ones worth enduring" (Harvey 1979:271).

Korean elderly women are venerated by their children and grandchildren who will also become leaders for their ancestor worship ceremony in appreciation of their sufferings for their children. Children are expected to make their parents happy in three ways: by exalting themselves, by contributing to society, and by direct veneration of living and deceased parents. Filial piety is encouraged for parents who sacrifice themselves for their children's sake. According to Covell (1982:120-121). King Chongjo in the Yi dynasty (1777-1800) wrote a plaque about Confucian teaching of filial piety and exemplified himself as a filial son. The following passages written by this king in particular convey the ways a mother demonstrates her profound loving care of her children:

1. The baby is in the womb for ten months
2. The mother suffers at childbirth
3. The mother suffers because she needs a son to carry on the family
4. Parents eat poor food so that children can have the best possible
5. The suffering of breast feeding
6. Taking the most difficult place (this is illustrated by a mother covering up a place where her child had urinated)
7. The mother suffers to keep the child's clothing clean
8. The father suffers as he must leave the house to earn money for the child's maintenance
9. The parents' suffer pains of separation when travel is required
10. Suffering when parents must leave their children through death (This was illustrated by a 100-year-old mother with her 80 year old son. She turns to him, almost at the moment of her own death, to warn him not to misstep under the slippery bamboo.) (Quoted from Covell 1982:120).

How the child may repay the parents are written in two parts:

1. Study with diligence
2. Diligently cause others to study
3. Repent one's own errors
4. Pay obeisance to religious leaders
5. Serve one's fellow men

1. Perform filial duty to parents, such as a morning and evening bow
2. Inform parents on leaving the home, as well as on returning
3. Provide parents against want
4. If they are sick, nurse the parents personallly (illustrated by cutting off a finger to flavor the broth, since this was the only thing available)
5. In case parents are not living properly, correct them cautiously
6. Live in such a way as to be a paradigm for others to follow (Quoted from Covell 1982:120-121).

Korean women become free from household responsibilities upon attainment of the sixtieth birthday. They have privileges such as leisure. They may love and indulge their grandchildren (Harvey 1979:271). Their wisdom is sought and their wishes are indulged by their children. Korean elderly women's sixtieth birthday is celebrated with "great pomp and ceremony" (Vreeland et al. 1975:88). Particularly low ranked Korean elderly women are allowed to be less restrained in manners and social conduct. Osgood describes this: "Once a woman passes the menopause, which is no secret, she becomes somewhat sexless in the eyes of the population and may do much as she pleases within the restrictions of lifelong habit" (Osgood 1962:114).

It seems to be essential for Korean elderly woman to have children and grandchildren to enjoy a full old age life. The "golden period" in a traditional Korean elderly is described by Osgood as below:

> If the old couple has a living son residing in the house which he will inherit, and if there are a number of grandsons playing about, the ancient ones who enjoy good health will probably be happy enough. A reasonable leisure will be theirs and the satisfaction of reflecting on lives with the principal goals achieved. For them, only death lies ahead, but they have little fear. To become one with the ancestors they have worshipped for decades is a proper conclusion to the pains of the world and they are certain that in the unbroken and endless chain of clan obeisance they will not be forgotten. Thus they prepare for their decease (Osgood 1962:114).

It should be noted that in order to understand Korean culture as a whole, one has to know both Yangban (nobility), upper ranked families and Sangin (commoners), lower ranked families. Yangban families are politically, socially, and economically superior to those of Sangin. Usually Yangban families live in urban area and Sangin families in rural area (Ibid.) Yangban family women are more secluded from society and segregated from men than the Sangin family women (Osgood 1962:145). Stricter rules are applied to the women from Yangban families than those of a Sangin family background.

For example, remarriage is unthinkable particularly for women
from Yangban families (Osgood 1962:148). Most of the women in
the upper rank families adhered to Confucianism while the women
of lower ranked families tended to be interested in Shamanism
(Osgood 1962:152). The Yangban women enjoyed more leisure and
material affluence, so they could pursue personal hobbies such
as games, literary interests, embroidery than Sangin women who
were usually busy with daily labors (Osgood 1962:145).

CHANGES IN SOCIAL STRUCTURE, CULTURAL VALUES, AND ROLES
OF ELDERLY IN TRADITIONAL KOREA

Changes in Korean Women's Status

There have been efforts to changes Korean women's
status. Rhim states that under the influence of Christianity,
there were three notable emancipatory movements for Korean
women although none of them was fully successful. The earliest movement was Tonghak, Eastern learning. This movement was
influenced by Eastern philosophy and Roman Catholicism and it
began in the 1860s. This movement demanded human rights and
equality of the sexes. The first of the six Tonghak teachings
states: "Revere your wife as a god. Love your daughter-in-law.
... If not, Heaven will get angry" (Quoted from Rhim 1978:25).
The leaders of the Tonghak movement established a formal school
for women (Ibid., 25). The second movement was organized by
an American-educated physician and Christian, Philip Jaisohn,
and the third movement was initiated by a Protestant missionary

through means of education (Ibid.)

Western influence, industrialization, and education accelerated massive urban migration, and consequently this has brought changes in the social structure from extended family households to nuclear family households. This independent family setting has changed the status of Korean women (Vreeland et al. 1975:101-102). However, D. Son notes that the traditional women's status has not been improved fundamentally although different efforts have been made to enhance women's status. The laws of inheritance and other areas still disregard women's rights (Kim and Strawn 1979:94-98 and Son 1978:257-282). Vreeland et al. state:

> ... the father is recognized as having an overriding right to the custody of children; laws defining the extent of family ties and obligations treat men and women differently; women have no right to demand the distribution of property in divorce proceedings; a husband can legally register an illegitimate child as his own and his wife's without her consent; and a wife and daughter can inherit only half as much property of a deceased father or husband as the son, and when a daughter marries, her maximum share drops to one fourth (Vreeland et al. 1975: 102).

Lee states that Korean women face various types of discrimination. For example, there are inequalities in the areas of economics and work according to Lee: "Women receive considerably smaller wages than men. Women are restricted in advancement. When they get married, they give up their jobs. If women are not doing the simple tasks of daily life, they are usually assigned to the service industries of the economy" (Lee 1978:78). Vreeland et al. state that there is a growing women's consciousness in South Korea, urging that these legal barriers to equality be removed (Vreeland et al. 1975:102).

The Elderly in Modern Korea

Rapid social changes were brought to the agricultural traditional Korean society after World War II. The major reasons were: (1) industrialization along with urbanization, and mobility due to rural-urban migration; (2) the development of mass communications; (3) education with influence of American and European cultural values; and (4) demographic changes due to the prolonged life expectancy. The newly emerging issues for the aged in Korea are demographic changes, changes in the family life patterns, the working status of the aged, economic, and welfare considerations (Roh and Kang 1981:1-2).

Traditionally in Korea, old age had not been a serious problem (Roh and Kang 1981). Elders held positions of prestige, power, and status within the family, lineage, community, and society (Williamson et al. 1980:173). However, in the process of modernization and various transformations, questions have been raised as to whether these traditional concepts toward the elderly will prevail in all institutional functions (Decker 1980:80). Roh and Kang (1981) assume that elderly Korean people have everyday life problems and their position is undergoing rapid changes.

The Korean's average life expectancy has increased from 51,1 years for a male and 53.7 years for a female in 1960 to 66.1 years for a male and 70.3 years for a female in 1975.[19]

---

[19]Economic Planning Board, Republic of Korea, <u>Korea Statistical Yearbook</u>, Vol. 26. 1979. Pp. 26.

The reasons for the prolonged life expectancy are a reduction of the infant mortality rate, advanced medical technology and a general improvement in the standard of living (Harris and Cole 1980:29-30).

In 1955 there was a total of 520,713 or 3.4 percent of the population who were 65 years or older. This increased to 950,059 in 1960 and further to 965,961 in 1966. By 1970 that specific age group passed over one million or 1,039,378 and reached 1,201,599 or 3.8 percent in 1975.[20] It is projected that by the year 2050, the life expectancy for a male will be 71.7 years and 77 years for a female.[21]

The traditional Korean household is an extended one typically composed of grandparents, parents, and grandchildren. This type of family has favored the high status of older people. The aged were well integrated in to the total family life (Kart 1981:149). While there are still people, especially in rural areas who adhere to the traditional concepts of family life, the majority of urban people are undergoing significant changes from the traditional life patterns (Roh and Kang 1981:7).

According to the 1981 Park report on aging based on the data sample survey jointly conducted by both the Research Institute of the Aging, associated with the Korean Elderly Association, and the Dong-a Il Bo newspaper, it was found that 51.6 percent of the respondents lived with an elder son while 15.3

[20]Economic Planning Board, Republic of Korea, Korea Statistical Yearbook, Vol. 26. 1979. Pp.41

[21]The Dong-A Il Bo (Newspaper), July 2 and September 3, 1981.

percent lived with other sons or grandsons; 5.3 percent lived
with daughters, while 26.9 percent of the elderly lived independently. These living arrangements were different from what
the elderly wanted in terms of the kind of living situation.
The study indicated that 40.1 percent desired to live with
elder son, 18.6 percent with any sons or daughters whomever
they favored. Furthermore 29.2 percent preferred to live independently and 11.3 percent to stay in nursing homes or homes
for the elderly. Among those children who lived with their
elderly parents, 52.9 percent responded favorably toward living
with their parents, 24.9 percent expressed no clear opinion
and the rest 17.8 percent, responded that they preferred not
to live with their parents if they had alternatives. Thus, the
traditional attitudes toward the elderly have been changing.[22]

Park's survey further indentified the most difficult
problem that the elderly faced: the survey showed that 37.6
percent responded that they did not have economic security.
It was also reported that 55.7 percent of the elderly were
simply unable to plan for their future due to already heavy
day-to-day living expenses even while they were employed.
In addition, 23.2 percent replied that they had already transferred their properties to their children and only 16.7 percent
of those remaining responded that they planned economic affairs
ahead of time for their old age. The elderly Koreans in this

---

[22]Jae Gan Park, Director of the Research Institute of
the Aging attached with the Korean Elderly Association in Korea
in conjunction with the Dong-A Il Bo (newspaper) studied 600

research experienced serious economic insecurity.

In the nation as a whole data show that four fifths of the elderly age 65 and over are economically inactive even though 82 percent of the total elderly Koreans sampled in Park's survey (1981) indicated that they wished to work. Besides this employment condition in Korea, early retirement plans presents economic problems because these individual lose their basic income sources while they are not ready to assume financial responsibilities for themselves after retirement (Roh and Kang 1981).

The enactment of the "Old Age Welfare"[23] drew attention to the welfare problem which exists among the Korean elderly. The main functions of the "Old Age Welfare Law" are: (1) to revive the spirits of filial piety in the family and society in general, (2) to establish counseling centers at various government levels in order to provide guidance services and activities for old people, (3) to provide the care facilities for the elderly who are not able to take care of themselves, and (4) to provide the elderly Koreans different free and discount services. I am not aware of a systematic report

---

sampled rural and urban elderly residents aged 60 to 85 years and also sampled 550 youth and adults 20 to 40 years of age who were currently living with their parents regarding different life patterns and attitudes toward life of the old and opinion surveys of the young adults toward their elderly parents. The finding were reported in a total of 26 series in the Dong-A Il Bo (newspaper), Seoul, June 30 to September 2, 1981.

[23]"Old Age Welfare Law" (No. 3,453). The Government Announcement Paper. Republic of Korea, No. 8857, June 1981. p. 89-92.

on the impact of this law thus far.

The Immigration Experience

The immigration process signifies disruption of a familiar life style. It may involve disintegration of the persons' familiar patterns of role relationships, loss of social identity, and major shifts in the value systems and behavior patterns. It is an upheaval which can be considered as a crisis. For the immigrant, the process is stressful and it challenges all her resources in order to cope with this process. It places her in a vulnerable state which may require varieties of social intervention (Kim 1976:140). The situation confronted by immigrants who have left their own country to settle in a new one is basically the problem of learning to adapt to an unfamiliar culture. The need to adapt to new situations is part of life. No two situations are ever identical and adjustments must continually be made to changed circumstances. Usually, changes are dramatic and force extreme and wide ranging adaptations if an individual is to cope effectively with the new situation. When the elderly migrate to new settings, they often have to face the challenges of adaptation to sociocultural change and moderation with few resources (Rosow 1973:82-87). Myerhoff has shown that some common problems of the aged immigrants in the United States are separation from the culture that socialized and nutured them into adulthood, partial alienation within their present cultural environment, and often intergenerational ties are severed (Myerhoff 1978).

Yang points out the hardships experienced by early
Korean immigrant women in the United States in his article
"Korean Women in America: from Subordinate to Partnership,
1903-1930." These women had to live in a harsh unfamiliar environment. Also, they had to adapt to a different cultural
milieu such as different "language, customs, foods, clothes,
values, and standards." They had to do intolerable physical
labor to which they were not used. Besides, they faced "poverty, loneliness, and discrimination." The 1903-1905 wave of
Korean immigrant women contributed significantly to family economy and stability (Yang 1983:1-8).

The 1910-1924 wave of Korean women immigrants were
picture brides who were different from the wave of 1903 in
areas of age, socioeconomic level, socio-political experience,
educational level, participation in the nationalist movement
at that time. These women were influenced by social change. They
were relatively young in age ranging from 17-25. They were from
low socioeconomic families, but they were educated in modern
newly opened schools, and participated in the nationalistic
movement during the Japanese occupation from 1910 to 1945 (Yang
1983:8-9).

After migrating to the United States, this group of women became Americanized more quickly than the group of women of
the 1903 immigration wave. The picture brides learned English
and wore clothes like Americans. They actively participated
in the family economy by working outside the home as well as
assuming thier original responsibilities such as child rearing,

homemaking, and creating a harmonious and hopeful family atmosphere. These women also contributed and participated significantly in the Korean community especially in their ethnic
churches. They continued to assist the movement for independence from the Japanese occupation by raising funds (Yang 1983).

Yang notes that their pioneering life as immigrants was
courageous and successful. Yang believes that their young age,
Christian background, pro-American spirit, relatively high educational level, and contact with Western influence as were
sources of a successful immigrant life. However, according to
Yang, the single most contributing factor for survival and their
upward mobility as immigrant families was attributed to the op-
portunity-seeking spirit of this Korean family as a unit. Yang
elaborated on the background of pioneering spirit of these
Koreans:

> The rapid adjustment and upward mobility of the immi-
> grants can perhaps be better explained by examining the
> unique cultural traits and characteristics of Korean so-
> ciety. Koreans are essentially individualistic in their
> pursuit of opportunity--a trait which has evolved from
> the traditional social structure. Koreans are therefore
> predisposed to grasp economic and other opportunities
> whenever possible. Confucianism attempted to maintain an
> equilibrium between man and society by stressing harmony.
> But this equilibrium has always been disrupted by the
> egoistic pursuit of protection, security, and prosperity
> for an individual and his family, as evidenced by the
> factional strife that occurred among the Yangban elites.
> However, this individualistic pursuit of opportunity is
> closely connected to a family centered ethic, a moral
> which is equally stressed both Shamanism and Confucian-
> ism. It is the connection between the individualistic
> element and the family centered ethic that has allowed
> Koreans to rapidly adjust to different situations while
> still retaining their sense of ethnicity (Yang 1983:23-24).

Although there are few studies of the present-day
adaptation of Korean newcomers to this country, a few works

suggested that Korean immigrants have changed in economic and
sociocultural patterns due to their language difficulty and
cultural differences, particularly at the beginning of their
process of settlement in the United States. Yu states that
former professionals frequently engage in unskilled or semi-
skilled labor (Yu 1980:86). Yu also states that language
difficulty causes poor communication between Korean immigrant
parents and their children. Korean parents may have limited
competence in English while their children often do not speak
Korean. Thus, a harmonious parent-children relationship is difficult to establish (Yu 1980:89). Most of the second and third
generations do not speak Korean, while many of the first genra-
tions do not speak English (Choy 1979:245). Language difficulty
and cultural differences between generations cause strains. The
first generation holds traditional Korean values and beliefs
while their children are oriented to American values (Choy 1979:
245). These language and cultural differences do not only influence family relations, but they also affect their sociocultural
life beyond the family level. Community activities of the Korean
elderly tend to be centered within their own community. They
participate in the activities of Korean organizations such as
Korean churches. Yu states that while these Korean-centered sociocultural activities may preserve Korean cultural traditions,
they may cause social and cultural isolation (Yu 1980:89).

According to Yu (1980:90), the social and the intensive-
ly work oriented Korean immigrant life requires certain changes
with respect to traditional Korean life patterns and ways of

thinking. "Male dominant sex roles and the authoritarian position of parents in the traditional family cannot be maintained intact in the United States." These traditional aspects
of the Korean family values are changing. However, adult
Koreans tend to resist the transition and try to maintain
their traditionally oriented family values. This results in
conflict between parents and children (Yu 1980:90).

Kim (1980:153-154) states that between generations,
the parents' "familism" and their childrens' "individualism"
are confronted with each other. Koreans are very concerned
with family unity as a whole based on Confucian ethics of
family relations which emphasize respect, support, and obedience to one's parents and seniors. For example, it is a "duty
for sons and daughters to have aged parents live in their
own home for an indefinite period of time." However, in
American society, individualism, freedom, and equality are
highly valued. Thus, dependence on others presents strains
in interpersonal relations among siblings, and in-laws.

Elderly Korean immigrants try to live independently
from their adult children as soon as they can establish their
financial independence or support from Social Security (Yu 1980:
81). According to Luhmann's research in Washington, D.C. and
New York City, elderly Korean immigrants have problems with
lack of English familiarity, lack of mobility, and lack of independence. For elderly Koreans in an independent group home
setting, which is separated from the children, lack of communication with society, distaste for non-Korean food served in

their group home, and the "process of aging" were identified also as problems, while residents in their children's home responded that they experienced homesickness for Korea, lack of communication with people around them, and health problems. Significant differences were noted in responses identified by elderly Koreans living independently and the Koreans living with children in the following problem areas: housing, difficulties with children, food, and income. The Koreans who live with their children tended more frequently than the informants of the group home setting to express concern about difficulties with their children, problems of housing and matters of income. However, elderly Korean living independently expressed a much higher degree of concern than the people living with children on distaste for non-Korean food (Luhmann 1978:57-58).

In researching Japanese Americans in California, C. Kiefer described how acculturation undermined the authority of the Issei (second generation), both men and women, over their children's generation. Under the traditional value system, dependent elders were not regarded as subordinates, because what they received from thier children was considered repayment. However, now dependent elders are a burden to their children. C. Kiefer further observed that the growing command of American cultural skills has probably weakened family relationships more than any other factor. It has made the Issei heavily dependent on their children for information about the society in which they live and has reduced Issei authority. The lack of command of American skills of most Issei women seriously limited their

role in the family. Japanese mothers are supposed to provide
training and advice on social skills to their children through
out their lives, while fathers enforce morality and provide
economic and technical training. Also the major result of the
loss of traditional Japanese values and skills by acculturat-
ing generations has isolated the Issei emotionally from their
family (Kiefer 1974:197-199).

Invariably, the informants in the present study said
that they came to the United States to be with children and/
or to help their children looking after their grandchildren,
doing housework and cooking, and helping in business. All of
the informants were invited by their children except one person
who came with her husband. Thus, eleven informants in this study
were invited by their sons, seven were brought by married daughters, one by an unmarried daughter, and another informant came
with her husband. The experiences of informants in coming to the
United States are illustrated in the following cases.

The central kinship bond for the Korean elderly immigrant woman is the relationship with her children. It is meaningful and influential in her daily life and in the major decisions made. The most important reason why these women emigrated
to the United States was to be with their children, although
some of them mention other advantages such as freedom in the
host society, security from the invasion of communists, and
favorable economic condition, but when these points are compared with their desire for a close relationship with their
children, they are relatively unimportant. If it were not for

their children, they would not have come and could not have come.

Actually a number of informants said that life in Korea is better for the elderly Koreans than the life in the United States. "The United States is a heaven for a poor elderly Korean but not for the elderly Koreans who have money and people who care for them in Korea," said Mrs. Park and she elaborated as follow:

> "We lived comfortably in Korea. Things are cheap there except a few things such as meats and fruits. We had a maid so that I did not have to do anything. We prepared our burial ground in our family cemetery even including the tomb stones so that our nephews and sons will not have a hard time to bury us."

On the occasion of a child's one hundred day birthday celebration, Mrs. Park was asked by one of the elderly women guests about life in America as follows:

> Mrs. Baik: "How do you like living here in the United States?"
> Mrs. Park: "I am all right because my children are doing fairly well. I do not care for other things much."
> Mrs. Baik: "We do not know English or have transportation. We have to be interested in our children."

Mrs. Ahn expresses contentment by saying "I am very happy now. I live with my child. I depend on him and he looks after me." Issues about children seem to be most important for the elderly women. Happiness and sadness originate with children. Mrs. Baik and Mrs. Yun talked about a mother who killed herself with an insecticide after her son had been killed by a member of an opposing sports team.

The strength of the kinship bond between mothers and

children and the depth of emotion involved was commented upon
by all informants. Some believe it is an "innate" quality,
while others explain it as part of generational relations, as
noted in the following comments:

"It seems to be some kind of inheritance from parents
to children. Parents gladly sacrifice themselves for their
children. They do not go places where they like to, but
stay home to take care of the grandchildren and the house"
(Mrs. Baik).

"Parental love for children is congenital. There are
no filial sons. Parents make filial sons. This love is
from the older generation to the younger generation"
(Mrs. Ku).

"The older generation truly cares for the younger generation. It is not the other way around. Youth receives
from parents or grandparents, but they do not return the
love they had received to their parents or grandparents
but they care for the next generation as they were cared
for by their parents and grandparents" (Mrs. Song).

Mrs. Son is going back to Korea because there is no
meaning without children. She said the following as if it were
unquestionable: "All my children are in Korea so that we are
going back to Korea." There is no other central bond that at-
tracts them to this country. And this bond is a continuity with
ties they had with their children in Korea. They are only here
because the tie moved to this country.

Usually one of the children comes to the United States
and establishes himself economically, and then he invites his
parents. These parents invite the rest of their children. The
entry of their children to the United States is said to be
easier if they are invited by their parents rather than their
brother or sister. Mrs. Koh, for example, has nine children.
One of her children came to the United States and became a

physician. This son repeatedly invited his mother to come to America. However, she felt she had to take care of the rest of her children. Thus, she declined to come at that time. Then her son in the United States asked one of his friends to bring his mother to this country. His friend asked the mother to come out to see him because he had a message to give her from her son. She met him in a hotel. By that time he had prepared her visa and airplane ticket. He let her board an airplane with him and that is how she arrived in the United States. She knew something happened to her in the airplane, but it was too late to do anything by that time. At the beginning of her life in America She was miserable particularly when she thought of her children in Korea. Soon, however, she started to invite her children and they came one by one. At the time of this research, all her children had emigrated to the United States.

In the case of another informant, Mrs. Hwang, one of her daughters had been invited to come to America by one of her relatives in 1960s. She graduated from a local university and was employed by the State Department. She invited her parents to the United States. It was easy for them to decide to accept the invitation because they were in trouble after their life-long lumber business had failed and besides that, they wanted their children to be educated in the United States. It took less than two years to bring five of their children to America.

Mrs. Hahn's oldest son read an advertisement that skilled auto mechanics were wanted in the United States and he applied. He, his wife, and his children came to America under a job contract. Later he opened his own gas station and let his parents emigrate. Then his parents extended invitations to the rest of their children except one daughter who is settled in Korea with her husband.

Mrs. Kim's daughter came to the United States as a student and met a professor from Korea whom she married. She subsequently became a permanent resident, and invited her mother and sister to come to this country. The sister married an American lawyer who was a Peace Corps volunteer in Korea.

Mrs. Kal's daughter was married to an American soldier who was stationed in Korea. Her daughter's family had come to America and invited her mother. They all live together. All her other children care in the United States too.

With regard to the occupation of the children of the elderly women who had settled in the Greater Washington Metropolitan Area, fifty percent of the informants have children with a business such as a grocery store, a laundry, a restaurant, a wig shop, and a hot dog business. Forty-five percent have children who are professionals such as ministers, professors, and physicians. A few informants' children are students or laborers. Ninety percent of these informants had some children who owned houses.

A review of the limited literature on contemporary Korean elderly immigrants in the United States shows that lack of attention has been given to the social and cultural circumstances which influence their adaptation. To my knowledge, study

of their medical beliefs and practices or examination of the
nature of the Korean health care system has not been undertaken.
The following chapters present findings concerning the changing
lives of a group of such immigrants, within the context of the
Korean health care system.

CHAPTER IV

CHANGING LIVES OF ELDERLY KOREAN IMMIGRANT WOMEN

INTRODUCTION

Every human being grows old, and in this process, social and cultural factors are important (Kendis 1980). An un-
understanding of the old age life experience of an individual
should be studied with regards to the sociocultural context.
Keith emphasizes this point as follows:

> There is an emic emphasis, which attempts to under-
> stand the meaning of old age from the point of view of
> the old, or to observe old people among themselves. There
> is a holistic concern with the influence of cultural con-
> text. The concept of culture itself is central: What are
> the socially transmitted shared understandings that affect
> old people, or that are invented by them? (Keith 1980:343).

Kiefer states: "The terms 'aged' and 'minority group'
both refer to high-level abstractions covering complex, hetero-
geneous realities." The study of the aged among minority groups
appears to be ideal to explore patterns of conflict in complex
societies. He further points out that such research provides a
unique opportunity to study the interaction of social change,
acculturation, spatial and social mobility, and aging (Kiefer
1971:97 and 1974).

How do the elderly Korean immigrant women live, interact,

work, change, and react to their circumstances? Why do they
live and change as they do? By answering these questions,
their sociocultural background, persistence and change in
their lives, and their thoughts about these life experiences
will be explored. Their perceptions of life and old age, their
children, work, economy, social life, leisure, religion, death,
and world view will be the main focus of this chapter.

RECOGNITION OF OLD AGE

Old age is recognized in different ways by each individual besides the socioculturally recognized "rites of passage" from adulthood to old age which starts at age "60." To
these informants old age means a series of changes. Changes
occur in appearance, in behavior, and in social, physical, emotional, and intellectual factors. Spiritual and personality
changes also take place. These informants seem to dichotomize
these changes in old age into positive and negative aspects in
relation to their adaptation to old age life.

Negative aspects of changes in old age have been mentioned. Negative recognition of physical changes in the old is
described by Mrs. Rhim as follows: "One becomes weak and
diseased like an old car." Other remarks on appearance on old
age contain derogatory expressions of old person: "Look at this
ugly white hair," "Look at this leg, it is ugly, I have to fall
down (die)," "I live like a dead person," and "My body is weakening and wrinkling."

An informant comments about behavioral changes: "I no longer can mix with young people. What I say is considered as nagging. There is no job for me to devote myself." This informant realizes that she becomes socially alienated due to the generation gap and a feeling of uselessness. Mrs. Koh found herself not engaging in different activities in life such as social visiting and travelling, and said, "What would I do if something happened to me away from home? I stay near home all the time." At eighty she seems to respond according to her apprehension and perception of weakness.

Mrs. Chin expresses a sense of inadequacy and devaluation of self, which often discourages her from doing something: "I want to telephone my children and find out how they are doing. But, if I know how they are doing, what can I do for them? That's why old persons are told that they are absurd or nonsensical."

To some informants, experiencing old age means changes in the affective or emotional realm. Mrs. Lee expressed her feeling about moving to an old people's home: "I felt something I had not felt before when I went for an interview at a senior citizen's apartment, I thought I had become an old woman, I asked myself, 'Really do I have to live there far away from my children, my church, and my friends?" She reacted to inevitable changes required in order to adjust to her old age. Another informant shared the feelings of being "faint-hearted, discouraged, and miserable" for being an old person.

Some comments about intellectual deterioration are:

"I am just old and do not know anything," "I am unintelligent
and uneducated," and "The old person is useless. The old eat
three meals a day and rest." These remarks speak about their
low self-esteem. Mrs. Kim said that she was a useless person
because her children are not satisfied with what she does.Her
children like American things while she can only do Korean
things. Others disparaged her work due to her lack of knowledge of the American life styles. Her lack of familiarity with
American society affects her life with others.

An informant is concerned about her insensitivity in
the spiritual realm in her old age as follows: "The old become
too hardened and dull to accept, sense, and absorb beautiful
things in life like faith."

Some of the informants' views of personality changes
in old age are often compared with a child's mind and behavior.
The elderly people want to be treated as an elderly person and
and a child at the same time. Mrs. Kim explains it this way:

> "Although the body is getting old, the mind is young.
> Getting old is becoming a child. The period of youth to
> adulthood is physiologically the child bearing and rearing
> stage, so that adults tend to take care of others and
> consider others, but childhood and old age tend to be
> selfish."

Mrs. Yik commented: "An old person seeks attention from her
grown children and easily gets upset." Mrs. Choi put it "They
are old so that they do not think of a grand scheme in their
lives. They live day by day with small joys which mean a great
deal to them."

Mrs. Uh compared and contrasted the personality of old
age with that of the old people of the Western world: "Contrary

to the elderly people from Western countries, elderly Koreans
tend to give up activities in family and society thinking 'I
am old, What can the old person do?'" She added that lack of
confidence was noticed in her old age: "Even to do a small
thing, it provokes anxiety in me. For example, when I go somewhere, I have to get ready one hour or two hours before the
time arrives."

Some of these informants are concerned about their
personality changes in relation to others, particularly with
their children. How are these undesirable changes perceived
by others? How do others react to the changes? In turn how do
their responses affect the old people's lives? The informants
have these questions in their mind. They try to live up to
others' expectations, especially their children's. However, it
is not always easy.

Mrs. Kim explains a dilemma which results when the
child-like aspects of old people are ignored:

> "In a family, there are real children and 'old child-
> ren.' They are all 'children.' However, the real child-
> ren are treated as children by the adults, but not the
> 'old children.' For example, children are given food,
> love, and attention but not the 'old children.' Thus,
> the elderly feel that they are alienated."

Mrs. Ahn pointed out that an old person becomes se-
nile and indiscreet. These personality changes lead to their
behavioral changes. Ultimately, these negative aspects of
change affect others and themselves unfavorably. She states:
"They become talkative, particular, hard to please. That's why
people say, 'When people become old, they become childlike."
Mrs. Kwon explains about personality and behavioral changes

in old age in relation to daily life interaction:

> "Adult children do not tell us anything because we talk
> with others about what we hear from our children with-
> out proper judgment. In a very short time, the news will
> be spread to different elderly people over the telephone
> and soon everybody knows about it."

> "Old people tend to interfere with other's business
> without legitimate reason: young people do not like that
> and say something to the old person. The old person feels
> sad and alienated. For example, when an old woman sees
> that her daughter-in-law has bought something then she
> asks how much it is, where she bought it and so on, al-
> though she does not have money to buy one for herself.
> The daughter-in-law may get irritable and says something
> to her mother-in-law, then the mother-in-law may feel
> rejected. Thus, one has to be discreet."

Generally the informants believe that others do not

appreciate what they are and what they do. As Mrs. Hwang dis-

closed their plan for cooking a Korean delicacy, red bean soft

rice, during a social visit, Mrs. Ahn as a member of the group

herself responded, "Ghosts like old people gather and do such

worthless things." Mrs. Ahn meant that what they were about to

do was not important and felt ashamed of herself. She felt she

should be doing something worthwhile for others. Mrs. Ahn does

not think she meets the expectation of others and she assumes

that others think that what she does is worthless. When Mrs.

Ahn does something for herself and for her small social group

which "does not contribute anything to others in a direct sense,

she becomes uneasy and ashamed. This is because Korean women, as

mothers are always expected to do things for children and others,

but not for themselves. They know that they have to set good

examples for others. Otherwise, they feel that they are inade-

quate.

One informant said that she cannot persuade people al-

though she knows that she is right. She tends to say to others,
"I am not sure whether I am right or not." In her old age she
has developed a lack of assertiveness and confidence in herself.

Some informants find "good" aspects of aging and enjoy
them. What they mentioned were the changes in roles, or role reduction in a negative sense, in relation to disengagement. Positively, it could be said that they have gained a new status and
privilege in old age. The comments are: "I do not have to worry
because the young have taken over everything. All the responsibilities have been delegated so that I feel relieved," and
"It is good that I do not have to worry about anything because
my son and daughter-in-law do everything." However, some informants think this new role is their loss.

Some informants found in themselves behavioral changes
and emotional contentment which differ from those discussed.
Their expressions are "less restrained," "more relaxed and involved in activities with the opposite sex," "getting calm
about a difficult situations." Mrs. Yun experienced that the
old tend to say something which is usually not done by the
young. The old are less inhibited in speech and behavior. When
Yun was buying herb medicine with her daughter, she felt that
the price was higher than she thought. She was able to haggle:
"Why on earth is this so expensive? Make the price somewhat
lower!" Her daughter told her mother that she should not have
said that. Mrs. Hahn was able to join and laugh when her husband's friends visited her house. According to tradition, when
she was a young woman she could not do that.

HOUSEHOLD COMPOSITION AND RESIDENCE PATTERNS

A close tie between elderly Korean parents and their children seems to be evidenced by the patterns of household composition. Thirteen informants (65 percent) live with their children. Within this group, three informants (15 percent) with a married son, five informants (25 percent) with a married daughter, and five informants (25 percent) with an unmarried child or children as shown in Chart 1. In this study, living independently means that the informants are living apart from their children. They are either living with husbands or alone, if widows.

The household size of those who live with married children is usually four to five persons. A typical household may include an elderly woman, their son and daughter-in-law and one or two grandchildren. Most of these people live in apartments which are located in the county where Korean immigrants are concentrated.

Thirty-five percent of the informants who live alone or with their husbands live in senior citizen's apartments. Their residence is near their children, although they live by themselves. Their children usually drive 5 to 10 minutes to visit their parents. These informants who live apart from their children have been in the United States longer than 5 years; two of them have been in the area longer than 10 years. They are relatively Americanized and do not have family responsibilities such as the care of grandchildren. Most of their grandchildren have grown up. These informants seem to enjoy their independence as well as their contact with their children.

Twenty-five percent of the informants live with their unmarried children. With the exception of one informant, all of the informants who live with unmarried children have also married children. Korean women believe that they are responsible for their children until they are married. Living with unmarried children seems to have two functions: (1) the parents can fulfill their parental obligation by helping their children achieve independence and (2) the parents can secure a harmonious relationship with the married children's family. Mrs. Hwang cooks and does laundry for her five children. Mrs. Hahn lives with her daughter and she and her husband planned to live in a senior citizen's apartment when their daughter marries. Mrs. Park and her husband had lived with their married son's family and a mentally ill and divorced son in the household. However, Mrs. Park and her husband moved out with the son who was ill. Their "mentally disturbed son" interfered inappropriately with his brother's family especially with his sister-in-law. Mrs. Park and her husband said that "the unfortunate son" is their responsibility and they have an obligation to see whether or not harmony is maintained among their children.

The older and traditionally oriented informants also seem to live with their children. This situation is reinforced by their children's traditional attitudes and beliefs in the extended family household. Mrs. Ahn and Mrs. Chin live with their children. Mrs. Ahn did not understand why parents and children lived separately. When Mrs. Chin mentioned to her son about moving out to a senior citizen's apartment because her friends were talking about it, her son said "How shameful it would be!" and told her not even do think about that.

In summary, the data suggest that parents and children live together under the following circumstances: (1) when parents are traditionally oriented and less educated, (2) when their length of stay in the United States is relatively short as shown in Table 3, (3) when their children meed parents' help, (4) when parents are relatively old, and (5) when the parents and their children mutually desire an extended family structure.

CHART 1

HOUSEHOLD COMPOSITION AND TYPES OF RESIDENCE OF INFORMANTS
(N=20)

Household Composition	Residence
Lives with Married Son	
Ego (Mrs. Ahn, 75), son, daughter-in-law, granddaughter	Two story apartment
Ego (Mrs. Chin, 79), son, daughter-in-law, grandson (12)	House
Ego (Mrs. Koh, 79), son, daughter-in-law, granddaughter	Apartment
Lives with Married Daughter	
Ego (Mrs. Baik, 67), daughter, son-in-law, grandson (5)	Apartment
Ego (Mrs. Kal, 71), daughter, son-in-law, grandson (14)	Apartment

Ego (Mrs. Kim, 73), daughter, son-
    in-law, grandchildren (3,2,1)   House

Ego (Mrs. Suh, 72), daughter, son-
    in-law, grandsons (7, 5)   Apartment

Ego (Mrs. Yun, 68), daughter, son-
    in-law, granddaughters (3, 1)   Apartment

Lives with Unmarried Child

Ego (Mrs. Lee, 68), daughter   House

Ego (Mrs. Nam Kung, 72), son   Apartment

Lives with Husband and Unmarried Children

Ego (Mrs. Hwang, 62), Husband (72),
    2 sons (40, 25), 3 daughters
    (35, 30, 23)   Apartment

Ego (Mrs. Park, 70), husband (70),
    separated son (45)   Apartment

Ego (Mrs. Hahn, 63), husband,   Apartment
    daughter (25)

Lives with husband

Ego (Mrs. Choi, 73), husband   Senior citizen's apartment

Ego (Mrs. Sunu, 65), husband   Senior citizen's apartment

Lives Alone

Ego (Mrs. Kang, 79)   Senior citizen's apartment

Ego (Mrs. Myong, 79)   Senior citizen's apartment

Ego (Mrs. Rhim, 70)   Senior citizen's apartment

Ego (Mrs. Uh, 72)   Senior citizen's apartment

Ego (Mrs. Yik, 70)   Senior citizen's apartment

TABLE 3

RESIDENCE PATTERN IN RELATION TO

LEVEL OF EDUCATION AND LENGTH OF STAY IN THE UNITED STATES

	Level of Education		Length of Stay	
Independent Living	University	3*	More than 20 years	2
	High school	1	More than 10 years	2
	Primary school	3	More than 5 years	3
Living with Child	High school	3	More than 20 years	2
	Primary school	7	5-10 years	3
	No school	3	Less than 5 years	8

* Number of informants

RESPECT, RANK, AND STATUS

In Korea, due to the Confucian influence all aged are
treated with respect. The origin can be traced to patriarchal
authority in Korean society. Essentially, old people themselves
and their young relations know that elderly people should be
respected and supported. Koreans call their own grandparents
as well as others' grandparents "grandfather" or "grandmother."
In the Korean community where the informants live, this respect
for old age is reinforced through sermons, wedding speeches,
the granting of awards to filial daughter-in-law, and giving
a respect-age party by young people. Older people are addressed with honorific language by younger people while nowadays
elderly people talk to younger people with plain forms of
language with non-family members. Elderly people are given
priority in daily life. They are expected to enter first

so that doors are opened for them and served first.

A son shows utmost respect to his father and their relationship is formal. A son does not drink or smoke in front of his father. However, the relationship between mother and son is relaxed and a son does not always address his mother with full respect language. The father-daughter relationship is more lenient than that of father-son relationship although the two relationships are essentially the same. The mother and daughter relationship is mutual, understanding, intimate, and sharing.

Generally younger men and women show respect to older men more than to older women. In a church clinic, for example relatively young elderly people yielded their turn to older and more prestigious elderly people. An elderly man with a social position, such as Rev. Baik receives the highest respect.

Elderly women serve elderly men and tend to yield their turn to men although the men are younger than they are. Some of the men usually yield back to older women. Mrs. Park's husband was certain about man's superiority and unquestionably made a statement:"Man is stronger than woman mentally and physically. Man is determined and courageous. The evidence is that there are more male leaders than female leaders in the world and there are more male killers than female killers. A man's heart, which symbolizes 'courage,' is bigger than a woman's." Mrs. Park appeared to accept what her husband stated.

The Korean church club affairs seem to be executed by both men and women although crucial controversial issues are settled by seeking the advice of a man. An elderly minister's advice was accepted to handle crucial issues by the club members. Neverthless, women's participation in the club activities was high probably due to the changing position of women and the high attendance of women in these activities.

Rank and status are important in social relations among elderly women. One's status is determined by what her family is, what her children are, and/or what she is in the Korean society in which the informants are involved. If an indivudual has a kinship relation with a socially recognized person with social position or title, the person's rank would be raised and then his status elevated accordingly.

Koreans address or introduce persons with their social position or title as well as those of their kinship such as minister's mother, professor Lee's mother-in-law, and president of a certain association. For example, when I was introduced to one of the church groups, my personal name was not mentioned but the names and positions of my grandfather-in-law, a missionary and my father-in-law, a missionary, and my husband's academic degree and social position were.

When Mrs. Kim was visiting her <u>Hanui</u>, a traditional Korean physician, she expected him to associate her with her son-in-law who is known as an elite and who teaches at one of the local universities as a professor. The physician did not seem to be aware of the relationship. However, he acted as if he recognized the connection in order not to affect her prestige. She is also proud of the fact that she was the governess to one of the descendants who is related to the royal family of the Yi dynasty.[24] Mrs. Kim talks about this whenever she can.

Mrs. Chin is respected by most of her church group members for the following reasons: her old age, seventy-nine years old, her dignified behavior, her caring and harmonizing attitude with people, and her children's social and educational success. Her daughter holds an important position in one of the ivy league universities and is an author of a number of publications.

Mrs. Choi is known as a minister's mother or an elder but not by her name. If someone has more than one title, they are all used in introductions. The president of the church club is also an elder and she is called "president elder."

TIES BETWEEN ELDERLY WOMEN AND THEIR CHILDREN

Children's Selective Acceptance of Parental Assistance

The informants' assistance in the areas of child care housekeeping, which still allow for some traditional aspects seems to be appreciated by their children. The elderly women in this study assist their children mainly taking care of grandchildren, housekeeping, and cooking. In case of sickness of family members, they give nursing care so that the rest of the family members' work is not interrupted.

Examples of this type of help are shown in comments

---

[24]The time period of the Yi dynasty is from 1392-1910.

by Mrs. Baik and Mrs. Suh. Mrs. Baik comments on what and why
she does for her children and grandchildren: "I do not consider the care of my grandchildren work. This is something we,
grandmothers, want to do for our children. I do not want to
view it in terms of money but something our children will talk
about in terms of motherhood." Mrs. Suh said, "I feel good when
I see people who enjoy what I cooked or I did." Mrs. Nam Kung
went to the grocery store in the snow with her painful ankle
in order to cook vegetable and meat dumplings for her son when
he came home from work. Mrs. Song went to help her daughter's
family during a busy period by doing housekeeping, cooking,
and giving parties. When the family holiday season came, she
left for her own place lest she should interfere with her
daughter's time with her family.

In other areas, the informants' assistance to their
children seems to be accepted selectively by their children.
Parents' advice about everyday matters to their children is
ignored or resisted by their children. In some cases the informants' children and the informants themselves consider that
the informants are not qualified to give advice to their children because they are viewed as not keeping abreast with modern
technological daily life and trends. Consequently, they believe
that they have no authority to influence their children because
they lack up-to-date knowledge and economic power.

Generally these elderly women feel that their children
would not accept their advice although they have useful suggestions to offer. The elderly Korean women often pointed out that

they have experienced much more in life than their children.
Mrs. Suh remarked: "I knew a certain thing would not work, but
they insisted. They learned that I was right. Sometimes it is
too late."

Mrs. Kil comments from her experience that her children
did not pay attention to her ability to advice:

"There are very few who ask for parents' advice to make
major decisions in life. Husband and wife usually make decisions. We feel that we could advise our children in some
aspects, but they would not give us a chance. If we insist
on doing so, there might be a chance of endangering interpersonal relationships between us. Under the circumstances
the old feel alienated and most sad. Adult children include
their own children in the dicision-making processes and consider their children's opinion, but not their old parents'
view-points. They say they follow American customs, but
learned and considerate Americans obey and respect their
parents because they learned that from the Bible. When we
were selling our house, a family escorted their mother in
a wheelchair to see the house. I was impressed by them."

When Mrs. Kal said "Although I know the proverb which
says 'Do not discard old things and do not follow new things
blindly," she knew that her children would not listen to her,
but she comforted herself by saying, "Children are ahead of
me and I'd better follow them." Although Mrs. Kal feels that
her traditionally oriented advice might be useful for her children, she let her children follow their modern ways which might
have some valid aspects too. However, Mrs. Kal indicated that
her advice would be more effective then her children's ways.

Some informants stated that they have no authority
because of their poor economic status, as shown by Mrs. Baik
who stated: "I have no property and no authority. In Korea,
I distributed the money which I earned to my children, but I
can no longer do that."

Informants readily recognize their children's ability to manage the tasks of daily life and what they know is no longer useful in the United States. The following are comments about why they are unable to give advice. Mrs. Ahn said, "I am not able to advise my children because they are the experts in managing daily life." And Mrs. Baik commented: "I am going after my children. They go before me. They learn new things in this country. While they live in this country, my children know much more than I do."

There are some areas where children listen to the elderly particularly in the area of mothering. But it is difficult to advise them about marital problems, as shown in the following discussion:

> "When my daughter-in-law was about to give up her disabled daughter, I emphasized the responsibility of child rearing as a mother. My daughter-in-law listened to me. She did not leave home and ask me to take care of the child. She is settled now. I ask my children to look after their children well despite their busy life
> About my daughter's unhappy marital life, if I were a 'dog skinned' person (a person without dignity), I would demand a divorce from my son-in-law right away, but husband-wife affairs are different from other matters. My daughter, her husband, and their child might blame me later on. I do not like that. That's why I do not take any action in those problems" (Mrs. Baik).

Mothers Concerns about Their Children

The elderly Korean women share intimately in concerns about their children. Since their children are viewed as most important in their lives, their children's problems are faced with as much distress as if they were their own.

Mrs. Chuck is worried about her children because they

came to America with very high expectations, but "their health
is in terrible shape due to hard work and stress." When their
children are ill the women are particularly distressed because
the death of children before parents' death is a tragedy. Their
initial reaction to this kind of event is "What terrible sin
have I committed to be punished like this?"

Mrs. Yik was sad because her daughter-in-law's mother
and sisters were "staying and doing nothing" at her son's home.
The increased number of household members means a financial
burden on her son. As a further illustration, Mrs. Baik is
distressed because her daughter's married life is miserable.
Her husband beats her often and the expected his wife to work
during the last trimester of her pregnancy. Mrs. Yun is saddened
about the fact that her daughter works as a housekeeper which
is considered a low ranked job. Her daughter's "fate of being
poor and disrespectable" distresses Mrs. Yun. Mrs. Ahn is
anxiously waiting for her younger son and his family to join
her. Whenever she sees "plentiful material goods" in America,
she thinks about her son and his family, and sighs because
she is not able to share that with them as she would like.

The elderly Korean women are concerned about their
children's welfare. This issue is very significant for them.
They would rather die than to face the misfortune of their
children. Their comments in this respect reflect these thoughts:

> "I would be happy if I could die before some kind of
> misfortune occurs. Misfortune might be the death of my
> children or a grandchild's accident" (Mrs. Kwon).

> "I want to die in order not to know of my children's
> sufferings. If I die I would not know If they suffer or
> not" (Mrs. Yun).

Mrs. Nam Kung and Mrs. Hwang criticized Mr. and Mrs. Park, who were visiting their son and daughter for two months at their children's request, because they left a middle aged "mentally disturbed son" at home. The son is able to take care of himself in terms of daily living. He goes to the library to study and goes shopping. The perception of other's parenting is as follow:

> Mrs. Nam Kung: "They should not stay with their other children that long. They have gone for over a month already."

> Mrs. Hwang: "They said that they moved out for their sick son. Now, they left the son all by himself and took off by themselves."

> Mrs. Nam Kung: "If they moved out for their son, they would get a two bed room apartment. The other day I saw him in a dark corner of their living room separated by a screen."

Their concerns about children are not limited to their own children. It often becomes a subject of peer review of one's performance. There exist negative sanctions and when one deviates even slightly, gossip develops easily. Child care among these elderly women is considered absolute and a sacred priority which is part of maternal duty. If a mother does not behave this way, shame is brought to her easily. There is saying: "A child is worshipped as God." A child is always viewed as a child by parents even he becomes an adult. Leaving a sick child alone is inexcusable.

Being an Example for Their Children

The elderly mothers engage in unceasing efforts to teach their children by setting themselves as examples of ways to attain a respectable and harmonious family life. This is only possible by sacrificing individual wishes and interests which is the central theme of Korean moral and ethical teaching based on East-Asian philosophy.

Thus, the elderly Korean mothers discussed the principle that they have to be a good example to their children. Mrs. Rhim never skips going to church because she feels that she has to teach her children "dignified ways of living." She manages financially by herself so that she is able to "maintain her dignity."

Mrs. Baik participates in activities planned by her children although she is not particularly interested in joining them. She does not care much to dine out because it is expensive and the food in restaurant does not impress her. She believes, neverthless, that she could hurt her children emotionally by not accepting their invitations. That is why she wants to involve herself in her children's activities as much as possible.

Mrs. Ahn had been living with her younger son and his family almost all her life. Since her arrival in America two years ago, however, she has been living with her older son. She is always grateful toward her older son because he is very kind to her although she feels that she has not done anything for her older son for 35 years because of an unfortunate separation between mother and son due to an international political situation. One day her older son asked his mother jokingly, yet seriously, with whom she wanted to live when her younger son came to the United States. She answered with her older son, although she really wanted to live with her younger son. Her decision was based on the moral and ethical principles of the traditional Korean family value system. According to the patriarchal Korean society, the oldest son is supposed to support the parents. Also, since her son took "all the risks in the world" to bring her to America, she does not want to hurt him by making decisions which would bring shame on her family because of her "narrow and selfish love for her younger son." She knows that if she behaves righteously, others in the family will react accordingly.

CONFLICT WITH CHILDREN

Conflict between parents and children can develop in various types of sets of kinship relations. Conflicts between a mother and her own children may occur more overtly and frequently than between a mother-in-law and son-in-law or daughter-in-law. However, the conflict between a mother and her own children is usually rather quickly resolved by mutual understanding, but a troubled relationship with a daughper-in-law or son-in-law is not easily settled. There is a saying indicating degrees of comfort in different kinship ties: "When you live with your son, you can eat comfortably in a sitting position, with a son-in-law in a standing position, and with a husband in a lying down position."

The informant who lives with a son and his family, seems

to face a much more direct and strained relationship with a daughter-in-law than the informant who lives alone or with a husband. An informant with a husband is more respected by a daughter-in-law or son-in-law than a widow. An informant's husband is viewed as the patriarchal authority of his extended household and protector of his or her mother-in-law and also he is known as generous and understands the two parties without bias. A mother-in-law and daughter-in-law or son-in-law usually make an utmost effort to avoid direct confrontation as long as they can tolerate each other. However, once they challenge each other, it is difficult for them to reconcile. The mother-in-law and son-in-law relationship is believed less restrained than that of the mother-in-law and daughter-in-law. This is so because there is a close relationship between mother and daughter, and this daughter is usually on good terms with her husband. A son-in-law is considered easy to reconcile with in case of a conflict because a man is believed to be more generous and resonable than a woman. Besides, her daughter manages their household details which often are considered causes of conflicts. This factor also contributes to the reduction of conflicts between mother-in-law and son-in-law.

The strains that exist between a mother-in-law and daughter-in-law appear to be much more intense, serious, and persistent than those between a mother and her own children. The kinship relationship between mother-in-law and daughter-in-law causes these strains rather than any problems they might face in daily life. The mother-in-law and daughter-in-law re-

lationship is based on a connection between two strangers. The
mother has been the closest person to her son. However, nowadays in the United States, after the son's marriage, the
daughter-in-law becomes the closest person to her son. It is
very difficult for them to agree even on small matters due to
a basic "antipathy." Furthermore, the mother-in-law in present
day society does not have any household authority, but the
daughter-in-law does. However, to some degree, the matter of
creating and sloving a conflict situation depends on the nature
of the issue and the people's perception, understanding, and
ability to adapt or manage complex human relationships.

The common cause of conflict between an elderly mother
and her son seems to be related to family responsibility and
welfare. When elderly mothers perceive that their sons neglect
their family members, they become disappointed and unhappy. Mrs.
Baik stated: "Children cannot be perfect always. Even jade has
a flaw. My children cause me sadness. I say to them that they
will regret it when I die." Mrs. Baik feels that her son should
be interested in his disabled daughter instead of absorbing
himself with a strange woman.

Lack of financial support is definitely one of the factors which make parents sad. The elderly Korean women who gathered for a social visit spoke ill of the son of one of their
friends who, they say, does not look after his 79 year old
mother properly, although he is a physician and owns a very
large house which was known to be "so big one that one cannot
find one's way around."

A son's behavior toward his wife could be viewed with jealousy by the mother-in-law and a husband's behavior toward his mother could be envied by her daughter-in-law. The strains in these relationships can contribute to conflict situations among the elderly. Mrs. Hahn talked to her friends in her neighborhood about the anger which she experienced toward her son based on these strains:

"Sometimes I regret that I did not throw him out during the Korean War. I protected him in dangerous situations. At that time we could not have light in fear of being bombed so he would cry. I placed a light under the Ibul (a thick Korean style blanket), and he played. I had to wash his diapers when bombers were passing over me very closely with loud noises. Now, the very son bought his wife a heavy gold necklace, a diamond ring, and other expensive jewelry. Yet he will not buy me the medicine I need."

There are different ideas about easing this strained relationship. Some elderly Korean women believe that the traditional approach by the patriarchal line of authority should be used in order to maintain harmony in a household. Mrs. Myong emphasizes that harmony in her family is dependent upon on the adult son. In this process, no direct transactions are seen between mother-in-law and daughter-in-law, but only through male authority as noted in her comments:

"The mother-in-law and daughter-in-law relationship is an instinctively antipathetic one. Blood is thicker than water. The mother-son relationship is essentially close. If a son is filial to his own parents, he should influence his wife so that she follows proper behavior with his parents. A son should be responsible in case his wife does not contribute to family harmony. A son should be a successful negotiator between his mother and wife. Sometimes he helps his wife to recognize the importance of his parents and he may need to advise his wife when they are alone. The wife and his mother should know each other. The son can let his mother know his wife's merits and vice versa. When a son is in a superior position to his wife in terms of education, income, and authority in a household there will be harmony in family and the son's parents will be respected."

There is an opinion that if mutual understanding and effort are shown in this relationship, family harmony will result. Mrs. Ahn expresses her opinion on how harmony in a family is possible: "If a daughter-in-law is kind and understanding, son and parents will be happy. It is still essential for parents-in-law to be understanding and generous with a daughter-in-law."

Most women find that the traditional Korean values of filial piety have become weakened in the Korean family in the United States and consequently, elderly parents are less respected than they were. Mrs. Kim is saddened as she expresses her fellings about this issue: "I feel I am useless. There is not much difference between the old and the young in terms of respect and authority. People talk back." Rationalizing and explaining are considered talking back. According to the traditional Korean value system, the young should not utter a word to the elders, even when the elder is wrong. Disappointment and unhappiness result because parents and their children have different expectations of each other in this changing society.

Mrs. Uh commented that if an elderly woman expects a traditional Korean way of life with children in the family, the person would not be happy at all. The person should try to understand the conditions of a changing society. They should not expect to be served. Mrs. Uh went on to say that intergenerational value differences result in different expectations from each other. For example, parents expect to be respected and supported by children. On the other hand, children expect their parents to help them by working around the house. When conflict arise, parents feel that their children do not appreciate what they do for their children. All these combination lead to interpersonal conflict between the generations.

The traditional household structure contributes to strains and conflict. When parents and children live separately in a nuclear family structure, intergenerational conflict situations appear to arise less than in the case of an extended family structure. Also, if independent daily life is possible between parents and children, again there will be less intergenerational conflict than in the case of interdependent situations. Economic independence seems to be particularly important. Mrs. Rhim was convinced economic and residential independence brought the two generations close together in harmony. She thought she was fortunate enough to be in this position.

The elderly Korean women are aware of role reversals which they face particularly in this country. One of the Mrs. Kim's comments reflects this points:

> "These days the husband and wife relationship is more important than the parent and child relationship. The roles of mother-in-law and that of daughter-in-law are exchanged these days. Young women work outside the home and old people stay home and do housework, meal preparation, and raising children, which were traditionally done by daughter-in-laws. Nowadays, young people are bosses."

The children's attitude toward an elderly parent in terms of duty of support and attendance is also changing. The

following observation was made in interaction between mother
and daughter: During lunch time, Mrs. Kim's grandchildren were
served hot noodles first by her daughter while Mrs. Kim was
told to fix whatever she liked. Mrs. Kim mumbled something and
fixed herself a cold sandwich with a cup of cold milk. In a
traditional Korean family, grandparents are served first before children. One day Mrs. Kim said that if she were economically independent and had another source of support such as a
son, she would not be treated without "respect and dignity."
Her son died a few years ago. The presence of an alternative
close kinship support person such as a son or a husband seems
to be important to counterbalance conflict in another set of
relationships.

In a transitional period, it is difficult for a traditionally oriented elderly Korean woman to accept changes in the
division of labor in her very own household. Mrs. Myong talked
about the case of one of her friends which reflects this situation. It is shocking to some of the elderly women to notice
that "a son is controlled by a wife" or that he is doing house
work. Once Mrs. Myong's friend saw that her son was doing house
and kitchen work. She immediately went back to Korea after she
called her son "a puppy" because to her only a puppy is controlled and protected by a housewife.

When parents and a daughter-in-law are not in good
terms, a son cannot do much but sympathize with his parents.
Mrs. Hahn stated that she could not reprimand her daughter-in-
law as was done in the past because in the first place it

would not work. Moreover, she believes it would only endanger the relationship between her son and his wife. Mothers-in-law feel that divorce is not recommended because of their upbringing. The solution they follow when they note strains between their children and spouses is to avoid anything that might cause disharmony in the household. There are two prevalent opinions about dealing with children. One opinion is that old parents should accept their children's opinion especially those of a daughter-in-law in order to keep peace in a household. The other opinion is that old people should take the role of "enforcing the law and righteousness."

CHANGES IN TRADITIONAL KOREAN FAMILY STRUCTURE

Residence Patterns

There is a marked tendency for elderly Korean immigrant women who live with married children to do so with married daughters rather than married sons in order to promote harmony in the family and in order to avoid strains particularly with a daughter-in-law as mentioned earlier. At the time of the present research, only three informants (15%) lived with their married son and daughter-in-law. Five informants (25%) lived with their married daughter and son-in-law. Another five informants (25%) lived with unmarried children. Seven informants (35%) lived apart from their children altogether as shown in Chart 1.

Two of the five informants, who lived with their married daughters, also had a son in the United States. Furthermore two

of the informants, who lived with unmarried children also had
a married son in the United States. All of the seven informants,
who lived apart from their children, had a married son or sons.
Thus, altogether fourteen informants (70%) had a married son
or sons in the United States including the three informants
who lived with their married sons. If these informants would
have been living in traditional Korean society, it is quite
probable that most of them would have lived with their married
sons. Before they came to this country, the majority (70%) of
them had lived with married sons. According to the traditional
Korean family value system, a married son lives and supports
his parents and unmarried brothers and sisters.

Upon arriving in the United States, most of these elderly Korean women lived together with their children. Then, some
of them moved toward independent living and some of them continued to live together with their children. The informants
who live with their children tend to be responsible for the
care of their grandchildren and unmarried children. These
Korean women appear to be traditionally oriented and to have
limited formal education or primary school education. Another
characteristic seems to be that they have resided in the United
States a relatively short time as shown in Table 3. These women who live with their children as well as their children
appear to have a mutual desire to reside in the same residence.
These informants seem to have a greater continuity of the
Korean way of life than informants who live by themselves.

Some of the informants who live with their children are

adamant about leaving their present residence pattern and quite
content about the arrangement. Mrs. Ahn and Mrs. Nam Kung expressed their opinions. Mrs. Ahn is sure that she will live
with her family always. She said, "I live peacefully with the
children because it is fun to watch children live. They are
always kind to me." When she was told by Mrs. Suh's daughter
that she was looking for a senior citizen's apartment for her
mother. Mrs. Ahn asked Mrs. Suh's daughter almost in a tone of
protest, "Does she have to move out?" Mrs. Nam Kung said that
she does not understand why her friends live alone and sit
around doing nothing. Mrs. Baik commented: "What is the joy of
living in this world without getting involved or sharing the
life of one's children. Also while the children are busy, they
let them visit you every once in a while."

The informants who live apart from their children, tend
to be the more highly educated informants with a university
education as shown in Table 3. They are more socially involved
and have an effective social network outside of the family.
They possess knowledge about the utilization of public welfare
and other facilities and an orientation toward change. These
women have had a relatively long length of stay in the United
States as shown Table 3. They have no unmarried children, and
have no need to care for grandchildren. This group of informants
believes that elderly Korean parents should live by themselves
to attain independent living with privacy in areas of child
rearing, decision making about family affairs, preparation and
preferences of food. These women like to choose their recreation,

to develop hobbies, to become "boss" of their own household,
and ultimately to attain harmonious and mutually respectful
relationships between elderly parents and children. Women who
lived in independent residence arrangements thus believe that
this pattern makes it possible to maintain a good relationship with their children. They seemed to have started an ad-
venturous life on their own in a strange country.

However, in most cases, these elderly independent women have moved through earlier phases of residence with married
children. The pattern is clearly shaped by the ages of grandchildren as shown in Mrs. Myong case. Mrs. Myong has been living in the United States for longer than twenty years. She has
two sons in America. She took care of her older son's children,
then her younger son's children who are presently high school
students. About seven years ago, she moved to her present senior citizen's apartment from her younger son's residence. Mrs.
Myong explains why and when elderly people should live by themselves:

> "If possible, elderly parents should live apart from their
> children especially when the parents are not needed any
> longer. When adult children have small children, it is prop-
> er to stay with children and care for grandchildren, but,
> when grandchildren grow up, grandparents should leave. The
> elderly people want to rest quietly, peacefully, and inde-
> pendently. By living separately from children, they can
> avoid conflicts between parents and children so that they
> maintain a mutually caring relationship."

Living alone requires certain steps. A certain length
of time of residence in the United States of about three to five
years is required while giving help to children by caring for
grandchildren, and doing work around the child's house; the

elderly also need to get to know the American belief and value systems; and they need to become part of effective social networks and get information about living separately from the family network. Once the decision to move is made, they apply and wait until they are notified that desired housing is available.

There were exceptional informants who did not go through the stage of attainment of living alone mentioned above. For example, Mrs. Yik did not wait until her grandchild grew up. She moved to a senior citizen's apartment about a year after she emigrated to the United States. She is a university graduate and a socially active person in connection with her church, the Korean Elderly Association, and is interested in elderly Koreans' welfare issues. Mrs. Yik did have a hard time deciding whether she should live in the senior citizen's apartment or take care of her infant grandson. She found it difficult to take care of her grandchild and stay home especially because she had been socially active. Finally, she moved out although she realized that as she fulfilled a duty looking after a grandchild she had conflicts in choosing between the two roles of the woman who lives apart from her children and the woman who lives with children. She knew that her family members and friends would talk about her if she lived independently. However, she added the Japanese proverb, "Do not worry! A child will grow well!"

It seems to be important for some of the informants to move towards an independent living arrangement while elderly parents and their children have a good relationship. It is obvious that they want to keep their parent-child bond intact

by doing everything possible. Mrs. Sunu commented: "It is ideal
to start to live separately from children when we are in good
terms. It gives us bad feelings if we moved out when we are
not getting along." However, some informants were trying to
move out after the parent-child relationship had deteriorated.
For example, an elderly woman, who said that she was having
a very poor relationship with her daughter-in-law, was determined to live alone, although she was told by one of her
friends that she might be found dead alone in an apartment.
She replied, "That's good! If I could die that easily. How
can I live with her (her daughter-in-law)? She asks me to take
care of my grandchild, even when I am gravely ill."

Some traditionally oriented informants felt that children had forced them to live separately by degrading what they
did and by emphasizing their lack of knowledge and experience
with American society. Sometimes, the customs of an elderly
mother were classified as old fashioned discipline of children,
"poor quality of housework," and "out-dated cooking." Mrs. Kang,
who lives by herself, comments: "Children make the elderly people live away from them. It is a shame when we think of our
tradition. Nobody wants to live with their parents."

There seems to be no essential difference in causes of
strains between the informants who live with their own children
and those who live with daughters-in-law. Characteristics of
these informants are generally to be protective of their children including daughter-in-law or son-in-law so that it is difficult to obtain adequate information about a sensitive issue

such as a conflict situation between mother and children or children-in-law. However, strains generally are seen between mother-in-law and daughter-in-law are a daughter-in-law's "inconsiderate attitude" toward her son such as not helping him through employment, not serving him properly well cooked food, and interfamilial differences in household management, and child rearing. Due to the basic strained relationship discussed earlier in the Section, Conflict with Children, once mother-in-law and daughter-in-law have confronted each other, it does not seem to be easy for them to reconcile themselves to each other.

On the other hand, mother and children are close, understand each other, and protect each other. They have a similar belief and value systems because they have lived together at least 20 to 30 years. They have faced each other with conflict, strains, and disagreements. However, they can reconcile easily because of their basic understanding and mutual affection and caring. During the social visit at Mrs. Ahn's house, Mrs. Hahn, Mrs. Hwang, and Mrs. Nam Kung and the hostess agreed that animosities toward their children can be forgotten easily, but not toward a daughter-in-law.

Since the independent living residence pattern is fairly new among the elderly Korean women, they are concerned about what others think of their change in family structure. They tend to defend themselves from negative remarks about their independent living by their family members, friends, relatives, and others they know. Mrs. Myong comments:

"Most children and even elderly people themselves
tend to think that there are conflicts between parents
and adult children when they see an elderly Korean who
lives alone. But it is not true. They do not understand."

Some of the informants who live with their children
were actively getting information about moving into senior
citizen's apartment. Mrs. Hahn and Mrs. Hwang who live with
their unmarried children, plan to move into senior citizen's
apartment so that they could live independently as soon as
possible after their children start to live independently from
their parents.

However, according to Mrs. Yik, who has lived alone for
a few years, only a small percentage of the elderly population
live alone. Mrs. Yik stated that generally the Korean elderly
people are not courageous enough to live alone due to their
traditional family orientation of an extended family residence
pattern. One of the friends of Mrs. Yik informed me that she
had been encouraging other Korean elderly people to live
independently. She added, "Some elderly Koreans cannot think
of living separately from their children."

Independent Living

Essentially the apartments of those who live independently have basic Western furniture such as a bed, sofa, table,
and chairs although some of them do not use them but live on
the floor as they did in Korea. For example, in Korea, in winter time, they lived and slept on a papered warm rock floor
called O'n Dol and in summer they used the cool wooden floor.
Even Western style houses in Korea have one or two O'n Dol

rooms and usually this room is occupied by elderly parents.

Their apartments are decorated with art objects from Korea and the local area. They love to grow plants and keep their apartment clean and attractive. When I visited Mrs. Rhim's apartment, for example, it looked like a miniature Korean museum : Art and other objects were displayed such as, mother-of-pearl wall pieces, a mother-of-pearl lacquered dresser with a big mirror with many different cosmetics on it. There are a red sofa and an arm chair, an Oriental carpet, many green plants, and many other small and big decorations.

The most acute problem which the elderly Korean immigrant women face when they live by themselves is loneliness. The common complaints is that the women do not have an appetite when they live alone. They do not cook meals regularly.

They are concerned about safety within the home and the unpredictable nature of sudden accidents. Informants feel that they may accidentally fall down and become unconscious or die alone during a shower, sleep, or while using the bathroom. These health and age-related problems cause fear of living alone. A minister encourages them to ask their children to call them frequently and to try not to take a shower while they are alone.

One of their other major questions is about residence patterns when they get older. They anticipate that they will need people around them because they will become old and unpredictable in terms of health and life. The majority of them think that they can manage until the age of seventy, but after

that they might have difficulty to manage by themselves. All of
the independently living informants in this study are over the ag
of seventy except Mrs. Sunu. No one clearly said that she would
go back to her children's family, but they expect to live in a
government-owned nursing home. One lady said, "Here in America,
people do not seem to depend on their children in old age. They
go to a nursing home. If necessary they are sent to a hospital.
I do not think the majority of old people will bother their
children in their late age." Two women, Mrs. Myong and Mrs. Rhim
are saving their money to go to a private nursing home.

Independent Living, Friendship, and Leisure Activities

A group of elderly Korean immigrants who live in a
senior citizen's apartment have a close relationships among
themselves. They are interdependent in affairs of life. Their
friends seem to have replaced family members. They often eat
together, work together, shop together, and solve problems
together. When one of them is sick, they give her nursing care.
When someone who does not read English receives a document in
that language, she goes to the person who is known to understand English best among themselves. There is a viable exchange
of goods. For example, they often visit each other bringing
dishes of food or wine, if they can drink. They also share medicines with one another. When a person has to be in bed because
of illness, the person is usually visited by friends and church
members. Yellow flowers or gifts in yellow color are not usually
given to an ill person because the color symbolizes illness or
death.

These patterns of closeness have created a lack of
privacy so that they finally made a rule that they should visit
only at certain hours during the day. Thus, they can take care
of individual needs such as taking medicine, getting in touch
with the family, developing individual hobbies or just having a
quiet time.

Generally, independent living informants have much time
for themselves because they do not have the responsibility for
caring for grandchildren and the family. The time is spent for
different matters such as leisure activities, volunteer work,
tasks of personal interest, and social activities. Telephone
conversations are frequent among friends. Since the means of
transportation to get together, are not easily available, they
call each other frequently. Usually telephone conversations
are long. There is a long greeting with discussions on old
age and health, children, cooking, future get-togethers and
so on. Mrs. Rhim received five telephone calls during a two
hour long interview period. They were all from her friends.

Different games are played such as cards and Korean
stick game called Yut. Mrs. Sunu commented on the popularity
of playing games among her friends. She explains that this is
done "in order not to gossip" because gossip is discouraged.

These independently living informants do volunteer
work a couple of days a week. They make stuffed animal toys,
decorations, and other objects for orphanages. They also work
in a hospital laundry room and some of them work for their own
Korean churches. Their other leisure activity is gardening.

They are provided a small piece of land and they cultivate vegetables and flowers. They appreciate this opportunity for physical exercise also.

Informants who have time, education, interests in enhancing the family and social condition of elderly Koreans, and in insturcting American way of life, seek active opportunities to realize their interests. Mrs. Yik is concerned that there are some elderly women who are not treated kindly by their children. She wants to involve herself and reflect on the situation of the elderly Korean community in a legal agency for the elderly. She also has been trying to teach American ways of life and Western forms of etiquette to other elderly Korean women. She pointed out that some of the elderly Korean women need to learn American manners for eating and patterns of sitting. Korean elderly women are used to sitting on the floor in a broad and long skirt which is different from American style.

During the weekends the women visit their children or they are visited by their children. They seem to value this opportunity most and wait for this moment all week long. Two informants are planning to visit Korea soon. Almost everybody longs for this opportunity, particularly, the people who left their family members and relatives there. Two of the informants have been back to Korea. These independently living informants frequently join a tour group arranged by the Elderly Korean Association to see different part of the United States independently from their children.

LIVING WITH CHILDREN

Family Living

The family life of the informants who live with their children is very casusal. The privacy of an individual does not seem to be very important and it does not appear to be required. These informants generally sleep with one or two grandchildren in a room. For example, Mrs. Yun slept with her toddler granddaughter in the twin bed and her infant grand- daughter slept in the crib. The only decorations in the room were the children's framed pictures on walls.

Mrs. Ahn slept alone in her own room. There were two twin beds in the room, and a sewing machine which she uses frequently. Her friends came to visit during the sewing. They all sat on the two beds and talked together. Mrs. Ahn responded and occasionally consulted with her friends about her sewing, and then they gave frank opinions about it. Mrs. Ahn tried on the pants she was making and they often commented jokingly: "You can wear this to go to a nice party." The room also had a pile of boxes. On one side of wall, a framed picture of Jesus Christ was hung. Mrs. Ahn's living room was decorated with a screen with Oriental drawings and calligraphy, Korean tradi- tional art objects and green plants. There was a display cup- board too. A new dinner table set was conspicuously placed. Mrs. Ahn volunteered to comment about this set: "My grand- daughter bought this, but not my son." Her son is a minister. A display of wealth in a minister's residence is considered

shameful among Koreans. Mrs. Ahn added that her son would use
all the available funds for his service center.

Living with Children, Friendship, and Reciprocity

The daily lives of these informants are regulated mainly by the activities of their children. Also, friendship activities among these informants take place as an essential part of
daily life. Friendship does not only contrubute to their social,
but also to daily life matters such as family economy and mental
health. It is a pattern of reciprocal relationships.

The elderly women who live with their children work
mainly in their household. They care for their grandchildren,
cook, wash, and shop at the store. A typical day begins after
their children go to work. The elderly Korean women finishes
washing the dishes, house cleaning, and she does the laundry
or similar chores. After these tasks are completed, she may go
for a visit. These visits last for half a day sometimes or at
other times they stay all day until about two hours before
their children come home from work. The elderly women then
prepare dinner for their children.

The informants who live with their children, eat Korean
food together. In a particular neighborhood, the elderly gather
mainly at Mrs. Ahn's. She shares lunch with them. Sometimes
other ladies bring lunch to share among themselves. Mrs. Ahn
and two other elderly women are seen together all the time.
They are called by their friends the "Three Musketeers." Some
of the other women want to visit Mrs. Ahn's but they cannot

because they care for their grandchildren. At the end of this
field work, one more woman joined the group of three women.
They help each other and tell each other of their whereabouts.
These elderly women's children assist their mother's friends
when they can.

When these elderly Korean women meet someone new, they
are interested in knowing her age, whether she lives with sons
or daughters, children's occupation, and how long they have
been in the United States. Their conversation usually centers
around family, and their neighbors. They talk about family
problems and suggestions to ease the situation are given.
Thus, a form of psychotherapy or group counseling is done. When
someone is ill, they usually find out what might be wrong and
what should be done, and particularly whether or not one should
go to see a health practitioner. They consult each other in
the decision making process.

Much material sharing takes place mainly in the area
of food items. When there are limited goods or opportunities
the person who is not offered this opportunity expresses dis-
pleasure toward the person who has had a chance. For example,
Mrs. Baik's son wanted to sell one of his shops downtown. Mrs.
Baik informed Mrs. Yun so that her son-in-law can offer to
become a manager. Later when Mrs. Hwang heard about this, she
looked unhappy about this matter and said, "I already asked
Mrs. Baik to tell me about it so that my daughter could become
a manager." Mrs. Hwang was particularly critical of Mrs. Yun
because she felt that she was kind enough to give her different

opportunities to earn money, e.g. baby sitting and introducing
house guests so that she should have reciprocated rather than
taken away the business opportunity.

Friendship, matters of economic interests, and patterns
of reciprocity are closely intertwined. Mrs. Yun shared bean
sprouts which she grew with Mrs. Ahn and Mrs. Hwang. Although
Mrs. Yun knew that Mrs. Nam Kung came to Mrs. Ahn's everyday
for visit, she did not prepare a bag of bean sprouts for Mrs.
Nam Kung who has not contributed to her in any way and is rather
critical about people. However, Mrs. Yun told Mrs. Nam Kung:
"If you like some, come to our place and get some." Mrs. Nam
Kung replied, "I do not need bean sprouts. We do not have
family members who eat that."

The patterns of reciprocity among these elderly friends
are seen in their mutual conceptions of each other, and their
exchanges. Mrs. Ahn is known as a generous and understanding
woman. Mrs. Ahn's daughter-in-law introduced housekeeping work
to Mrs. Yun's. Mrs. Hwang took Mrs. Yun to different places for
recreation when Mrs. Hwang's children gave her a ride. Mrs.
Hwang introduced a couple of visiting scholars from Korea to
Mrs. Yun. Mrs. Yun's family was able give them room and board.
and they earned somemoney. For this, Mrs. Hwang was given a
large bag of rice by Mrs. Yun's family.

When the informants invite friends to different occasions such as birthday parties, they usually try not to let
the invited guests know why they are invited unless it is a
modernized formal invitation. They might say, "Just come over

for a chat", or "Why don't you come over? It will give you
chance to have fresh air or take a walk" or "Why don't you come
for a while." When it becomes more obvious that there is a celebration they say, "Why don't you just come over and have dinner with us?" without giving the reasons for the invitation.
When I was invited to the one-hundred day old celebration for
Mrs. Yun's granddaughter, Mrs. Yun called me and said: "I have
not seen you these days. Why don't you come to our house for
dinner about 6:30." When I asked what the occasion it was, she
hesitated at the beginning. When I insisted that I wanted to
know, then she told me what it was. Similarly, a wedding invitation card was not given to me directly, although there was a
chance but through another person. It seems to be this way because people bring gifts for the occasion, and party givers are
neither supposed to burden guests in any way nor make their family or private affairs big. Some of them are very strict about
it to the end and some of them let the people know the nature
of the occasion with a gesture of reluctance. It appears to be
a trait related to etiquette, modesty, and humility about self
and family.

People brought different gifts to the 100 day birth
celebration such as money in a white envelope, baby clothes
and other gifts for the baby, and a bottle of wine. For the
celebration, a Korean style white cake and a red cake were
steamed. The white cake is supposed to be ditributed to 100
houses to please a child's guardian spirit in each household
in the neighborhood where the child is growing and the red

cake is to drive away evil spirits. A long many folded white
thread is hung around the child's neck to symbolize a long life.
In olden days, when the infant death rate was very high, this
custom was observed very carefully. This ritual is said to
have originated from animism.

For Mrs. Baik's birthday, all the elderly ladies in her
neighborhood were invited. Three of them ("The Three Musketeers") were about two hours late. Mrs. Baik said in a dis-
pleasing tone of voice, "At least they could have telephoned
us and told us." But the ladies appeared not to have been concerned much about being late. Time orientation differs according to the individual. On the day before the party, when I
called Mrs. Hahn, who was also invited to the party, and asked
her to tell Mrs. Baik that I would be a little late, Mrs. Hahn
said, "Do not worry about that, you will not be late."

The main theme of Mrs. Baik's birthday was that life is
vain and short like morning dew, so that they'd better enjoy
what is left. After the birthday breakfast, all the invited
persons danced, and sang. Some Korean music and dancing were
introduced as well as American music and dancing.

Gifts were given, but they were not opened and shown to
guests. Money was given by grandchildren. Adult children sometimes ask their children to present gifts to their grandparents.
It is done this way to teach child to show respect, care, and
reverence and to give the "message" that "What I present you is
trifle," to solidify their relationship including the grandchild, and/or to show affection indirectly without presenting

oneself. Other gifts from guests were a bottle of home-made rice wine, a package of cigarettes, and red carnations.

The party was essentially given by Mrs. Baik's eldest son's wife. Her eldest son lives with a woman other than his wife. Since he is a Chinese style cuisine cook and owns a restaurant, he brought a large amount of Chinese style food. Among the family members, Mrs. Baik's daughter-in-law was the only person who used language with endings of respect to her mother-in-law . In some families, highly correct language is not used with mother by her children, because the mother and children's relationship is considered close and informal. However, children are expected to use respectful form of language with their father. Her sister-in-law, her husband's sister, gave orders to her elder brother's wife even though she does not live with her husband any longer. The dauhgter-in-law, in turn, obeyed the commands from her mother-in-law and sister-in-law with apparent pleasure. She is still her husband's legal spouse, and she has a disabled child from this marriage.

Assistance by guests at the party was not accepted. One woman said, "If you do work, when you are invited, the host family will live poorly." It seems to be the principle that a guest should be treated correctly and with respect. In Korea, up to recently, physical labor was considered for "low class" people.

Constraints in Living with Children

Those Korean elderly women who live with their children want to help their children as much as they can. However, they are physically and mentally exhausted due to their old age. Generally, they wish that there was not so much house work for them to do although they know that working is physically, mentally, morally, and socially. Some of their comments are: "I dread to go into the kitchen" and "I avoid it as much as possible." They say that their feelings toward work are different from the feelings they had when they were young. For them working around the house seems to be burdensome psychologically and physically. It might be interpreted as signs of disengagement in old age. Seventy-nine year old Mrs. Chin talks about her experience which reflects this main concern:

> "My grandchildren and their friends came to us one day from out of town. I was alone at that time. I thought they would stay for supper at least. I was planning supper for them. Unexpectedly they said that they had to leave for somewhere. I am always glad to see them, but it is too much for me to prepare food and do their laundry and cleaning so that in a way I was glad to hear that they were leaving."

The majority of the informants said that they did not work hard in Korea. They enjoyed activities of elderly people, such as visits, sightseeing trips, and just plain leisure time because their daughter-in-law did the house work and child rearing. During their first few days in the United States, parents are usually taken to different places for sightseeing and then the parents start doing housekeeping and babysitting.

They find the care of grandchildren particularly hard and it
is even harder because some of them do not think their adult
children fully appreciate what they are doing. Mrs. Kim who
has 3 grandchildren, ages of 3,2, and 1 shares her thoughts
about the delicate situation related to the care of her grandchildren:

> "It is hard work to care for children in old age due
> to the deterioration of physical strength. Some of the
> adult children do not know how hard it is and how much
> their parents save them money by caring for their child-
> ren. Sometimes I think of moving out to an apartment, be-
> cause it is so hard, but I wonder whether I would really
> be happy there or not, because moving out means not show-
> ing parental concerns in time of their need."

Their adult children's appreciative attitude toward what their
elderly parents do for them seems to affect their spirits positively.

When these elderly women feel that some of their friends
are unusually burdened with their children's work, they suggest
to their hard working friends that they slow down. Still, some
of the elderly women have different opinions about that and say,
"You have to do it until you can." The majority of the informants have this attitude and continue this pattern due to the
traditional parental obligation of helping children. In addition, it is required in changing society.

These groups of informants who live with their children
rarely join in leisure activities such as trips or tours which
take usually more than one day, and other social events, due
to their work in the household. They consider work for their
children as their priority. Thus, when they have time to join

leisure activities, they really appreciate it. If they go to
church or the elderly university,[25] they do not hesitate to say
that they are there for relaxation, but not much for worship
or study. Mrs. Chin said that she enjoys church because she can
talk with other aged people. She added that children are too
busy and tired to be expected to spend time with her even in
evening.

Mrs. Suh, who has two grandchildren who need Mrs. Suh's
attention almost all the time, goes to an elderly university
on Saturdays. She takes her grandchildren even to her university with her because her daughter expects her to do so. For
Mrs. Suh, going to an elderly university is her valuable leisure activity and she elaborates as follows:

> "I thought I was the only one who went to the elderly
> university to have my own world away from children and
> to see friends and exchange information, but all the
> others are like me too. I am not much interested in
> learning English because I do not understand it and if
> I learn something, I forget it right away. I have vaca-
> tion until March and I already miss the school. I enjoy
> the social opportunities there very much. We can exchange
> information about daily life, the life of the elderly,
> children, grandchildren, cooking, and our past and future.
> Saturday is my best day in the week. I enjoy going there
> immensely."

A social worker in the Korean service center encourages
the elderly people to come out to the center to participate
in the activities planned there. She found that they seem to
be happier and complain less of health problems after they

---

[25]This particular elderly university is run by a Korean
church to help the elderly Korean immigrants to adjust to the
life of immigrant family and society. They mainly teach English
and American ways of life. The university also provides social
and recreational opportunities.

take time out. Mrs. Yik who has a leadership role among the elderly Korean immigrants commented that talking, singing, and dancing with her same age group, ethnic group, and sociocultural background relieves anxieties and strains caused by the different sociocultural realities expressed by the Korean elderly, such as loneliness, alienation due to intergenerational conflict, the language barrier even among family members, confinement caused by cultural and social unfamiliarities, and transportation limitations. It should be noted neverthless that the two informants, who are more highly educated and who are also devout Christians, despise the above mentioned public group singing and dancing which they think is "shallow" and in "poor taste."

INCOME, WORK, AND ENGLISH SPEAKING ABILITY

Income

All of the informants regardless of patterns of residence, depend on their children and/or the United States government for partial or total living expenses. The eight informants living with married children and a single informant living with an unmarried son do not have to worry about their daily living expenses because their children pay as family expenditure. Also, the eight informants living with married children receive Social Security pensions and the informant living with an unmarried child receives state aid.

Four informants who live with unmarried children have different income sources from the cases presented above. These include: income solely from children, a pension solely from Social Security, combined income from children and Social Security, and combined resources from children and income from employment.

Mrs. Lee, who lives with her unmarried daughter who takes extensive trips abroad, is responsible for paying all living expenses by herself. She receives a Social Security pension and food stamps. Mrs. Park and her husband live with their "mentally ill" son with financial support from other married children. Since they came to America recently, they are not eligible for government aid. Mrs. Hahn and her husband have two sources of income; from their children and Mr. Hahn's work. Mrs. Hwang's household finance is managed by Mr. Hwang's Social Security pension and some contribution from their five unmarried children.

The informants who are supported mainly by children seem to experience financial difficulty. Mrs. and Mr. Hahn had to move to a cheaper apartment than they were used to living in and Mr. and Mrs. Park were about to discontinue their health insurance subscription. According to these informants, part of the reason is that they receive the same fixed amount regardless of rising expenditures.

As the elderly Korean immigrant women settle in their communities, they are being oriented to economic independence from their children. Mrs. Kim evaluates the trends as follows:

"My friends are facing acute economic and social problems during this transitional period. We were not prepared for the neccesity of independence from our children. But I think your generation is preparing for independent life from your children. We devoted everything
to our children with the thought that if we raise our
children properly, we would not have any worry in our
old age."

The informants who live apart from children have

achieved financial independence from their children in order

to maintain a harmonious relationship with them by not burden-

ing them economically. Neverthless, they are dependent on the

government. These informants' economic dependence has shifted

from their children to the government. All the informants who

live in the senior citizen's apartment building are recipients

of Scial Security pensions. One of them receives a govern-

ment retirement pension because her husband worked for the

government. Another lady, Mrs. Myong, also receives $200 from

her two sons monthly and she commented that she appreciates her

sons' support very much because it helps her financial situa-

tion a great deal.

The possession of money and material security among

these women gives them a feeling of security in daily life.

Mrs. Rhim elaborates about this point as follows:

"Having money means a sense of security. The old people
desire money. Having money is happiness. It is better than
a husband or son. If one has money, she is able to maintain
a good son-mother relationship, a good mother-in-law and
daughter-in-law relationship, and a good relationship with
friends. One can have happiness in giving. Economic dependency is a sad thing. When a person is poor, she becomes
oversensitive."

Mrs. Rhim is happy about her economic independence from her

children. She does not depend on her children economically. Sometime ago, all of her children had a meeting and decided to collect money from each of them in order to give mother a monthly pension, but she declined their offer. However, she receives occasional gifts from her children and she also gives them gifts on different occasions. A reciprocal relationship is maintained.

People who receive monthly government pensions are more or less financially independent. These people cannot save, however, because of the many expenditures they have and government regulations against saving. This pattern is seen in Mrs. Myong's case. She lives in a senior citizen's apartment and receives a monthly Social Security pension and extra support from her sons. She describes her economic situation as follows:

> I live with the money $275 per month from the nation and $200 from two of my sons. I have to pay $75 for rent and $115 for meals. I buy tapes to record sermons to distribute to family members and friends. Also I need money for family members' birthdays, Christmas, and other occasions. I pay offerings to church. I try to live within my budget. I am thankful to my children for giving me monthly support."

The informants, who live in the senior citizen's apartments, receive a Social Security pension, and Medicare benefits. They are very grateful to the government. Here is an example of their gratitude for the support:

> "Who would give me this lovely and comfortable place to live in? They give us money monthly. We can go to a clinic or hospital everyday if we want to. Of course, transportation is a problem. However, if we really have to go somewhere we can call our children. We can go to a nursing home when we cannot take care of ourselves. Even a good filial son cannot do that well for his parents. They do not delay even one day in sending us the check on the first day of each month."

Some of the recipients of state or federal assistance
expressed feelings of inferiority in receiving the assistance
and they said they questioned themselves whether or not they
deserved to be supported by the government for allowing them
to have emigrated in their old age. Examples of their feelings
and opinions about this issue were given by Mrs. Myong:

> "At times I feel inferior to the people who live by
> themselves without receiving assistance. Sometimes I am
> not sure whether I deserve a low cost apartment or not.
> So I comfort myself with the thought that my sons pay
> a large amount of taxes."

Even indirect thoughts of their own sons' support seem to comfort
these ladies because most of them have been supported by their
children in Korea.

Volunteer Activities, Work, and English Speaking Abilities

Nine (45%) informants hold honorary or volunteer positions in the Korean community. These include seven women who
give their services to churches and two women do volunteer
work for the elderly Korean community. There seem to be some
continuity in the patterns of activity held by some of these
informants in relation to their formal education and experience
in Korea and in the United States. For example, three informants who have primary school education, did not have any
apparent occupation outside the home in Korea and in America.
They are paid for occasional child care which does not require
formal education. Two of them also work sometimes as housekeepers. Their child care work is arranged through their friends.

TABLE 4

COMPARISON OF INFORMANTS' OCCUPATIONS

IN KOREA AND THE UNITED STATES

Occupation in Korea	Number of Informant	Occupation in U.S.	Number of Informant
Honorary and volunteer work	6	Honorary and volunteer work	9
Orphanage director	2	Babysitting	3
Librarian	1	Housekeeping	3
Government employee	1	Staying home	5
Staying home	10		

Informants with relatively high formal education hold
responsible voluntary or honorary positions although what they
do is limited to the Korean community and it is different from
the kinds of professions held in Korea as shown in Table 4.
This pattern is probably due to their age and the language
barrier. Seeking honorary or volunteer position might be at
least partly related to acquiring recognition or status. For
example, Mrs. Yik who is a university graduate and was a
director of an orphanage, was the president of the Korean
Elderly Association and is an advisory member of the association. Mrs. Myong is a graduate of a seminary school in Korea.
She was active as a minister's wife in Korea, and in this country, she assists her minister in a Korean churches in America.
Some informants who were educated and professionally
active in Korea seem to feel alienated since they have not been

utilizing their skills according to their professional ability. Mrs. Uh who is a university graduate was a librarian in a leading university library in Korea. Although she is active in church work, she often says, "I do not know why but since I came to the United States I have not been feeling confident." Mrs. Yik frequently also comments that she has not been engaged in activities in American society. She attributes this to the language barrier and "transportation paralysis."

Some of the informants who live with their children desperately want to help their children who are not settled financially: Mrs. Yun has accumulated about $1000 by working as a babysitter for a couple of young Korean parents. She hopes to give this money to her children when they start a small business. While these people seek job opportunities eagerly, a few work due to their age, language barriers, and transportation problems. Some of the informants wanted to earn some pocket money for themselves and they are constantly considering ways to do so. The following conversation took place during a neighborhood visit about job opportunities and the problems of language and transportation which make it difficult for them to work:

> Mrs. Nam Kung: "I wish I could rent one of our rooms to a male student or worker. Perhaps I could cook him dinner. In Korea we received work from sweater factories and did it at home."

> Mrs. Hwang: "If we look for it, there should be something like that. There are no babies these days to take care of because so many people came over here. If I spoke English, I could sell flowers."

> Mrs. Nam Kung: "I heard the Oriental grocery needs some help, but how can I get there."

Mrs. Hwang: "You can take a bus."

Mrs. Nam Kung: "I do not know how to get there."

Fifteen informants (75%) do not speak English except for
a few English such as "sale," "grocery," "car," and "doctor."
Arabic numerals and gestures are helpful means of communication.
Five informants (25%) are in English classes. Some learn through
voluntary tutors, and some go to classes offered by a voluntary institution. One informant is learning by herself. These
students want to learn more conversational English than other
types of lessons. In the elderly university, they learn important
medical and biblical terminology. They were particularly interested in learning English to carry on a telephone conversation.
Some women, like Mrs. Suh, feel that is is hard to learn
English in old age: "I cannot learn English, I listen and I
forget right away. I came to America before my grandchildren
were born, however, they speak English very well, but I do not
know anything."

Twenty-five percent of the women go to the bank, travel
by themselves, exchange greetings and manage very simple interviews. However, even a simple telephone conversation is hard
for them   to handle. They need an interpreter for different
kinds of written English material.

Some informants do not seem to feel acutely the incon-
venience of not speaking English. For example, Mrs. Kal coped
with a situation with minimum knowledge of English as follows:

"I can communicate, although I do not speak English.
I use gestures and let one of my children talk with
Americans over the telephone. When I was in the hospital,

I could not express myself to the nurse in English. I let the nurse speak with my grandson and the problem was solved. When I wanted to have soup, I used the English word 'soup' but the rest was Korean. They could understand me and they got me soup."

Mrs. Ahn also said, although she does not speak English, she does not feel very uncomfortable because stays mostly at home. Some of her grandchildren do not speak well, but they can manage. Mrs. Rhim does not study English, but she said she copes with it fairly well:

"I do not study English. It gives me a headache. I manage buying things. I could say 'Good morning!' and 'How are you?' Surely I can say 'problem' when I need to have something to be fixed, as I point to the object. Do you think I can expect to have a conversation with Americans? If so, I expect too much of myself. When I need to go somewhere I need to speak English, I go with my children because I need the ride any way. My significant people are my children and friends who speak Korean."

Still more different methods of communication were mentioned. In the case of shopping, the women read the totals on the cash register. In order to ride the bus alone, the number of the bus and directions are written on a piece of paper and given to the bus driver. When a repairman comes, he is shown the object which needs to be fixed. When aspirin is needed, the empty aspirin bottle is taken to the pharmacy. Grandchildren point out what they want to eat after they take their grandmother to the refrigerater. Television programs are watched with the sound turned off and they interpret the program among themselves according to their perception of the scenes on the screen

Informants, who are relatively more educated and were active socially, voiced the discomfort and inconveniences due to lack of facility with English. Some of their complaints are about not being able to communicate with grandchildren, inability to get a job, to function as the president of the Elderly Korean Association, to read and to fill out important documents, to write a check, and to obtain and to give information. They referred these kinds of difficulties to me on numerous occasions. They also added that there are only a few elderly Koreans who are American citizens because the elderly Korean population does not have the English proficiency which they believe is required to become a citizen of the United States.

Some of the informants, like Mrs. Yik, express their fellings about not being able to communicate with others in English as follow:

"Ifeel like I am a fool. I cannot speak and go any-where " (Mrs. Park).

"It is sad that I am not able to speak English" (Mrs. Myong).

"In Korea I was perceived by others as an educated and socially active women. However, in America I feel I am treated as an unintelligent and uneducated person. That's why I am learning English. When I was holding an office in the elderly immigrant Korean community, I could not do much because of the language barrier" (Mrs. Yik).

The majority of the informants depend mainly on their children for transportation. The women with higher education and self-confidence tend to use public transportation. Sometimes these informants express their inability to get a job and to engage in activity everyday due to lack of transportation as follows: "How can I do that without 'feet' (means of transportation)?" Often visits to clinics are delayed until their children can take them. Many other different visits such as going to church or shopping cannot be carried out as they wish. The elderly Korean immigrant women's social activities are also limited due to the inconvenient transportation situation in the suburbs. One of the informants furthermore lives in an isolated area where there are no Koreans. She said that she felt as if she was trapped.

Another obstacle which prevents the elderly Korean women from engaging in activities outside the home is related to their traditional value system. Their children usually do not help them to find an activity because it is against their traditional family value system. The children are supposed to help their parents to live as comfortably as possible. Thus, they do not volunteer to find work for their parents. Mrs. Yun's son-in-law did not permit his mother-in-law to work for others, but once she started to babysit, he took an attitude that he could not stop her working. However, she could not let her son in Korea, know about this. If she did, filial piety would have led him to be distressed about it. She commented on numerous occasions what a marvelous son she has. When some of the informants in this study learned that the elderly parents of economically well-off children were in some type of work, they blamed their children for this shameful situation.

RELIGIOUS LIFE

Almost all of the informants (85%) said that they went to Christian churches. This included thirteen Baptists, two Methodists, one Presbyterian, and one Catholic. Two women wor-

ship their ancestors, and one is a Buddhist. Most of the informants can find common elements among the different religions
so that they do not reject any particular one. Some of the informants and other Korean Christians I met in this research
point out that many Korean immigrants go to Christian churches
for social reasons particularly because they are lonely. Churches are important especially at the beginning of their settlement in the United States.

Mrs. Hwang identifies herself as a Buddhist although
she goes to a Christian church here. She stated that ultimately
Buddhist monks and Christian ministers are the same in terms
of helping people to have faith based on spiritual beliefs.
Mrs. Yik commented that both Mudang and minister heal sick
people based on the patient's faith.

Twenty-five persent of the informants (five informants)
have been devoted to one religion for a long time, and they
excluded other religions. Occasionally, one of the informant's
religious view is not related to the recognized world religions,
but to the thoughts of an individual. Mrs. Baik expressed her
religious views as follows:

> "I never believed in any god seriously. I prayed in
> front of Buddha when I had problems in family such as
> sickness. They say illnesses can be cured but it is all
> psychological. Some people feel that they become healthy,
> but that's again all psychological. I have been to church
> for about six months now, but I do not think I am serious.
> I think god is your own thought and reason. I take nobody's
> way but mine. If I think my way is right way, I take that
> way whatever others say."

This expresses her own individual religious meaning. Her religion lies in her thinking and judgment in her mind or heart.

In the neighborhood settings occasionally, the elderly
talk about religious beliefs in relation to their concerns
of life after death. Mrs. Hwang considers herself as a Buddhist
more than as a Christian although she goes to Christian church
with her friends. She poses the question: "Christians believe
that they go to Heaven after they die, but can anybody prove
that?" Mrs. Nam Kung, a Christian elder, answered, "Even
among Christians, it is very difficult to go to Heaven. One
has to do many good things in the world." She had not answered
exactly what Mrs. Hwang asked and the conversation did not
continue.

THOUGHTS ABOUT DEATH AND BURIAL

Informants reflect their close parent-child bond in
their discussions about death and burial. The elderly Korean
women in this research want to die quickly and peacefully
when the time of death comes in order not to trouble their
children and themselves. After death, they desire to be buried
near their children so that they can maintain their parent-
child relationship as long as possible.

In the Korean ancestor worship tradition, ancestors
are served with utmost reverence and care like their elderly
parents. They believe that their ancestors' souls are in contact with their living children and maintain an interdependent
relationship. After death, the deceased elderly's body is laid
out on his back in order to keep a proper body alignment for

shrouding and placement in the coffin. Koreans believe that
dead souls are taken care of by three messengers sent by
Buddhist rulers of the underworld so that after positioning
the corpse, three bowls of rice and three pairs of straw shoes
for the three messengers are left in front of the main gate.
Relatives and neighbors came to help with different tasks
of the funeral. They pay their respects to the deceased elder.
Some of the tasks are preparing food, and sewing burial clothes
for women. For men, they hold a vigil through the night, carry
the funeral bier, and dig the grave (Janelli and Janelli 1982:
58-61). Both men and women family members and relatives wail as
a part of the mourning process.

Generally, funerals are expected to last three days:
the day of death, the following day, and the day of burial. This
time span may be changed depending on the wealth and prestige
of the deceased persons family, and at times because of a cosmological reason for selecting an auspicious day for burial
(Janelli and Janelli 1982:61).

According to Janelli and Janelli, the corpse is shroud-
ed on the second evening after death. Through this ritual, the
deceased becomes an ancestor. An ancestor tablet is made to
signify the deceased's new status as ancestor. It serves as the
object to rites for the new ancestor. The mourners, the deceased family and other relatives, wear mourning clothes made
of coarse hemp cloth. The clothes worn by the sons of the
deceased are the most elaborate. They include an outer coat, a
hat, and leggings made of hemp. A straw rope is tied about the

waist and upper part of the head; and a cane is used (Janelli and Janelli 1982:62-63).

These authors explain why the mourners wear coarse hemp clothes particularly the chief mourner, usually the de- deased's eldest son:

> The chief mourner's clothing is said to resemble the dress of a prisoner. He is guilty, say informants, of not providing better care to his parents and thereby not prolonging their lives. Thus the mourning costume is viewed as a tangible expression of guilt for inadequacies in the care and support of one's parent's (Janelli and Janelli 1982:64).

After wearing the mourning cloth, the first ancestor ritual is performed. On the burial day, several rituals are performed: before the coffin is taken out of the house and load- ed onto a bier, before it is carried out of the village, before it is lowered into the grave, and before the mourners return home. "Each ritual includes a formal address to the ancestor, written and recited in classical Chinese...." Janelli and Janelli 1982:65). Women do not attend funeral processions be- cause they hold peripheral positions in the agnatic descent group (Dredge 1978:19).

The funeral procession is accompanied by singing and rhythmic bell ringing. According to Janelli and Janelli, the funeral song contains a number of themes evidened: "...the sacrifices of parents and the love and care they shower upon their offspring; the indebtedness to parents; the soul's dif- ficult journey to the land of the dead and its understandable reluctance to depart the world of living; and the inevitabili- ty of aging and death" (Janelli and Janelli 1982:69-70). The

search for favorable grave sites, geomancy, is practiced for
the well-being of ancestors and their generations. Geomantic
theory is based on cosmological principles such as vital forces
(Janelli and Janelli 1982:71-75).

The elderly Korean immigrant women accept death naturally. They view it matter of factly as a natural last stage of
life. Mrs. Ahn made a statement about old age and death: "An
old person is like an old tree. It dies natually and slowly."
Elderly women often talk about the old burial custom called
Koryo-chang. Mrs. Kil, a woman who attended the medical clinic
along with the informants, explains it as follows: "There
was a custom called Koryo-chang which means that parents over
seventy year old of age were buried alive with a little food,
so that they would die sooner or later. If I were living in
the olden days, I would have been buried already."

The informants unanimously say that one should not live
a long time. If one has lived a reasonable length of time, she
should die. Mrs. Suh added to this issue: "My father lived
exactly 86 years old. He could not live like a man. Most of
the time, he had to lie down. It was difficult for himself
and for others."

In order not to prolong life miserably at the time of
death, some informants tend not to take ginseng, antler's
horn, or other tonics which are believed to give longevity.
Mrs. Suh said that she prays everyday: "When my health fails,
take me quickly and peacefully so that my children will not
be bothered because of me." They want to die in a very short

time without suffering so their children will not be burdened with pains and worries. Dying itself does not worry them
but how to die seems to be one of their grave concerns. Some
of the informants wish to die at home near their children, but
not in a "strange hospital."

The elderly Korean women in this study, have a strong
wish to avoid burdening their children with all possible means
within their power. Some of their comments regarding this are:

> "I do not worry about death itself but what I worry
> about is burdening my children" (Mrs. Suh).

> "My mind is still young, but I am physically old. I am
> weak and ready to die any time. I hope that I can die
> without giving agony to my children and my self. I do not
> want to bother my children because they have no time. I
> do not want to bother them because I love them" (Mrs.
> Myong).

The place of burial and sometimes new burial customs
are referred due to the new circumstances. It all seems to be
related to the desire of continuing long lasting relationships
with children or loved ones, even after death. Mrs. Chin referred to her reflection regarding death and burial:

> "I l ok at myself through a mirror rather often these
> days. I see myself getting ugly and weak. I know I need
> to die. I asked my son to cremate me and he said, 'How
> can I do that? How cruel it is?' I said, 'You do not know
> when you have to move again. Do you think you can take
> my body everywhere you go?' He told me that he plans to
> bury me beside my husband in Korea, but that is too
> troublesome."

Mrs. Park desires to be near her children even after death:

> "My children asked us where we want to be buried. We
> told them that we really want to be settled in Korea
> because it is my country and my ancestors' burial ground
> is there, But, we are afraid that we have to be buried
> in the United States because our children are living here
> so that they could visit us more often."

The understanding about ancestor spirits and worship
varies. Mrs. Hahn thinks that there might be ancestor spirits
because she dreamt about her deceased parents-in-law and one
of her family friends was sick until her ancestors' burial
ground was moved to a different site. However, most are not
clearly committed to belief in the existence of ancestor
spirits. Mrs. Park and Mrs. Yun commented about their ancestors as they understand and practice this worship. Mrs. Park
made the following remarks:

"Some people say that there is an ancestor spirit but
we are not sure about that. We venerate our ancestors as
descendants of them. We left all our ancestor's tombs in
North Korea. The country is divided into the North and
South, so that we cannot go back. Therefore, we bought
a piece of land in the country. We erected tomb stones
from our 15th generation back. They were alive 500 years
ago, by the way. We built altars for the ancestor worship ceremony. We prepared tomb stones already for our-
selves. We thought it would be easier for our children
and nephews to bury us if we prepared everything including
the tomb stones. That's why we did it."

Mrs. Yun expressed some of her doubts in ancestor worship in the following statements:

"Who believes in spirits these days. If you participated in the ancestor worship ceremony, you just felt
relieved because you did a kind of obligation. My mother
saved me from an acute disease but I have not participated
in a worship ceremony for her for years."

"My daughter wrote to me that her brother was pleased
to see that his wife prepared good food for his father's
ancestor worship ceremony day and everybody who participated in it was happy."

SUMMARY

It is evident that elderly Korean immigrant women's traditional life patterns have been changing particularly in areas of family life. The traditional family structure of the elderly Koreans has begun to change from the extended family to the individual or nuclear family pattern, or to the independent living arrangement. Children's economic support for these Korean women has started to shift as government pension programs have become available to some.

These aged informants recognize different changes as characteristic of their old age. They dichotomize these changes into positive and negative aspects in their life. Physical deterioration, personality change such as "indiscreetness" and alienation from young people are viewed as disadvantageous aspects. Some informants enjoy their disengaged status manifested in role reduction while other informants consider this phenomenon as a loss. Some informants find certain behavioral changes in old age convenient. They can be relaxed in social transactions including interaction with the opposite gender which was previously restrained.

These Korean elderly ladies view death in old age as a natural path so they tend to wait for it calmly. They wish to experience their last act in life as naturally as possible for their children and for themselves. These elderly women show their motherly concern for their children even in relation to their death, by avoiding everything which prolongs and makes

their life a burden. This outlook was evident in the tendency
of some of the ladies not to take restorative medicinals.

As thoughts of life after death are considered, these
elderly Korean women wish to be where their children are so that
they can continue to interact with them even after their death.
Their whole life has been for their children, by their children,
and with their children. In the changing American society, they
do their best to keep this special bond with innovative fashion.

In the following chapter, the concepts of health and
illness, with particular emphasis on Hwabyung, a popular
Korean construction of illness, and meaning of illness in old
age of elderly Korean immigrant women will be discussed.

CHAPTER V

UNDERSTANDING HEALTH AND ILLNESS OF

ELDERLY KOREAN IMMIGRANT WOMEN

In this chapter, conceptualizations of health and illness will be discussed based on the East Asian medical principles and religious backgrounds. The impact of old age on the meaning of health and illness will also be examined. Spiritual causes of illness will be dealt with in terms of religions such as animism, shamanism, Confucianism, and Christianity. Finally, focus will be placed on Hwabyung as a cultural construction of illness in relation to Korean sociocultural norms and traditional Korean medical principles.

CONCEPTS OF HEALTH

The elderly Korean women consider health the most important aspect of their life. Koreans frequently reiterate the saying about health as being the prime importance in life: "There is no treasure more important than health." The informants define health in various ways such as invincible strength, physical and functional maintenance, genetic inheritance, physi- activities and participation, freedom, independence, happiness, good appetite, and fate.

Mrs. Baik talks about health as an unchangeable force. To her, if a person is healthy, the individual is not affected by external factors such as a harmful substances to the human body. Mrs. Baik commented: "These days we hear that people were killed after taking tampered medicine, but I do not believe that they were killed by the medicine. They were killed because their basic health status was weakened." She views health as a real strength, energy, and power. In a similar vein, Mrs. Uh expresses the concept of health as an extraordinary positive condition of the body: "I do not particularly want to be healthy. As long as I live, I want to have an intact and functional body." To her, health is more than a whole working physical system.

In contrast to the above, Mrs. Park is satisfied with her definition of health as the optimum function of body organs. Mrs. Park's comments reflect this concept of health as functional physical maintenance: "Health is to have good working Ochang (five storage organs: lungs, spleen, heart, kidneys, and liver) and Yukbu (six working organs: gall bladder, small intestine, stomach, large intestine, urinary bladder, and triple warmer). This concept of internal anatomy, is part of the traditional medicine familiar to Chinese and Koreans.

Some informants have a genetic point of view of health. According to Mrs. Nam Kung, health is good physical inheritance, so that she does not emphasize patterns of health measures much. A genetic endowment is the primary health determinant to her.

Health is an ability to involve oneself in activities
with children, but when one is sick, it is not possible to do
so and one has to stay home alone. Mrs. Suh elaborates on this
situation from her experience: "Health is a necessary element
or requirement to be able to participate in activities with
children such as shopping, going on picnics, and travelling.
If health is lost, children ask you to stay at home, and then
I have to stay at home, when I would love to go out with my
children, I need diversion. Health means activity and participation."

One informant mentioned the need for freedom. According
to Mrs. Ahn's life experience, before she came to America, one
time her younger son's freedom was deprived. Confucius relates
harmony and order in society and harmony in human beings--
health. She felt that liberty is a necessary condition to
achieve health in mankind. For some informants health is independence. To Mrs. Ahn her health is "not bothering children."
When a person is healthy, she does not have to lean on her
children in sickness.

Still, there is the broad positive notion that health
is happiness. Good health means no interferences with daily
living. It gives a person a sense of well-being. As long as
they live, they want to be healthy. That does not mean that
they want to live a long time or that they fear death. They
want to live life fully.

The women, furthermore, are oriented to physical health.
They put a heavy emphasis on diet and its vital function as an

essential contribution toward a healthy state. These immigrants put a great deal of emphasis on good appetite or ability to eat and digest in judging a person's health status. When they greet each other, they say, "Have you eaten breakfast?", "Do you have a good appetite these days?", or, "Do you eat well these days?" Desire to eat is a criterion to measure a person's health status. When someone presents her own physical complaints, one always inquires about his appetite and what he has eaten recently. The good quality of food intake is equivalent to taking restorative or tonic medicine (Lee 1982:71). Ki, vital energy, originates in the abdomen. Food as a source of energy is digested there, mixed with air or force, and transmitted to different parts of body.

When I visited the homes of the women in this study, they never failed to serve me or ask me to join them for their next meal. They also spent a great deal of time preparing food for the family. One of the important ways of showing affection is serving tasty nutritious cuisine such as rice with different grains and beans, broiled sea-weed with sesame oil, beef turnip soup, bean curd vegetable and meat dumpling, pickled vegetable, and ginseng tea which are believed to promote health.

Some of the statements they made about the importance of food intake for health are as follow:

"A healthy person eats well and is active. In order to be healthy, one has to eat good food and what he likes to eat" (Mrs. Hwar.g).

"If a person has a good appetite, he will be active physically" (Mrs. Suh).

"One eats well, sleeps well, is not often sick, but energetic" (Mrs. Hahn).

"If one eats well and is free, he will be healthy"
(Mrs. Ahn).

At least twenty-five percent of the informants said that
health, illness or other related matter are ultimately dependent
on fate. Mrs. Kal describes these fatalistic aspects of health:
"You are given your life span by fate. You live only the life
span which fate gives you. You try to live longer than what you
are given, but it does not work." This aspect of their attitude
towards health, illness, and death is fatalistic, as Metzger
has also pointed out for the Chinese (1980:7).

According to Mrs. Yun, everybody is endowed with a
certain fate from birth. Fate is related to the year, month,
day, and time of one's birth. It is understood that fate is
determined by the movement of vital energy in connection with
Ohang (Five Elements) and Ŭm and Yang principles of cosmology
at the time of a person's birth. The force of the macrocosm
affects a human being, a microcosm, with the force of the cosmos.
It determines one's fortune, number of children, wealth, social
position, and life span. Commonly, people say that one's life
is dependent on heaven. If a person dies despite all different
kinds of good remedies, they believe that it is because of his
Palcha (fate).

THE MEANING OF OLD AGE AND ILLNESS

Elderly Korean women have a classification system to
dichotomize all their different health problems: (1) natural
signs of old age which do not require their children's care

so that they accept them relatively calmly and (2) signs and
symptoms of illness which usually require their children's
attention and care so that it provokes anxiety among them because they wish to avoid burdening their children as much as
possible.

Elderly Korean women equated old age with deterioration of health. They have a subtle dichotomy in the concepts
of health and illness in old age. First, old women have increased malaise, but they still have the ability to participate
in the activities of daily living independently particularly
from their children. The second, complementary concept is that
old women have illnesses. Two different sets of illness beliefs
and practices seem to apply in the two states.

Their commonly accepted expressions for old age, related
to increased malaise, are loss of vital energy, poor appetite,
general physical weakness, easy fatigue, dizziness, poor eye
sight, hearing difficulty, memory loss, and missing teeth.
Thus, seventy percent of the respondents complained of old age
as fatigue or general physical weakness, thrity-five percent
about poor eye condition, ten percent about missing teeth, and
five percent about senility.

They frequently present their symptoms of old age in the
following terms:

>"I know I have loss of vital energy because of a slow
>and weak pulse, and difficulty in singing in church"
>(Mrs. Kim).

>"I have no appetite. It means that a person is close
>to death. Legs are heavy. I feel like I carry huge rocks
>while I walk" (Mrs. Yun).

"I become inactive so that I do not go out often"
(Mrs. Koh).

"It gets burdensome to work around the house due to
lack of vital energy" (Mrs. Suh).

"My eyes are woozing and getting dim" (Mrs. Yun).

"The first sign of old age seems to be blurred vision.
My eyes are very tired. I cannot read the Bible so that
I listen to my tape instead. During the sermon this morn-
ing I closed my eyes because they were very tired and un-
comfortable. Others might have thought I was sleeping"
(Mrs. Chin).

"I always look for my key. I don't seem to remember
things any more" (Mrs. Nam Kung).

These changes are accepted as natural phenomena of old

age. Thus, usually nothing is done unless their children urge

and assist them to have treatment. Mrs. Yun remarked: "Treat-

ment would not do much good because there is the force of

aging," and Mrs. Hahn commented: "My children asked me to fill

missing teeth, but I found that I have to go to the dental cli-

nic many times and the expense is very high. That's why I deci-

ded not to bother. Any how, how long do you think I can use

them? Sooner or later I will be going (death)."

A second aspect of deterioration of health among these

women is illness which to them is inability to participate in

everyday life independently, and the fear of burdening their

children with their inevitable dependency. They consider this

situation very unfortunate for them and for their children. Ill-

ness means to some elderly Korean women "burdening the children"

or "bothering the children," which they abhor and wish to avoid

at all cost. Their discussions of these points are as follows:

"To die peacefully without prolonging the state of sickness, so that I would not bother my children. This is my last wish" (Mrs. Uh).

"It affects one's ability to work. But frankly I do not have worries. All my children are grown up. If I die now, I do not have worries. My only worry is that if I do not die quickly during an illness, my children suffer. It would be a sad thing if I become incontinent" (Mrs. Sunu).

"When I am sick I am afraid that my children will notice that I am sick. My children and husband consider me as the main pole of their house" (Mrs. Hahn).

"When I could not see very well, I covered my bad eye so that I could see better with the other eye, but it did not work very well. Finally I decided to have an eye operation to live with sight so that I can help my grandchildren and children. Because, if I do not die and cannot see, then I would be only a burden to my children. It is all right for me not to see and die If I were alone" (Mrs. Baik).

"When I am sick it is difficult to get around. I often think how good it would be if my husband were alive. He could get me water to drink and so on. He is my husband, so that I do not have to feel particularly bad about troubling him. It is difficult to bother others even my own children. I was not able to carry out house keeping. On the contrary, I have taken their time while they are busy. Althoug my daughter thought that there was risk involved in the operation recommended, I underwent the operation because I did not want to bother my children any longer. But I did not die as I secretly wished" (Mrs. Kal).

Their reasons why they received treatment are mainly for their children. Their motivation for curing an illness is their children. Usually operations are not recommended for these elderly people. Mrs. Kal had surgery for her gall bladder problem although her internist and daughter had some hesitation about carrying out this plan. Elderly Korean informants tend to delay informing their children about their illness. Sometimes they do not inform them at all. In order not to let their children know that they are ill, they continue to carry

out daily chores and behave as casually as possible. Mrs. Wang
made an effort not to show her signs of illness by not lying
down although she was very sick. She tried not to take a sick
role as long as possible in order not to interfere with her
children's life. However, children usually recognize the illness of parents when it is obvious.

When the elderly women are ill they tend to try to
solve the problem by themselves first. If care is still
required after self-help, some informants refer to their
friends before their children. When Mrs. Ahn diagnosed herself
having arthritis on her knee joints and legs, she came to
Mrs. Yun and told her about it and Mrs. Yun took her to Mrs.
Park who practices moxa burn. Mrs. Ahn received moxa burn
treatment and had obvious burns from the treatment. When she
limped, her children asked to examine her legs and then her
children found that she had moxa burn treatment. Her children
were gravely concerned about her original leg problem as well
as the burns from the moxa treatment, and told her not to have
moxa burn anymore. They took her to a biomedical clinic immediately.

The elderly Korean women, who live in the Senior
Citizen's apartments, are interdependent while they are sick in
terms of nursing care and daily living as much as they can.
However, when they think their condition is serious enough,
then they let their children know. Mrs. Uh did not let her
children know about her back pain until she could not get
around any more. She went to her daughter's house for a week
for rest and returned to her friends' care in the senior

citizen's apartment. In Korea, there is an old saying: "There is no filial son for a long sickness." This proverb seems to reflect the elderly Korean women's fear of bothering their children. More than half of the informants reiterate this theme whenever they can.

A few of the informants refused to have extensive laboratory tests for symptoms of the digestive system. They felt that those are not necessary for in their opinion. There is nothing much that can be done even when they learn the results of the tests. They do not want to bother their children for those problems. Mrs. Kae, well educated and well informed woman, who attended the church clinic along with informants, for example, was not happy to learn that her physician discouraged her from having an excision for an irregular painful walnut size mass on her left flank because of her diabetic condition and old age. She felt that she has been treated differently because of her old age.

It is clearly evident that in the United States there is a much stronger feeling about illness as a burden to children than in Korea. In order to settle down as immigrants in new country, they need to mobilize all their resources. If a member of a family is not able to work, it almost manifests a chain reaction. At least one more family members worry about the ill family member as well as the absence of the person from the job.

There is a change taking place in traditional relations in the family here in the immigrant situation in the United States. Koreans seem to be adopting the patterns of the larger

society which are a diminished respect and concern for the
elderly, and a priority for children in family care. Mrs. Rhim
commented on adult children's attitude toward a sick elderly
in the family as follows:

> "When young children are sick in the family, immediate
> action follows such as taking them to a physician. How-
> ever, care for elderly people is done differently. Usually
> a certain medicine in the house is recommended by the adult
> children to take and one is told to see how one feels."

In this connection, Mrs. Choy said that true affection
among generations is directed downward. Thus, parents take
care of children, but not the other way around. One receives
from her previous generation, and then she does not pay back
directly, but to her next generation. Due to Confucian influence, in Korean society, elders are expected to be respected
and venerated. However, in today's family, the elderly Korean
women believe that a child receives immediate attention but not
the elderly.

According to Korean tradition, a son and a daughter-in-
law have responsibility to take care of elderly parents in a
family. This custom is based on a patrilineal kinship system.
When daughters are married, they become members of her husband's
household. Traditionally the daughter-in-law is responsible
to look after her parents-in-law. Mrs. Ahn says that it is
more comfortable to talk with her daughter-in-law about her
health matters than with her son. Traditionally it is awkward
to talk about "body" matters with the man of a household. Mrs.
Ahn feels that she tends to be formal in interactions with her
son. She thinks it is something to do with a thirty-five-year

long unfortunate separation. Anyhow, health problems of women
are customarily kept among women unless it is beyond their
power to help. Mrs. Ahn and her daughter-in-law have a harmonious relationship. When Mrs. Ahn is on medication, Her daughter-
in-law telephones her to remind her to take medicine. Other
elderly ladies, who have witnessed Mrs. Ahn's good relationship with her daughter-in-law, are envious of Mrs. Ahn.

Although, son and daughter-in-law are responsible for
the care of their elderly parents, elderly Korean women share
the recognition of their illness with a person who has a close
emotional relationship with them. This person seems to be
usually their daughter. The reason behind this illness behavior
appears to be: (1) the elderly ladies desire to be comfortable
and peaceful while they are ill, and (2) they want to avoid
any possible chance of developing a strained relationship with
their daughter-in-law.

The two informants who live separately from their
married sons and daughters, tend to inform their daughters
of their illnesses instead of their son. Mrs. Uh had a backache
and she stayed with her daughter's family, for example.

One additional factor of importance is that in traditional Korea, there were intracultural differences according to
rank. Lower ranked families from farming communities were not
as strict in the observance of "ideal principles of relationship" as were higher ranked families. It is of interest to note
that Mrs. Yun who is from a lower ranked family in a farming
community has a relaxed but less formal relationship with her

son-in-law. This pattern is different from a family which con-
serves the traditional formal relationship which can be seen in
upper ranked families. Thus, when Mrs. Yun had a skin eruption,
she was able to show her bare foot both to her daughter and son-
in-law and her son-in-law bouhgt her a tube of ointment. She
also says that she is here in America to help her daughter's
family to improve economically by baby-sitting with their children. She does not feel that she should be treated like a burden.
She relatively spontaneously expresses her opinion and behaves
without strong inhibition.

COSMOLOGICAL CAUSES OF ILLNESS

The conceptualization of illnesses is holistically
(Lock 1980:217) or synthetically (Porkert 1976:65) oriented
based on East-Asian cosmology and Confucian principles. The
concept of Ki, a universal energy or a vital energy in the
universe plays a central role in understanding the etiology
of illness. Illness occurs when the flow of life energy is
interrupted by its own difficiency due to a disharmonious
state caused by lack of physical and emotional care and a failure to observe proper social conduct in daily life.

There were several causes of illness in regards to Ki,
vital energy, expressed by the elderly Korean women in this
study. This includes causes related to a lack of regularity
and control of patterns of daily living, lack of control of
food intake, a lack of blood, influences of cold, dampness,

wind, and heat; and a disharmonious state of emotions.

Ki, life energy, and blood are particularly important in understanding states of health and illness. Generally, the cause of illness is related to the poor or absent flow of Ki, vital energy, in the body. The flow of Ki is composed of life energy and blood. This energy is called Yang amd blood is called Ŭm (Sunu 1983:435). Thus, a healthy state of person is described as a harmonious state of flow of Ki or Ŭm and Yang.

There were several causes of illness in regards to Ki, vital energy, expressed by the elderly Korean women in this study. These inluded causes related to lack of regularity and control of behavior; a lack of blood; lack of control of food intake; and influences of cold, wind, and heat; and disharmonious state of emotions.

Regularity and Control of Patterns of Daily Living

Daily patterns of living require regularity and control and these patterns should become a habit. This to Koreans is what The Yellow Emperor's Classic of Internal Medicine has emphasized from ancient times and was spread throughout East Asia. Following these principles, it is believed that reckless daily living causes illness. "Poor hygiene, overeating, and lack of mental readiness," are areas which directly relate to causes of illness. Mrs. Byon, a patient at the Korean church clinic, confidently explained: "Statistically man has a shorter life span than woman does, because he tends to neglect hygiene. Man also has to avoid overindulgence in drinking and sex."

Physical exertion from over work or heavy exercise is
said to be a cause of sickness, because regularity and control
are not exercised. Sunu, a traditional Korean physician and an
author, specifically points out that sudden physical exertion
in particular, causes poor flow of Ki, vital energy (Sunu 1983:
435). According to Cheong, in the section of Plain Questions
of The Yellow Emperor's Classic of Internal Medicine there are
five injuries caused by physical exertion: (1) blood is injured
by staring for a long time; (2) vital energy is injured by lying
down for a long time; (3) muscle is injured by sitting for a
long time, (4) bone is injured by standing for a long time; and
(5) tendons are injured by walking for a long time (quoted
from Cheong 1977:45).

The following illustrations by Mrs. Sunu and Mrs. Yun
reflect on this pattern:

"I really do not control myself in relation to work
habits. I know if I overwork, I will be sick. But when
I see work, I forget my health and finish the work. Then
I get sick. My children ask why do I have to overwork"
(Mrs. Sunu).

"In Korea we do farming so that there is a great
deal of work. Although I am an old woman I tend to work
even if I know certain work will be too much for me because I could not just sit around in a busy season when
others work very hard. Sometimes I work first and get
treatment next" (Mrs. Yun).

These two women came from a farming background in Korea. In
a farming family all the hands are needed in order to have
a good harvest. Without collectivism, it connot be managed.
"Esprit de corps" is vital to the survival of the group
as an extended family. In order to encourage family members
and others to work, these women believe that the best approach

is by being an example and so they work with relatives as an elder of the family.

According to Mrs. Yun, physical exertion causes neuralgia:

> "In Korea, I lifted and carried heavy bundles of twigs. After that I had a very severe neuralgia. It was painful particularly on my shoulders and all over my body and I did not have any appetite at all. Neuralgia is from hard work. I used my right arm as an ax. When my husband passed away thirty some years ago, I was alone with small children so that I had to do all the farm work. When the rice paddy band was destroyed by water, a skillful able-bodied laborer threw two shovels of dirt, I did three to five shovels."

Table 5 shows the distribution of symptoms related to physical exertion among informants. With regard to neuralgia, Mrs. Nam Kung is not exactly sure whether arthritis or neuralgia developed from much walking when she was a young mother. During the Korean War and afterwards she became a peddler to support her children and she had to walk all day with a heavy load on her head. She is sure that her long hard walk with heavy burdens caused her knee and ankle pains.

Mrs. Lee is well educated. She is a deacon in her Korean church and also a committee member of the Elderly Korean Association. She worked as a housekeeper in an American house in the United States which is a five story building. She had to climb up and down the stairs several times a day. Her knee joints are "torn apart" because "arthritis is developed."

Mrs. Hahn who cares for her three grandchildren all day, says that she is exhausted physically and mentally. She complains of weight loss and poor appetite. She describes her situation as follows: "I feel as if I am going to die because of the grandchildren. You do not know what a hard time they

give me. They fight each other all day and they put the house
upside down. That's why I am so sick."

TABLE 5

DISTRIBUTION OF CONDITIONS RELATED TO

PHYSICAL EXERTION AMONG ELDERLY KOREAN WOMEN

Condition*	Number of Informants
Neuralgia	3
Arthritis	2
Backache	1
Colds on throat	1
Hepatitis	1
High blood pressure	1
Immobility of neck	1
Tired and red eyes	1

*Conditions are those described by informants.

Mrs. Suh believes that hepatitis is caused by physical
exertion. She told in tears: "I truly wished that my mother
would appear in my dream. However, she does not. She was a hard
working lady on a big farm with big responsibilities. She worked
too hard. She died of hepatitis."

Other conditioned mentioned which are believed to be
due to physical exertion are being unable to move the neck,
"colds on throat," high blood pressure, backache, and tired
and red eyes.

Control of Food Intake

Maintaining a well functioning gastro-intestinal system is viewed as very important in controlling related diseases. This system is responsible for the digestion of food intake and absorption of nutrients. It is said that a weakened digestive system can cause many diseases. However, it is difficult to regulate the amont and frequency of food intake because food has a special personal and social meaning.

Mrs. Lee says that the cause of her diabetes is an excessive intake of sugar. She added also that when she goes to a party, in particular, she is resentful about the necessity of dieting and occasionally, she does not follow her diet. The popular notion of diabetes mellitus in a group of four informants, Mrs. Ahn, Mrs. Hwang, Mrs. Kal, and Mrs. Nam Kung, is as follows: Diabetes is a rich man's disease because this disease is common among the wealthy people, who eat all good food items such as meat, honey, and other rare delicacies and they do not work hard physically.

Mrs. Hahn believes that high meat consumption is harmful to humans. She is concerned about her husband's high blood pressure:

> "Many people say that vegetables from the mountain are good for health. Pure water and air are also good. I do not like meat much. It was the same in Korea. I eat mainly vagetables. However, my husband loves meat. He eats it everyday in a large amount. He says that he perspires if he does not eat meat. They say meat is not good for health. I worry about my husband's health. Also, his blood pressure is high and he takes medicine for that. He cannot wear the clothes he brought with him from Korea."

Twenty-five percent of the informants say that overeating is hard to control. Lack of control of food intake leads to poor flow of Ki, vital energy, due to blockage caused by too much food and gas from this food. Consequently, a person can suffer from fainting spells, cold sweating, and cold hands and feet.

A Lack of Blood

The concept of blood is important in understanding the conceptualization of illness of elderly Korean women. Blood and nerves are often equated in their medical language due to a synthesis-oriented approach to body functions instead of an analytical approach. Blood is explained as the most important part of vital energy in the body system as follows:

> Ch'i [Sic] is the vital energy for all parts of the body. It has its main origin from the stomach which grinds foodstuff into minute particles and transforms them into 'energy.' When this energy is combined with the air ('energy' from the surrounding air) from the lings, Ch'i (vital energy) is formed. Ch'i is circulated sequentially via all the meridian tracts to provide nourishment and vitality for all parts of the body. Blood (hsüeh) and the cardiovascular circulatory system in the modern sense are regarded as the more substantive parts of the Ch'i circulation system. Blood is viewed as mainly containing 'constructive' energy.... (Lin 1980:100).

Responses about vital energy focused particularly on blood. One reason might be that blood is rather concrete and visible. Some respondents believe that blood and nerves are the some. They say that neuralgia is involved with nerves. A lady at a Korean church clinic explained to me: "I am not sure how neuralgia develops but I think in old age blood is dry and circulation becomes poor in blood vessels and this causes

neuralgia." Mrs. Nam, an elderly Korean lady at a church
clinic, believes that her legs are swollen due to bad nerves.
All four women associate their problems with a loss of vital
energy. A biomedically oriented physician told Mrs. Nam that
her leg condition is associated with bad blood vessels. She
asked him back, "My tendons are bad you mean?" Actually Mrs.
Nam and the physician do not have a common language to understand each other's medical concepts.

"Drying blood" is a common expression used among elderly Koreans. They had expressions such as "Cramps are due to
lack of blood. Blood is dry in old people," or "The most important causes of illness such as neuralgia and indigestion are
drying blood like in a big old tree." The expression of "hardening blood" besides "drying blood" exists and this is believed
to cause pain. Mrs. Baik remembered her reaction after surgery: "After awakening from anesthesia, all my joints were very
painful because of hardening of the blood." Mrs. Baik had an
eye operation for cataracts under general anesthesia. She
believed that under general anesthesia, circulation stopped or
at least it became inactive, so that the blood hardens although
the heart continues to palpitate.

The concept of "bad blood" was also used. In one case,
it was believed that fright causes _Dahm_, a lump of phlegm and/
or congested blood with pain, and ultimately it develops into
bad blood and then neuralgia. Mrs. Nam Kung remembers the
effect of poor _Ki_ flow caused by _Dahm_:

"When I was an infant, my sister dropped a small bronze
bowl on my abdomen, It startled me so that _Dahm_ developed

on my left knee. Sometime later, a large amount of bloody
pus ruptured out. I was limping until I was ten years old.
Then I was able to walk gradually but pain remains. Some
people say it is enuralgia.

Mrs. Yik shared her understanding of arthritis as

interference of free flow of Ki, vital energy, by lingering

blood:

"It is from a woman's disease. Women get venereal
disease from men. The venereal disease spreads all over
the complex reproductive organs. It produces bad blood
and it coagulates and arfects the joints. It gets worse
in winter. This bad blood is eliminated at the time of
delivery."

It should be noted that Mrs. Yik was highly educated in Korea

and overseas, and she also had a midwife training course in

Korea.

Mrs. Lee had an empirical explanation about pathophysi-

ology of headaches which involved aching blood or aching nerves.

She commented: "It feels like my blood is aching. Or maybe,

a line of nerves is aching. The shoulder pain and headache

seem to be connected because when I press one part, the other

part is also affected."

Some informants tried to be analytical about the func-

tions of blood and nerves. However, it becomes fuzzy maybe be-

cause they are used to a systemic and synthesis-oriented prin-

ciples in understanding illness. Blood is seen as a core com-

ponent of Ki, vital energy. In old age various explanations

of illness are related to blood.

Cold, Dampness, Wind, and Heat

Cold and dampness by themselves or through wind are
believed to enter the body through the pores of the skin and
then attack different body organs and different other parts of
the body such as bones. Cold, dampness, and/or wind interfere with the flow of Ki, vital energy, by themselves (Sunu
1983:439) or by weakening Yang and if this condition is not
treated, fever develops (Lyu 1975:2). During the summer, when
Yang energy comes out of the body, a person becomes "hollow."
According to Sunu, restoratives are recommended for this condition (Sunu 1982:467). Pung, wind, is considered as a cause of
illness among Koreans. Lin (1980:96) associates wind with power-
ful pathogenic forces which could cause an acute illness or
unpredictable result. Wind is often accompanied by cold and
dampness. All the informants are familiar with the concept called Pung, wind, as a cause of illness. Pung means "wind" in
Chinese characters. There are differences in interpretation
about the meaning of Pung in relation to illness. For example,
Mrs. Yun associates wind with a rather rapidly progressing
allergic or inflammatory illness, as noted in her comments:
"Pung is not really the wind, but it is something from inside
the body. It causes pruritis and toothaches which bring edema
on the face. It also causes an acute febrile sickness with
inflammation and redness of the skin." On the other hand, Mrs.
Park says: "Pung is a real wind with moving air in the body and
blood vessels. One could see the wind with one's fingers when
a person did not have good postpartum care. The wind causes

high blood pressure, neuralgia, and stroke." Mrs. Suh talks
about her experience with wind as a cause of illness: "I had
'wind teeth.' I could push them up and down with my tongue
and then I pulled them up completely with my fingers." According to Mrs. Yun, in the case of postpartum neuralgia, cold is
accompanied with wind.

Cold is interpreted as chillness, cold air, or a cold
place. It is commonly accompanied by dampness and wind. Thus,
Mrs. Kal is sure that cold air causes arthritis. A lady in a
Korean church stated that neuralgia is caused by coldness and
overtiredness with mental and/or physical strain. She continued:
"The prevalence of neuralgia among the Korean immigrants will
increase because they wear short sleeves and short skirts in
America and they tend to work more in America than in Korea.
They are responsible for the raising of grandchildren, house-
keeping, and cooking."

Neuralgia is believed to be caused by poor postpartum
care and inadequate protection of the mother from the cold. Mrs.
Yik explained: "One lives in a cold environment without proper
heating and with cold water only available. Symptoms of cold
diseases become worse in winter." Mrs. Yun's daughter complained of coldness and pain in her knees in the postpartum period.
Mrs. Yun thinks that her caughter's condition is from her exposure to the cold environment while she was in the hospital for
delivery. She wanted her daughter to have her baby at home
so that she could help her since she delivered many babies of
her own, relatives, and neighbors. However, she was told that
in the United States it is illegal to have baby at home.

Mrs. Koh has complained of indigestion and abdominal
pain. She believes that her condition is caused by coldness.
The condition is worse in the winter. In the summer she does
fine. Mrs. Rhim complains of a headache when she is exposed to
cold air, coolness of the air conditioner, and winds. Mrs. Hahn
told me that she was suffering from summer heat. She complained
of insufficiency of vital energy, loss of appetite, and loss
of body weight. Her physical condition was weakened because
her Yang, positive energy, came out of her body.

SPIRITUAL CAUSES OF ILLNESS

Spiritual causes of illness expressed by the elderly
Korean informants in this study are related to different
religious backgrounds: animism, shamanism, Confucianism, and
Christianity. However, regardless of the religious denomina-
tions, the elderly Korean informants believe that if they do
meet their spiritual being's expectations of them, they will
be punished with illness. Neverthless, most of the time they
are given opportunities to correct or compensate their mis-
behaviors by themselves or through a medium for their recovery
from illness.

Four informants have had experiences with animism
and shamanism. One common aspect among the four informants
was that their associations with folk beliefs have been mainly
recollections of past events. These four informants are from
rural areas in farming communities. They have not had much

formal education and have had serious hardships in life. Three
out of these four informants became widows early in their
lives. Nevertheless, they have been economically competitive
and independent enough to raise and educate their children.
They are rather fluent verbally. Mrs. Yun is a Catholic. Mrs.
Baik goes to a Christian church once or twice a year. She
believes "What she thinks within herself" is faith to her. The
other two ladies do not go to a Christian church. Mrs. Kal
goes only when she is very ill. Mrs. Hahn says she does not
attend a Christian church because her husband worships his
ancestors.

Mrs. Hahn knows that one of her friend's family had
misfortunes associated with a business failure and family sickness. This family was told by a Mudang, a female shaman, that
their ancestors were not pleased where they were buried. After
consultation with a geomancer, they chose another burial ground
for their ancestors to appease them and then this family did
not suffer from those misfortunes. Mrs. Hahn's husband has been
observing the ancestor worship ceremony only for his parents
since they came to the United States because it is much work
to worship his other ancestors. Prior to his emigration to the
United States, he bought a piece of land for one of his relatives and asked him to perform the ancestor worship ceremonies
for the rest of his ancestors. This concept is important to
maintain family well-being. Gallin (1978:175) pointsout that
in Chinese society the patients or his family, in order to
avoid the recurrence of the illness, attempt to deal with its

causal factors by rectifying the breaches in filial piety,
ancestor worship, and mistreatment of ancestors.

In animism, people believe that spirits are everywhere.
Generally, people are careful in order to avoid the wrath of
the gods, e.g., illness in conducting their life. A house
garden god was angered because a profane act was performed
in the god's realm so that one of the close relatives of the
person who misbehaved was stricken with a sickness. Mrs. Hahn
elaborates on her experience with her child's illness from
an animistic point of view:

"We were very poor after the Korean War and our
children were small. We lived on a farm. One day when
our middle daughter was young, she suddenly started to
have watery diarrhea. However, I had to carry her on my
back and went to school for my son. When I was waiting
for a bus, a woman approached me and asked me what
happened to my baby. I told her that she was sick with
diarrhea. She asked me whether a hog had been butchered
in the front garden of my house and I told her that
we had. She told me that the front garden god was angry
because of that. It was impure to the god. The woman,
who apparently was a Mudang herself, told me that she
would pray for us and asked me to prepare a food offer-
ing. I told her that I could not do it because we were
poor. Then she advised me to invite a grandmother from
my village and let her pray. I did and the diarrhea
stopped right away."

In a similar vein, a local deity was indignant, because
the god's shrine was transgressed and demolished by a young
man. The god punished a relative of the violator with an illness. Mrs. Baik talks about her folk spiritual explanatory
model of her illness:

"Something funny happened when I was about fifty
years old. At that time, I led a busy life in Korea.
My children were relatively young and I was selling
vegetables. One day I had a busy schedule. I was also
concerned about my younger son who was away from home

to study at a Buddhist temple in a mountain. I was ironing. I did not have an electric one. We were living very
poorly in a small place. I used a charcoal iron. While
I was ironing, I felt I was getting smaller and I was
going down into the dirt ground, so that I asked my
other son who was beside me, 'How are you doing?' and he
replied, 'All right.' I told him that I was not feeling
well and he told one of the neighbors. I was taken to a
hospital. Later the neighbor told me that my eyes were
rolling back. I had all the tests in the hospital and I
was told that I was all right. My son came home earlier
than he planned because he felt that he should go home.
When I told him about that episode, he said that he did
something wrong. He had demolished a rock pile shrine
in the country road. Usually a local rock pile shrine
is located under trees by a village road and decorated
with colorful strips of cloth. There is a custom that
a person picks up a rock and adds it to the rock pile
by tossing it as they pass by."

Mrs. Baik did not mention that any ritual was performed to make

up to the spirit for her son's transgression. She was sick

but recovered and her son was all right. Perhaps she thought

the whole matter was eventually settled between the spirit and

her family.

Mrs. Hahn is from a rural Korea. When she was young,

she suffered from a gross abscess in her chest cavity. Her

parents were told by a local Mudang that she was sick because

when their house was remodeled in order to increase one more

room, a pole god in the storage was neglected. Mrs. Hahn was

healed by a healing ceremony which was conducted by a Mudang.

Informants, who are professed Christian, believe that

lack of faith and negligence of religious practices are re-

lated to disease occurrences. Mrs. Suh commented that she

suffers from insomnia due to nightmares. She said, "When I

have a bad dream, I know that I did not pray hard before I

had gone to bed. Evil wants to try me." Mrs. Myong, who is

known as a very religious person points out that lack of faith
in God is an important cause of sickness.

Concepts of causes of illnesses are related to origins
of popular, East-Asian traditional professional, and folk sectors. The natures of causes of illnesses are physical, emotional spiritual, and social. The conceptualizations of illness
are synthetically oriented particularly in the cosmological
dimensions. Different religious influences such as Confucianism,
animism, and Christianity are reflected in understanding the
concepts of causation ot illness of elderly Korean immigrant
women.

HWABYUNG: A CULTURAL CONSTRUCTION OF ILLNESS

Koreans are taught to relate to other persons with
an attitude of benevolence, high-mindedness, restraint, understanding, and faith. Traditionally, obedience and submission
are great virtues particularly for women. Osgood states that
among Koreans since no individualism is allowed, repression
of emotion is required to adjust to the traditional complex
hierarchical Korean society (Osgood 1962:38-39). Koreans keep
emotions to themselves. They are not expressed openly. When
these emotions go beyond a certain threshold level and they
cannot be kept under control, they are manifested physically
as a form of illness called Hwabyung. Hwa means "fire" and
Byung means illness. Thus, Hwa and Byung become "fire-ill-
ness" (Kang 1981:84).

Koreans believe that there are seven emotions. These
are joy, anger, sadness, worry, fear, fright, and depression.
When these seven emotions are stimulated excessively, they
become causes of illnesses (Kang 1981:86). Frequently, changes
in emotions injure five organs. Overly stimulated emotions can
cause sickness; anger injures the liver; excessive joy injures
the heart, worry or excessive thinking injures the spleen;
depression injures the lungs, and fear injures the kidneys.
However, all seven emotions can cause heart ailment. Once the
heart is affected heart illness may interfere with other organs
because the heart is viewed as the center of all organs (Kang
1981:44 and Ho 1966:743).

The liver, the gall bladder, the heart, and the kid-
neysare particularly influenced by anger. In a state of anger,
Yang is stronger than Ŭm. This excessive Yang easily invades
the heart and then affects the kidneys. Liver and gall bladder
have a close relationship, so when the liver is affected, so
is the gall bladder (Kang 1981:87).

When anger injures the liver, considered an organ for
the storage of blood, this injury interferes with liver functions, so the liver is not able to store blood due to an ab-
normally high liver energy. This liver energy causes vomiting
of blood. Poor eye sight may occur when the liver fire goes
up, because liver communicates with the eyes. Frequently it is
believed that when the blood supply is not sufficient to the
liver, various eye diseases occur (Kang 1981:48)

When a person is severely depressed, circulation of

vital energy is interfered with and the interrupted vital
energy injures the lungs and the spleen. Excessive thinking or
worry injures the spleen which is related to thinking or worry.
Sadness is understood as overly stimulated states of anger,
depression and thought. Sadness affects the liver, the heart,
the spleen, the lungs, and the kidneys as well as other parts
of body. In excessive sadness, vomitting blood, unconsciousness, crying, and states of panic can be observed (Kang 1981:
87).

The Plain Questions in The Yellow Emperor's Classic of
Internal Medicine explain: "When anger is excessive, vital
energy rises up; when joy is excessive, vital energy is relaxed;
when sadness is excessive, vital energy is wasted; when
fear is excessive, vital energy goes down;... when excessive
fright occurs, vital energy scatters;... and when excessive
thinking takes place, vital energy is hardened." These altered
states can cause various bodily illness (quoted from Kang 1981:
86 and Hong 1972).

Hwabyung is a familiar illness among elderly Korean
immigrant women. It is understood among them as physical
symptoms which have developed by emotional distress or anger
provoked by troubles in life. One informant, Mrs. Koh and
a woman from a Korean church clinic, Mrs. Kil, talked about
their understanding of Hwabyung:

> "Hwabyung is caused by Hwa. Hwa comes up from the
> abdomen and one gets sick. Business failures can be the
> cause of Hwabyung. This illness has to be cured early
> or otherwise it is difficult to cure. It can be done by
> either a Western physician or a Hanui. Also one has to
> know how to control one's Hwa, overly stimulated emo-
> tions" (Mrs. Koh).

"Hwabyung is an illness which is caused by troubles
in life. For example, it may occur when a young girl is
deserted by her fiance, or a woman with a husband who
engages in extra marital affairs. A business man who
fails in business might be affected by Hwabyung. These
illnesses are manifested differently in different people.
Some might have this like a mental illness while others
might develop heart disease or indigestion. To prevent
Hwabyung, it is important to control one's state of mind.
There are different therapeutic measures: modern medical
treatments or Hanbang methods. One can also lose one's
life by this illness" (Mrs. Kil).

Mrs. Koh used the word Hwa with two meanings: one is fire and

the other is a strong emotion. She presented a traumatic life

event as an example of a cause of illness. According to Mrs.

Koh, this Hwabyung is serious enough to require treatment

early. She also suggested two choices of treatment either the

Western physician or the traditional medical practitioner.

Mrs. Kil includes a few different physical symptoms, e.g.,

heart, gastrointestinal symptoms, and mental illness like

symptoms as manifestation of Hwabyung. Also Mrs. Kil's explana-

tion of Hwabyung, includes distressful life situations, deser-

tion, facing spouse's unfaithfulness, and business failures.

Different body organs, such as heart and gastrointestinal

organs are involved. According to these examples, Hwabyung

develops only when there are problems in life severe enough

to trigger emotional distress or an extraordinary anger. This

illness can be manifested in various symptoms. Both males

and females can be affected. It is treated by different ther-

apeutic measures. There seem to be individual differences in

terms of etiology, course, treatment measures, and prognosis.

In this study, all of the informants are familiar

with Hwabyung and eighty percent of the informants admit that
at one time or another they have experienced it. Some of them
belonged to a high educational and socioeconomic group. Common
life problems which are related to Hwabyung are strenuous interpersonal relationships, financial difficulty, the insecurity
of children's welfare and health, the death of children, the
illness of children, the death of spouse, separation from
children, disloyalty of one's spouse, negligence by child,
physically and psychologically demanding work, illness of
spouse, incompatibility in marriage, contempt by others, and
unfair treatment by others as shown in Table 6.

TABLE 6

COMMON LIFE PROBLEMS RELATED TO HWABYUNG

BY NUMBER OF INFORMANTS

Life Problems	Number of Informant
Strenuous interpersonal relationship	6
Financial difficulty	5
Insecurity of children's welfare and health	5
Death of children	3
Illness of children	3
Death of spouse	2
Separation from children	2
Disloyal of spouse	2
Negligence by child	2
Demanding work	1
Illness of spouse	1
Incompatibility in marriage	1
Contempt by others	1
Unfair treatment by others	1

Some informants suffer from a cluster of life stresses.

For example, if one faces the death of a spouse, financial problems and the insecurity of children follow. Some have concerns mainly about children. The largest number of informants indicate various interpersonal relationships within the family and community as sources of emotional distress. The concept of the relations are based on hierarchical principles and interdependence, which discourage open communication, they learn to suppress their feelings and needs, and to express or channel them instead through Hwabyung

The most frequent symptoms which are interpreted as Hwa (fire or troubled emotions) or Hwabyung (illness from troubled emotions such as anger) are the following: gastrointestinal problems such as chronic indigestion, poor appetite, abdominal discomfort or pain, constipation, and diarrhea; cardiac symptoms such as palpitation, pounding of the heart or throbbing heart; musculoskeletal symptoms such as "neuralgia," and pains on thighs, legs or knees; vascular circulatory symptoms such as loss of vital energy with cold hands and feet, a sudden hot feeling in the face, vomiting blood, and "dizziness" in relation to hypertension; sensory neurosymptoms such as "blindness" or poor eye sight, and altered sensory perception, hearing impairment, and nightmares; respiratory symptoms such as shortness of breath; genitourinary symptoms such as decreased urine ouput and weight gain with generalized edema; and endocrinological condition such as hyperthyroidism. Table 7 presents the medical symptoms identified as Hwabyung. The relatively high frequency of abdominal complaints reflects the

the view that the abdomen is the center of body which produces
and supplies vital energy, Ki. Besides this, other important
organs mentioned are the heart, and the kidneys in relation
to decreased urine output. The liver is identified in relation
to low blood pressure and dizziness.

TABLE 7

MEDICAL SYMPTOMS IDENTIFIED AS HWABYUNG

BY NUMBER OF INFORMANTS

Symptoms	Number of Informants
Gastrointestinal symptoms	7
Vascular circulatory symptoms	4
Neurosensory symptoms	4
Cardiac symptoms	3
Muscuoskeletal symptoms	3
Respiratory symptoms	2
Genitourinary symptoms	1
Endocrinological symptoms	1

The informants did not identify all symptoms as
Hwabyung. For example, Mrs. Uh complained of hypertension,
hearing impairment and backache. She related only high blood
pressure and poor hearing to Hwabyung while she has another
explanation for her backache. She slipped down and was pinned
between the front and back seats when the car in which she was
riding stopped suddenly. Mrs. Chin complained of poor eye sight
and hypertension, but she did not link them to Hwabyung at all.
She explained her poor eye sight in relation to her old age
and hypertension with a biomedical explanation, the thickness
of blood vessels with fat substances and other material. She

did not talk about life problems in relation to troubled
emotions.

The majority of the symptoms associated with Hwabyung
were of a chronic nature probably because the informants in
this study had been experiencing emotional and physical distress for a long period of time. Most of the informants related Hwabyung with their troubled life experiences taken
place in the past. The symptoms are presented in both lay and
biomedical terms. Some of the typical expressions for the
presenting symptoms are: "I have a lump here (as pointing to the
chest or abdomen) and it gives me a pressing and tightening
feeling. I cannot eat. My abdomen is always full even when I do
not eat. This is Hwabyung. This lump is Hwa, troubled emotions."

Another lady said, "It is because of my nerves (troubled
emotions). My chest pounds rapidly. Our family does not
agree; that is why there are troubles." Another woman associated Hwabyung with increased palpitations. Mrs. Nam Kung said,
"My heart throbs and my face suddenly gets hot." Still another woman stated, "Hwabyung is a spasm of the stomach. It
comes up like a lump. When people have troubles in life they
get this. A physical condition can be identified as Hwabyung
by the individual, family members, friends, or traditional
Korean physician in Korean sociocultural and medical framework.

In terms of a regimen of treatment, the women included
mainly traditional Korean medical treatment, Hanbang, and biomedical treatment. Some informants employed Christian faith

healing through their prayers. The main purpose of treatment
is to cure physical symptoms. They are accustomed to bodily
treatments but not to psychotherapy. It is important to note
neverthless, that most women suggest that at times it is difficult to cure Hwabyung.

The constellation of somatic symptoms called Hwabyung
is a cultural resolution of emotional distress by somatization. Physical symptoms are accepted and dealt with. It is
an important concept for elderly Koreans because it allows
them to deal with life problems linking together emotional
and bodily ditresses. Every culture has had its ways of re-
solving the emotional distress which originates from life problems. In order to see how elderly Korean women conceptualize
Hwabyung, twelve case examples which describe symptoms and
explain the meaning, causes, and practices will be presented.

Four other informants commented briefly on Hwabyung.
Mrs. Hwang explained Hwabyung in relation to her hyperthyroidism when her son was critically ill and her husband's
business was failing. Mrs. Koh was suffered from indigestion
when she was separated from their children. Mrs. Nam Kung
described a symptom of Hwabyung as a sudden hot feeling on
her face and a discomfort on her heart. Mrs. Choi had diarrhea when it was difficult to live with her parents-in-law.
Four informants, Mrs. Chin, Mrs. Kang, Mrs. Lee, and Mrs. Suh
had not experienced Hwabyung although they were familiar with
this Korean popular illness.

Case Studies of Hwabyung

The following twelve case studies will illustrate how the Korean sociocultural context influences the construction of Hwabyung and other medical beliefs among elderly Korean immigrant women. Kleinman's explanatory model serves as a frame of reference (1980:119-178).

Mrs. Yun (Indigestion, Constipation, Insomnia, and Lack of Vital Energy

Mrs. Yun tells of the hardships experienced in her life which caused emotional distress. She had to overcome a hard life without much support from others. She did not have anyone with whom to share her feelings. In addition, her social norms did not allow her to express her pent up griefs. She kept everything to herself. This caused poor flow of vital energy and eventually it interfered with blood circulation. Consequently, a phenomenon of "food accumulation" or "trapped ki, vital energy," was manifested as chronic indigestion. The poor flow of vital energy also affected her large intestine and it resulted in constipation. Although, she has had different treatments, some of them were effective only temporarily and none of them cured her permanently.

Sixty-seven year old Mrs. Yun had lived in a farm all her life. She came to the United States to help her daughter at the time of the birth of her baby. After her granddaughter was born, she decided to stay in order to assist her daughter and her family to be economically better off. She misses her

home back in Korea, and her other children in Korea miss her.
While Mrs. Yun takes care of her two granddaughters and two
or three other children, her daughter and son-in-law work outside their home. Sometimes it is a little hard for her to care
for four or five children at the same time, particularly because they live above a real estate rental office and they are
not supposed to make noise. She often says, "I have to help
her because even a daughter is one of my children. In olden
days daughters were not considered important."

Mrs. Yun is known as an example of a healthy person.
She is active and sturdy. She has a tall body structure with
a straight back. However, she often complains of a lump or
mass in her chest which gives her pressing and obstructing
feelings. It is difficult for her to eat an adequate amount of
regular food, particularly starchy food. If she drinks soda,
beer, or wine, she is somewhat relieved with the feeling that
the lump has gone away but sooner or later it comes back. She
calls this lump Hwa, disharmonious emotions. She says she has
Hwabyung, an illness caused by troubled emotions. Sometimes
she complains of the lump in her upper right abdomen. She often
says, "How can I describe what I went through?" In order to
ease her burdensome life, she said that she started to smoke
and drink wine. She continues as follows:

"I never can finish talking about the terrible things
I experienced. My husband was good at just spending what
we had but he was not a good farmer nor a good financial
manager. He was very ill for three years. He poured out
blood with pus and stool everyday for a long time due to
an unsuccessful hemorrhoidectomy. I used all the remedies
known. He had modern Western treatment, Hanyak, traditional
Korean medicine, popular remedies, and Mudang healing rite.

I had to sell everything. At the beginning all the farm
products and later on land and even the house we lived
in were sold in order to pay the medical expenses. However, everything was of no use. He passed away. Soon one
of my daughters died because I neglected to take care of
her while I was taking care of my husband. My neighbors
and relatives did not help us but looked down on us. My
husband died before all my children got married, I had
nobody to discuss different matters. This is a sak and
a long story. Thanks to my sensible son, we live rather
well in the farm area. We have much to eat and enjoy,
but I cannot eat and enjoy food because of this indigestion. My fate was so bad. Misfortunes were all
around me."

These days she eats a small amount of cereal and milk.

She complains of insomnia and constipation. Sometimes she

cannot sleep for two or three days in a row and she does not

have a bowel movement for a week. However, at other times

she is able to eat, sleep, and move her bowels well.

Mrs. Yun views family economy, the sickness of her

husband, the death of her family members, and raising child-

ren without a spouse's assistance as her major troubles in

life. She also recognizes that she still experiences emotional

pains from the memories of the death of her daughter and the

unsympathetic attitudes from their neighbors and relatives when

she was in need of help. These are her sources of emotion-

al distress. She said that she felt so hopeless and helpless

that she thought of taking some medicine to take the lives of

her children and her own life. She believes that her emotional

distress from these sufferings has been transformed into physi-

cal symptoms such as indigestion with pressing and blocking

feelings on her chest and abdominal area combined with insomnia

and constipation. She somatized her agonizing experiences.

When she was advised to have X-rays and other tests to

find out what was bothering her, she declined the offer saying
"Why should I go to a hospital to go through with those when I
know what it is that caused my illness?" Although she refused
diagnostic tests because she is confident with her own diagnosis, she accepted drug therapy by a biomedical physician for
her chest and abdominal discomfort and for constipation. She
also tried moxabustion on the abdomen for chronic indifestion
and on the head for insomnia. This moxa burn was suggested by
an elderly Korean friend. She tried home remedies such as
drinking cold water and drinking soda in the morning. These
brought temporary relief for her constipation. She also took
Nokyong, deer horn, and other herbs to restore her appetite
and strength. This was taken everyday for about a month. Her
son-in-law and daughter bought her the medicine for two hundred
fifty dollars and the daughter stewed the medicine everyday
with great care and served her mother. Her physical discomforts
are well attended for by her family members.

Mrs. Hahn (Hypertension, Poor Appetite, and Lack of Vital Energy

Sixty-three year old Mrs. Hahn is a thin and exhausted
looking woman who is busy running after her three grandchildren.
Her chief complaints are lack of vital energy and poor appetite
with indigestion. Her comples family situation contributes to
physical as well as mental exhaustion. She also cares for her
active grandchildren. She complains of troubled emotions. These
stagnant emotions interfere with the flow of vital energy and

blood circulation and cause indigestion so her appetite has decreased. Ultimately general malaise results from weakened vital energy and blood flow as well as low food intake.

She mentioned that her blood pressure is high although she is not much concerned about this symptom at present because she does not feel any discomfort from this condition. According to traditional Korean medicine, the factors leading to the occurrence of hypertension are tension and strong emotional stimuli such as worry and anger, for these can lead to an imbalance of Ŭm and Yang, and eventually this state interferes with the circulation of vital energy and affects the liver, the heart, and the kidneys (Ebrey 1981:404). Her blood pressure has gone up to above 200 systolic.

Mrs. Hahn is from a poor family. She was married to a man from a farming family. She said she had a hard time gaininf acceptance from her mother-in-law and getting familiar with her husband's family tradition because she had not had much opportunity to learn and to see "refined" ways of living.

She worked very hard on the farm and did everthing she could to raise her children properly with the hope that all her worries and hardships would be gone when her children grew up. However, her relationship with her children is a strenuous one. She and her husband lived together with their eldest son's family, but they moved out because of their "daughter-in-law." Mrs. Hahn and her husband have tried to be self-sufficient and independent from their children. They have an unmarried daughter who is 23 years old. This couple feels

that it is their responsibility to secure and protect her welfare and security until she is married. She goes to college
and they are doing their best to help her finish her studies
and even study further if she wishes.

She often states that it is too much to take care of
young and unruly grandchildren all day by herself after she
raised her own six children. It is a big responsibility to
look after their safety and physical care all day long. She often wonders whether her own children appreciate what she does
for them.

Mrs. Hahn says she is ill because of this combination
of worries. She complains of gastrointestinal symptoms and
hypertension. Once her physician told her that she had a
"dropped stomach." She barely eats and it is usually only vegetable and rice. Meat does not agree with her. She had a total
gastrointestinal examination. The result was normal. She was
advised to eat whatever she can and to take Maalox, an antacid
preparation. Mrs. Hahn was treated only unspecifically by the
biomedical physician because the physician could not find
serious specific evidence of illness by scientific diagnostic
methods different from East-Asian medicine which emphasizes
and respects the presentation of symptoms by patient, and
functional observation in diagnostic process (Porkert 1976:67).
Her condition did not improve by biomedical treatment. Finally
she said she took snake soup and it was efficacious for a
year. Her friends told her that she became a different person.
Her appetite improved remarkably. Mrs. Hahn believes that she

was ill although the biomedical physician could not find any pathological change.

Mrs. Hahn has had complex life problems. Her complaints are somatic problems, which have been treated with physically oriented methods. She improved remarkably with popular remedies and is content with the outcome. She added that her husband sympathized with her physical symptoms and recommended and helped her to take the medicine.

Mrs. Myong (Indigestion and Epigastric Pain)

Seventy-nine year old Mrs. Myong is well-educated, refined, and very religious. She has been in America over twenty years. She was a minister's wife. During the Korean War, her husband was taken captive and taken to North Korea. She had the total responsibility of raising seven children. And one of her daughters died suddenly. It is said that this was due to overwork. She comments about this incident: "My daughter was very talented musically. She taught many excellent music students. One day she collapsed suddenly and she died. If I had given her a little more attention, it would not have happened." She still experiences guilt feelings about her daughter's death.

Her symptoms are indigestion, discomfort of the abdomen, epigastric pain, and diarrhea. She was given a diagnosis of neurogenic gastric disease by a modern Western physician in a hospital in the United States. She controls her diet only. Although medicine was prescribed, she does not take it. She says she does not want to take medicine if possible. She seeks health

through prayer in Christian faith. She believes that her condition has been controlled. Mrs. Myong and her daughter-in-law
think that the cause of Mrs. Myong's illness is from emotional
distress from the daughter's death and they call this Hwabyung.

Mrs. Yik (Indigestion, Constipation, and Insomnia)

Mrs. Yik, another information, is very concerned about
her son's health. He has a back problem. The best possible
treatment is being sought among family members and friends.
She is very anxious and is praying hard. She also hopes that
this illness will help her son to have better faith in God.
She adds that she cannot stop thinking what would happen if her
son dies before she does because it is considered the most
tragic thing that could happen for an elderly person in Korea.
She is seventy- one year old, highly educated and much involved
with the works of the Elderly Korean Association in Washington
Area.

Her mojor complaints are indigestion, insomnia, and
constipation. She classifies her symptoms as Hwabyung, although
she explains them in analytically oriented-biomedical terms
probably due to her education and modernization. According to
her the pathological conditions result from an overuse of
nerves in the head. The nerves in the stomach and other parts
of the abdomen are affected also because they are related to
the nerves in the head. However, on the whole, she is synthetically oriented and her understanding of her medical symptoms
is close to the concept of vital energy and harmony in body
system.

Mrs. Ahn (Heart Ailment)

Mrs. Ahn is a seventy-six year old woman who has two sons. She was recently reunited with her older son after a tragic thirty-five year long separation due to the international political situation. During this period of separation, she lived with her younger son and his family. This younger son was imprisoned "unjustly." He has been released but this time she is again experiencing a separation from this youner son due to her immigration to this country.

Mrs. Ahn states that her heart started to beat fast when her younger son was taken to jail. This happened before she came to the United States. Since this incident, she often experiences a "pounding of heart" particularly when she is afraid or scared by something. It happens also when she lifts rather heavy objects including her great grandson. She went to a modern physician's office and was given "white pills." She is now exempted from taking care of her great grandson. Another elderly Korean woman was asked to babysit in her place.

According to East-Asian thought, the heart is affected by emotion. In Korea, when something regretable or a sad situation occurs, it is common to say: "My chest is aching." The sad events in Mrs. Ahn's life were transformed into emotional distress and somatized as a heart ailment. The insecurity of her sons contributes to her own insecurity. She goes to her biomedical heart specialist once a month and takes the cardiotonic, Digoxin, everyday because her son recommended this treatment. She also freely takes Hanyak especially Uhwangch'ungsimhwan which is believed to be good for "nerve ailments."

Mrs. Baik (Eye and Other Neurosensory Problems)

Mrs. Baik as well as her two friends, Mrs. Hahn and
Mrs. Yun label Mrs. Baik's condition as Hwabyung. Mrs. Baik
who is sixty-five years old had eye operations about three
years ago because she could not see very well. She also complains of a palpitating headache which is discussed as follows:
"I feel like my head is a fully clogged kitchen sink. When I
think of my complicated family affairs and I am alone without anyone with whom to talk, I feel like I am becoming small
and I am sinking into the ground."

Her husband, daughter, and mother-in-law were bombed
and killed during the Korean War. They died together at the
same time. She and her young surviving children buried them
because it was during the acute period of the war. She then
became a peddler to support her six remaining children.

Recently her youngest daughter's marital problem has
hurt her deeply. She lives with this daughter because her
grandson requires her care. Her son-in-law often beats her
daughter even in her presence. She has a congenitally abnormal
granddaughter who is "neglected" by her father, Mrs. Baik's
eldest son. The problems are further complicated by the fact
that her eldest son lives with another woman. Also, one of her
granddaughters who was attending university was killed by a man.

Before the eye operation, when she was deeply troubled,
her eye-sight got worse. She had frequent nightmares. At times,

things around her went "round and round." She takes Tylenol
for her headaches and Uhwangch'ungsimhwan for palpitations and
dizziness.

In troubled emotional states it is believed that
blood is not supplied adequately to the liver and this leads
to a weakened Ŭm, negative force, and an overly strong Yang,
causes headache and poor eye sight or even loss of eye sight
(Lyu 1975:78).

Mrs. Rhim (Dizziness due to Liver Problem)

Mrs. Rhim, who is seventy years old and rather emotionally sensitive, complains of dizziness and was told by her biomedical physician that her liver is enlarged and its function
has decreased. She was also given a blood transfusion for anemia. She takes a high protein diet and tests her liver functions
regularly to see her prognosis.

When she was in her thirties, her husband started to
live with another woman and he also had children by the other
woman. Mrs. Rhim has kept their own seven children. She became
indifferent toward her husband and educated their own children
all by herself.

Mrs. Rhim is the only informant who has a history of
depression. She has had numerous hospital admissions, numerous
electric shock treatments, and different antidepressants in
Korea. As she gets old, she tends to somatize her emotional
distress. In the East-Asian belief system, the liver is the
target organ of anger. When unresolved stagnant emotions linger,

these become fire (Yang energy). Consequently, this fire weakens the liver (Ŭm organ), so Ŭm and Yang harmony has been lost
(Lyu 1975:76-79). The liver functions are believed to have become poor and this results in anemia and consequently dizziness.

Mrs. Sunu (Kidney Problem and Related Symptoms)

Mrs. Sunu, a lady of rural origin, is sity-five years
old, and complains of shooting pains in the back and thighs
and decreased urine output. She is satisfied with her Hanbang
treatment such as acupuncture and herb medicine which are for
her interrelated dysfunctions. Her troubled emotions affected
the flow of vital energy and this then interfered with blood
circulation to the kidneys so that her urine output decreased.
The water from the lingered blood penetrated through to the
bones and muscles and caused pains. This pathophysiology was
explained to Mrs. Sunu by her traditional Korean physician
and Mrs. Sunu agrees with this explanation. Mrs. Sunu points
out that her psychological problems are related to kidney ailments.

Her mind has been troubled by her husband's behavior
which she describes as "irresponsible." This couple live together in an old people's apartment and their sons and daughters
also live near by. She tried to live apart from their children
in order to keep her husband from interfering with their children. She says that he has a "wild personality." She points out
that he did everything. He gambled, followed girls, and had
many business failures. She is deeply religious and is a devout

member of a Christian church.

The following two ladies, Mrs. Uh and Mrs. Park, identified their problem as high blood pressure which is believed to develop by tension and stimulation of strong emotions such as worry and anger which leads to imbalance of Ŭm and Yang.

Mrs. Uh (High Blood Pressure and Symptoms of Deafness)

Mrs. Uh is a seventy-two year old university graduate has worked as a librarian in Korea. She had been living in the United States over twenty years. Her major medical problem is hypertension. She says that her hypertension and hearing difficulty started when her son was taken prisoner by the communists during the Korean War. The symptom is developed by Shimhwa. Shim means heart or emotion. Hwa means fire or troubled emotions. Shimhwa is interpreted as emotional distress. Most of the time she is on a low salt diet, taking pills, and her blood pressure is checked monthly by a public health nurse. She wears a hearing aid for her hearing difficulty.

Mrs. Park (High Blood Pressure)

Similar to Mrs. Uh's situation, Mrs. Park who is seventy years old, was first told that her blood pressure was high when she was about forty years old. Although this symptom started about thirty years ago, when she was asked the cause of her illness, she answered, "I am concerned about my mentally ill son." Her son is 45 years old. He does not know where his wife and children are. He is staying with his parents and re-

fuses treatment. Mrs. Park is on a low salt diet and takes anti-
hypertensive pills from a modern Western health clinic. She
misses the sweat baths which she used to take for her high
blood pressure instead of antihypertensive medicine.

Mrs. Kal (Shartness of Breath, and Chest and Abdominal Dis-comfort)

Mrs. Kal was thirty-seven year old, when her seventeen
year old daughter ran away from her home in Korea. At that time
Mrs. Kal vomited blood. When fire of the liver develops due to
the stimulation of strong emotions, it invades the lungs. The
over-powering vital energy influenced by strong Yang, weakens
the lungs and furthermore one can vomit blood due to this
weakness of the pulmonary system (Lyu 1975:78-79). Also, this
affects the abdominal function with imbalance of Ŭm and Yang,
and it causes accumulation of food and then indigestion develops. When she was fifty years old, she had to deal with other
serious life problems, Her son committed suicide, her husband
died, and her daughter married an American soldier. As a consequence she developed Hwabyung or Sogari.[26] She suffered
from shortness of breath and pain in her chest. A "lump" has
been pushing up from the right abdominal area. She has been
resting and taking synthetic medicines for easy breathing. She
believes that her physical illnesses are directly related to

---

[26]The majority of the informants seem to consider
Sogari, an internal disorder manifested by a combination of
unbearable digestive, cardiac, and respiratory symptoms such

her many problems in life.

Mrs. Kim (Lack of Vital Energy)

Mrs. Kim, who is seventy-three years old, explains her Hwabyung in relation to an incompatible relationship between her daughter and herself. She comments about her daughter: "She is too strong, aggressive, and outspoken. She disagrees with me and talks back all the time." According to the traditional Korean value system, one should not contradict an elder, even if the elder is wrong. Mrs. Kim says:"My health is deteriorating because my daughter told me things which hurt me and which I will never forget." She explained about her health status that due to anger from this relationship. She lost Ki, vital energy, so that her hands and feet are cold and she is generally weak. She often carries her grandchild on her back. She is taking care of three grandchildren. Their ages are 3, 2, and 1. At times she feels exhausted.

Mrs. Kim went to Hanui, a traditional Korean physician, and she was given the diagnosis, Hwabyung, which was the same as her own diagnosis of her illness. Hanyak, traditional Korean medicine, was prescribed. Its main ingredients were blood warming herb and sliced deer horn. She appeared to be rather satisfied with her diagnosis and prescription, probably because her explanatory model and that her traditional Korean physician were

---

as shortness of breath. One of the informants, Mrs. Kal, used this sickness category interchangeably with Hwabyung. There is limited knowledge about this condition, but it appears to be a popular Korean illness.

the same.

Twelve case studies of <u>Hwabyung</u> have been presented.
Each informant explained how <u>Hwabyung</u> served as an explanation for her unique difficult life situation. This model reflects the Korean sociocultural value system and medical belief system. These elderly Korean immigrant women reflected
a synthesis-oriented or holistically oriented principles in
understanding their illness which brought together social,
emotional, and physical aspects in their life experience.
They somatize their emotional distresses caused by different
problems in life and resolve them with bodily treatments from
various sources as their culture prescribes.

CHAPTER VI

THE KOREAN HEALTH CARE SYSTEM:

PLURALISTIC HEALTH AND ILLNESS PRACTICES

AMONG THE ELDERLY KOREAN IMMIGRANT WOMEN

A person's cultural beliefs and values not only determine his general behavior and hence influence his health but,
more specifically, they determine what he does to promote
health, to prevent illness, and to find a cure when he is ill.
To whom he goes for care when sick is determined as much by
his congnitive framework and his perception of meaning and the
nature of a particular illness as it is by the availability of
various services (Kark et al. 1962:3) People are influenced by
their cultural, psychological, and social situations, when they
choose alternatives (Foster 1978:304). Health maintenance and
promotion issues have been important to immigrants, to health
professionals, and to decision makers. Cohen states that there
is an "increased recognition of the range of cultural alternatives of health care practices available to members of ethnic
groups in contemporary society" (1979:38).

In this chapter, I shall present the health beliefs
and practices of elderly Korean immigrant women which make up
the Korean health care system. As conceptualized by Kleinman,

this system includes the popular sector, the professional sector, and the folk sector. The illness behavior of the Koreans will be discussed in terms of their understanding of the causes, meaning, and interpretation of their illness in relation to the symptoms in referring and selecting a particular treatment approach. Differences in the health and illness beliefs and practices between patients and biomedical physicians, and between patients and traditional Korean physicians will be compared.

THE PROFESSIONAL SECTOR

Hanbang, Traditional Korean Medicine

Hanbang, traditional Korean medicine, is part of the indigenous professional sector. As discussed in earlier chapters, it has been influenced by traditional Chinese medical principles. The major Hanbang treatments include Hanyak, traditional Korean medicaments; Ch'im, acupuncture; D'ŭm, moxa burn; and Buhwang, cupping. These forms of treatment were practiced by the elderly Korean women in this study. Often an informant diagnosed her own, her family's, or friend's illnesses independently and treated, evaluated the results, changed previous treatment plans, and adopted alternatives. Not infrequently the women used Hanbang just to buy Hanyak material because they had a diagnosis and prescription already. In the present discussion, each Hanbang treatment will be dealt with providing an explanation, the medical conditions for which it is used,

how it is used, what result is expected, and how the results
of this treatment are evaluated.

Hanyak (Traditional Korean Medicaments)

Hanyak plays a very significant role in the Korean
health care system. It is particularly important in the management of problems of health of the elderly. Koreans are used to
managing their health problems mainly by themselves. They are
familiar with restoratives which are frequently recommended for
elderly people because they believe that older people suffer
from lack of vital energy. A Hanyak like Uhwangch'ungsimhwan
is in great demand as an effective home remedy for many different medical conditions. Hanyak has three different origins:
herbal, animal, and metal. Among the informants, Hanyak as
restoratives and a home remedy called Uhwangch'ungsimhwan are
commonly used.

The term Boyak is used frequently in regard to health
and illness among elderly Korean women. Boyak means medicines
to refill "hollow" parts in the body in order to restore the
original adequate strength, or vital energy to thrive and resist
the cause of illness. Also, it is simply described as "filling
up a lack." Elderly people are known to have a tendency to
lose vital energy easily. When the hollow is not restored, illness can recur even after being treated because the body is not
strong enough to maintain vital energy or resist illness (Sunu
1983:464-466).

The elderly Korean women in this study are familiar

mainly with the Boyak, restoratives presented in Table 8.
This table shows the kinds of Boyak and symptoms treated. These
include Insam (ginseng), Nokyong (deer horn), Siechondaebotang
(a commonly recommended restorative formulary of a mixture of
herbs). Elderly Korean women know when to take and how to take
these.

TABLE 8

KINDS OF BOYAK AND SYMPTOMS TREATED WITH BOYAK

Kinds of Boyak	*Symptoms Treated with Boyak
Insam (ginseng) Siepchondaebotang (mixture of different medicaments) Nokyong (deer horn)	Poor appetite Lack of vital energy Cold hands and feet Dizziness

* Symptoms are those identified by informants.

If one of the symptoms or all of the symptoms are present, they
take a Boyak or a combination of Boyak which is agreeable to
them. The symptoms are interrelated so that if one of them is
obvious, usually other symptoms follow or are already present.
Some of the women use an important term "lack of vital energy"
which encompasses other listed symptoms.

Insam, ginseng, is included in almost all restorative
medicines and is widely used. Koreans take ginseng in many
different ways such as tea, soup, medicine, candy, and cosmetics.
As Boyak restoratives, they are boiled in earthern ware with
water, jujubes and/or ginger. Also, raw ginseng powder is mixed
with honey and taken.

Korean women know which restorative is agreeable and
good for them. Mrs. Choi, for example, found that ginseng is
what she likes. It helps her from feeling weak and it gives her

a good appetite. Mrs. Suh took ginseng as a restorative in her
adulthood and she had good results. She was able to work for
a long time without fatigue. However, she does not take it anymore because she believes that the time of death is coming and
she wants to "go quickly and peacefully without prolonging it
and struggling." People believe that Boyak prolongs life at the
time of approaching death. Not all elderly Korean women want to
delay death. It is considered particularly significant when
women over the age of seventy make the decision to take Boyak.

Mrs. Yun was sixty-eight years old, when she decided to
take Boyak and commented:

> "I heard that many elderly women do not take Boyak in
> late life lest they should have a hard time at death. But
> I had decided to accept the restorative when my daughter
> told me about this. I have to take care of my own grand-
> children and two other children. I cannot eat due to in-
> digestion. That is the only reason I took it. What can I
> do? My daughter needs my assistance. Although I finished
> taking the medicine not long ago, I seem to eat better
> already. I think good appetite is the first sign of the
> efficacy of Boyak."

A Boyak called Siepchondaebotang, a mixture of traditional Korean medicines, is commonly taken for poor appetite
and a lack of vital energy. These symptoms seem to be significant to this group of people. The center of this energy is in
the abdomen and is generated with food.

Poor appetite and idigestion are alarm signals which
have the potential to break the harmony of the whole body system
because they believe in systemic functions of body organs and
ohter parts of the body.

The following is an example of Mrs. Nam Kung's concerns
about poor appetite:

"Sometimes I feel I chew sand in my mouth. At times I can go for three days without eating anything. I force myself to eat because my flank area is painful due to a flat absomen. Boyak is agreeable with me. It does not give me uncomfortable feelings in my stomach and it is effective for poor appetite. My daughter-in-law sent me Siepchondaebotang from Korea. I do not know exactly why I am taking this. People say it is good for your health. I do not know the detailed reasons. I have to go and stew my medicine. I do not have anybody to do it for me now."

Nokyong, deer horn, is viewed as a precious, highly effective medicine. Mrs. Ahn comments on the high value of Nokyong:

"When they cut Nokyong, deer horn, they let the deer drink wine and let them sleep a little and cut their horns during sleep. They put white papers around to gather even particles of the horn powder."

Nokyong is prescribed as a Boyak as well as actual treatment for certain illnesses. Mrs. Oh, a lady at the Korean church clinic, took deer horn when she was twenty years old, so she still feels strong and does not catch colds. Deer horn is also used to cure certain illnesses such as a cold stomach, neuralgia, a stiff neck, a backache, and it is taken during the pre and postpartum period for a smooth delivery and recovery.

Sliced stewed deer horn liquid mixed with stewed broth of Siepchondaebotang is taken often as Boyak. This mixture is popular among the informants. Mrs. Rhim took the mixture because she had symptoms of dizziness and particularly poor appetite. She also thinks that her vital energy has decreased. She takes it once a year because its particular efficacy is believed to last only for a year. She boils her medicine almost all day and drinks it three times a day for twenty-one days.

Several months after taking this Boyak, she begins to feel less tired and dizzy. She eats better and sleeps better as well. Mrs. Kim has taken the same Boyak as Mrs. Rhim. She comments about its efficacy and how this medicine works in the body: "In order to feel real improvement, it usually takes about five months, but my hands are beginning to be warm already. The medicine becomes effective through the kidneys and the heart. The whole body is working together toward restoration." When a person takes Boyak at a young age, the efficacy lasts for a life time."

East-Asian medicine places emphasis on prevention as indicated in The Yellow Emperor's Classic of Internal Medicine in order to restore the vital energy and holistic function of the body. According to the medical text, a good physician is supposed to prevent illnesses instead of curing illnesses. This idea continues to be transmitted at the individual or family level. Symptoms for recommending Boyak are broadly and systemically dealt with. Specific symptoms are not usually matched with specific kind of Boyak among the informants in this study. Korean women practice Boyak in terms of choice of medicine and dosage of medicine. They treat Boyak almost as food and they are not much concerned with side-effects.

However, as noted earlier, Korean older women generally feel uneasy and ashamed of doing something for their own sake. They are used to working for other members of their family: grandparents-in-law, parents-in-law, children, and other related people. They learned and practiced this all their lives and so they find it difficult to take Boyak, such as Insam, ginseng,

and Nokyong, deer horn, which are not considered an absolute
necessity among lay people but a privileged treat. Boyak is
considered a luxury to people because one its purpose is longevity and they are used mainly by higher ranked and wealthy
people. It should be noted, neverthless, that eighty percent
of the informants responded that they had taken restorative
medicines recently. Forty-five percent of the informants had
taken restoratives after they had reached the age of seventy.
This phenomenon might be related to the surge of individual
and independent life patterns to which the elderly Korean
women are exposed. As discussed earlier, thirty-five percent
of these informants live alone or with their husbands. Another
explanation is that their children encourage them to take Boyak.

Another Hanyak which is commonly used by elderly Korean
women is Uhwangch'ungsimhwan which serves as an indispensable
household medicine in Korean families. It is a soft redish dark
ball about one quarter of an inch diameter. The surface is often
painted with edible gold color. It is found in wax capsules
secured individually or in a small wooden box with elaborate
golden wrapping inside. There are ten balls in a bigger box. It
costs about forty dollars to one hundred dollars depending on
the "genuineness" of the salesman or the place of sale.

According to Sunu (1982:458), the main ingredient of
Uhwangch'ungsimhwan is calculus bovis which is an accumulated
substance in a hollow musk organ. The main function of this
ingredient is to facilitate the vital energy flow particularly
for cardiovascular insufficiency such as in cases of heart dis-

ease, atherosclerosis, high blood pressure, and especially for
acute severe symptoms which require immediate relief. A fast
recovery is expected from this medicine.

The elderly Korean women in this study used Uhwangch'ungsimhwan for the following symptoms, as shown in Table 9: low
vital energy, headaches, dizziness, fever, high blood pressure,
poor appetite, colds, and neuralgia.

TABLE 9

CONDITIONS FOR WHICH UHWANGCH'UNGSIMHWAN IS USED

BY NUMBER OF INFORMANTS

Conditions*	Number of Informants
Low vital energy	4
Headache	4
Dizziness	4
Fever	2
Colds	1
High blood pressure	1
Nueralgia	1
Poor appetite	1

*Conditions are those described by informants.

Uhwangch'ungsimhwan seems to heal many different symptoms from the acute to chronic and recurrent medical conditions.
The majority of the informants have quite a flexible attitude
toward the dosage of this medicine. In other words, they are
not concerned about side-effects because they believe that
Hanyak rarely gives adverse reactions. Uhwangch'ungsimhwan is

a valuable medicine which offers avenues to restore vital energy
and it penetrates through obstacles which cause physical disharmony. The specific situations under which Uhwangch'ungsimhwan is used among the informants may be seen in the following
quotes:

> "I felt that my head was full of garbage. And I felt
> as if room was moving round and round. I took Uhwangch'ung-
> simhwan and waited for about 20 minutes, then I felt all
> right" (Mrs. Baik).

> "When I catch a cold I take Uhwangch'ungsimhwan and
> rest. Then I sleep more than usual and recover from
> colds" (Mrs. Ahn).

> "Uhwangch'ungsimhwan is taken for headaches and general
> weakness. This medicine is for nerveous system disorders
> or discomforts" (Mrs. Ahn).

> "Uhwangch'ungsimhwan mixed with water is given to a
> child who has high fever and convulsions" (Mrs. Kim).

> "Surgery was recommended for my son for appendicitis,
> but I gave him Uhwangch'ungsimhwan, and brought him home.
> He is over forty now and fine" (Mrs. Chin).

> "I could not eat anything for days. How can I eat
> when I do not have an appetite? I drank some juice, that's
> all. I am going to buy some Uhwangch'ungsimhwan" (Mrs.
> Nam Kung).

Ch'im (Acupuncture)

Informants know that a Hanui (traditional Korean physician) who has truly excellent knowledge and experience could
heal with only one prickle of an acupuncture needle. Acupuncture
theory has been advocated and used for the treatment of virtually every disorder or disease in man. Acupuncture is done alone
or in combination with moxabustion and herb medicine. Some
examples of diseases commonly treated by acupuncture are pain,
neurological disorders, convulsions, deafness, blindness, tremor,

enuresis, alopesia, hypertension, bronchial asthma, diabetes, and psychiatric disorders (Bonica 1974)

The selection of the acupuncture points varies greatly. Some acupuncturists select points at or near the site of the disease, following the rule of treating local points; others select points remote from the disease site according to either meridians or nerves. The needle is inserted and advanced until the "take" is experienced by the patient, described as a feeling of tingling, distension, heaviness, and numbness. Stimulation is achieved either manually on through a "push-pull and rotatory movement" (Bonica 1974:1546).

There are currently some scientific explanations about how acupuncture works. For example, in The Handbook of Acupuncture and Moxibustion Therapy (Agren 1971), anatomic studies are cited to prove that acupuncture points are located at important nerve endings and that meridians are related to peripheral nerves. Moreover, recent research on humans is said to show that acupuncture has a tonic-rehabilitating, and anti-inflammatory actions, and that it influences peristalsis, increases leukocyte count in peripheral blood, and inhibits pain. In acute appendicitis, it increases the hydrocortisone level in the blood and thus enhances the anti-inflammatory response. According to Bonica, many disorders are due to an imbalance between the sympathetic and parasympathetic nervous system. Acupuncture is said to selectively stimulate one or the other and thus, to restore balance, and to have demonstrated beneficial endocrine responses and normalization of altered functions (Bonica 1974: 1549).

TABLE 10

CONDITIONS TREATED BY CH'IM

BY NUMBER OF INFORMANTS

Conditions*	Number of Informants
Indigestion	4
Neuralgia	3
Neck stiffness	1
Backpain	1
Sprain of ankle	1

*Conditions are those described by informants.

According to East-Asian traditional medical principles, which differ from the biomedical interpretation above, acupuncture corrects interferences of the flow of Ki (vital energy) and blood circulation and it ultimately creates harmony in the body system (Sunu 1983:434).

Fifty percent of the informants have had acupuncture treatment in Korea as well as America. The major problems for which informants received acupuncture treatment as shown in Table 10 are indigestion and neuralgia. The less educated informants tend to receive acupuncture treatments more often than the educated informants. Informants go mainly to the local Hanui (traditional Korean physician) for acupuncture treatment. The women are well aware of the efficacy as well as the dangers of acupuncture treatment. An informant, Mrs. Park, comments: "However, acupuncture has dangers too, if it is done without knowledge and experience. I saw a person became a hunchback after acupuncture treatment."

Mrs. Kae, a <u>Hanui</u>'s wife, was proud of her husband's medical skill and she, herself, possesses rather detailed knowledge about acupuncture practices:

"My husband can do acupuncture. Some diseases cannot be cured by Western medical methods. For example, facial paralysis and other paralysis can be cured very well by acupuncture. Also, when someone has indigestion, so that the lips become white as paper, and when the person has cold sweats, acupuncture will cure the symptoms right away. Circulation returns and nerves start to work. The lips becomes pink and the person becomes lively again."

Mrs, Kae also introduced an acupuncture method without using needles:

"While you travel, say, you have indigestion. You press the spot where the index finger bone and thumb bone are fused with your thumb tip as hard as you can until the two finger bones are no longer separated. You do the same thing on the other hand. Also, apply the same technique on the spot between big toe and the next where the two bones meet and do the same on the other foot. This whole process is called <u>Sakwan</u>. Western medicine for indigestion is not as effective as acupuncture. In the first place the indigestion is not completely healed and can recur, but acupuncture cures it up completely."

The explanation given by traditional Korean medicine about indigestion is that food lingers in the digestive system because of inadequate flow of vital energy and acupuncture generates optimum level of circulation of vital energy and blood circulation. Meridians in hands and feet are to supply vital energy to digestive system (Sunu 1983:434-435).

Early stages of recurrent indigestion can be cured very well through acupuncture but according to an informant, chronic indigestion does not respond to acupuncture treatment. This lady believes that efficacy is related to the chronicity of the symptoms. Neverthless, another informant, Mrs. Yun, believes

that a gold acupuncture needle itself yields greater efficacy
than other kinds of needles. She said, "I even had treatment
with gold needle, but it was of no use because it is an old
case of indigestion." This concept might be related to the
alchemy of Taoism. People believed that precious metals are
good for health. Cha states: "Among the Taoistic beliefs was
the one that eating food out of a bowl make of gold which was
transformed from mercury would promote longevity" (Cha 1978:
76). There are different types and sizes of needles. Steel
needles are usually used.

Among this population, acupuncture treatment is frequently chosen for neuralgia. Sunu (1982:502-503) believes that
neuralgia is caused by poor blood circulation due to a poor
vital energy system in the body so that acupuncture is the
choice of treatment to correct the general circulation systemically. In most cases, with a single treatment pain dis-
appears and the individual can move around freely. An informant used a local Hanui for neuralgia. She received acupuncture combined with massage.

At the church clinic, Mrs. Won recalls various treatments she received for her neck problem from three different
health care sectors--the biomedical, the popular, and the traditional professional--until she reached a "cure." This seems
to be the typical pattern of illness behavior of this population who have access to a pluralistic medical system. The last
resort is usually acupuncture. A Hanui believes that this phenomenon is related to economic factors. The elderly Koreans

have Medicare coverage for cosmopolitan medical treatment while they have to pay for Hanbang treatment, the traditional Korean medical system, out of their own resources. Sometimes this is quite a large amount, for example, three hundred dollars in cash. Mrs. Won, a lady who also attended Hanui clinic, shares her pluralistic medical treatment experience as follow:

"I packed many boxes one day because my son was ready to move. The next morning I could not move my right neck at all. I went to a doctor who practices Western medicine. I was given some medicine, but, they did not relieve my pains and stiffness. A friend of mine told me that Uhwangch'ung-simhwan, a traditional Korean medicament, is good for my symptoms. I took about thirty of them, but still I could not feel any difference. Someone suggested taking honey, so I took honey. It did not do anything for me. I finally wernt to a Hanui upstairs and had acupuncture and moxa burn every week for about two or three months. Everytime I had these treatments I could feel improvement. It was very painful. Look at these moxa burn traces on my back, arms, and legs. He charged me five dollars each visit. He charged the lady down stairs ten dollars. She had an indigestion problem. It takes more needles. An American woman who was in Korea had a sprain problem or something, so she had acupuncture treatment. I did not see her any longer there. I heard she got healed after one treatment."

She described acupuncture treatment in detail. Sites of acupuncture and moxa burns, pains, scars, and efficacy were mentioned in relation to different symptoms and persons. Mrs. Won's symptoms disappeared after weekly treatment which lasted two to three months, while the American woman's sprain was healed in a single treatment.

D'ŭm (Moxa Burn)

D'ŭm is another treatment which is part of traditional medicine in Korea. A mugwort, artemesia, fire ball is made by crushing a small quantity of the stalk and rolling it between

the palms of the hands, after which the ball varying in size
from a pea to a walnut, is set on fire and placed on different
portions of the body. The pillow D'ŭm is made by heating the
wooden block on which Koreans rest their heads while sleeping
an applying it to different portions of the body for various
ailments (Borman 1966:111). The principle and purpose of D'ŭm
treatment is to stimulate interfered circulation of life
energy and to restore blood circulation and bodily harmony.

D'ŭm treatment is often used in combination with acupuncture. Acupuncture is done first and then on the site of
the acupuncture, D'ŭm is applied to enhance the total efficacy.
D'ŭm is recommended for the conditions for which acupuncture
is recommended. Moxa burn is given by the informant to herself,
by a family member, by a friend, or by a practitioner.

Among the informants, D'ŭm treatment was applied for
arthritis, indigestion, insomnia, and back pain as shown Table
11.

TABLE 11

CONDITIONS TREATED BY D'ŬM

BY NUMBER OF INFORMANTS

Conditions*	Number of Informants
Arthritis	1
Back pain	1
Indigestion	1
Insomnia	1

*Conditions are those described by informants.

Mrs. Park does D'ŭm on herself, and on her family members. She learned D'ŭm from one of her friends informally. She
supplies moxa burn material to her friends in her neighborhood
and she practices this on her friends also. She has been practicing this for a long time. When she emigrated to this country she prepared and packed medicinals, instruments, and other
necessary material to do D'ŭm, Buhwang (cupping), and Ch'im
(acupuncture) because she had been concerned about the health
care and illness treatment which she would find a strange country. She has a gold acupuncture needle made out of her eighteen
carat gold wrist watch. She feels secure about possessing these
self-treatment supplies. Not infrequently she cures herself,
her husband, and her family members, particularly her daughter-
in-law, who is a professional nurse in this country, as well as
her friends in her neighborhood.

Mrs. Park comments about her experience and understanding about moxa burns as follows: "My son had a pot belly with
indigestion by eating coarse food, and he had diarrhea. After
three D'ŭm treatments on the lower abdomen it became flat and
he digested well because his digestive organs were stimulated
by moxa burns with a resultant medicinal effects." She diagnosed
her son's symptoms and treated tham based on her beliefs. She
evaluated the efficacy and explained how D'ŭm worked.

Mrs. Yun lives close to Mrs. Park. Mrs. Park sympathized
with Mrs. Yun's chronic indigestion cause by Hwa, emotional distress. Mrs. Park gave Mrs. Yun moxa burn material, mugwort balls
and instructed her how to use them. Mrs. Yun had moxa burns on

her lower abdomen. They looked black on top and red on the
bottom of the burns. They were ring size. Some time later
Mrs. Yun complained to Mrs. Park about insomnia. For this problem, she suggested moxa burn on top of Mrs. Yun's head. Mrs.
Yun carried out this suggestion. After this therapy, she tried
herb medicine with deer horn. She looked much relieved from
ailments when she said, "I eat better these days. She believes
that Hanyak, traditional Korean Medicaments, contributed most
toward her improvement.

Buhwang (Cupping)

The principle of Buhwang treatment is to facilitate the
flow of Ki,vital energy, which is the vital condition to maintain or to recover from illness. Non-circulating bad blood or
other body secretions such as phlegm are some of the examples
to be removed by the principle of suction. Buhwang is practiced
by individuals or it can be obtained locally in a Hanbang, a
traditional Korean clinic.

Cupping was practiced by one informant in this study.
Whenever Mrs. Park has aching or painful spots, she does Buhwang on herself and her husband. Her husband had a yellowish
spot on the side of his neck which is where cupping was applied
the previous day. She learned to do cupping, moxa burn, and
acupuncture from a grandmother whom Mrs. Park knew. Mrs. Park
Mrs. Park was modest about her traditional medical skills by
saying: "I just do these without original or deep knowledge."
Mrs. Park explains how Buhwang is practiced: "Buhwang sucks

out bad or dead blood, so that a blockage by bad blood will be removed and circulation will be restored. I will show you how I do Buhwang."

She demonstrated Buhwang on her leg. She brought out a baby food jar like small glass bottle, a cotton ball, a small bottle of alcohol, a box of matches, and a gold acupunc- needle. She moistened about an inch radius on her outer lateral mid leg so that the bottle would stay better and then she prick- ed it several times with the gold needle which was dipped into the bottle of alcohol. Next, she pulled a piece of cotton from the cotton ball. She lit the cotton and put the burning cotton into the bottle and attached the opening of the bottle over the pricked skin area. She added a detailed explanation about suc- tioning of bad blood according to her belief: "The smoke from the cotton helps to form a suction and pulls out the bad blood. Let it stay there for about five minutes. Sometimes the skin area gets really red because the blood was sucked."

She was certain about the efficacy of Buhwang and she provided an example: "I saw a breast cancer which was cured by cupping after the Western method failed. The root of the cancer, a blockage, was removed. It has not recurred. In case of a chronic boil, the root of the disease could be removed by Bu- hwang.

Patient and Hanui in the Traditional Korean Medical System

In a Hanbang clinic the client and practitioner ther- apeutic relationship is important. The Hanbang, which is the traditional Korean medical system must be understood. Some of the features such as the personal and educational background of participants, the setting, types of patients, types of problems treated by the Hanui, kinds of treatment services offered and therapeutic approaches such as communication patterns will be discussed because these aspects directly influence the initiation of the therapeutic relationship as well as the outcome of the treatment.

The elderly Korean informants believe that efficacy depends on the Hanui's wisdom, knowledge, experience, and ability to heal the sick. Often they comment: "When sickness is healed there should be a mutual harmony or a unity between patient and physician. Somehow they agree, they trust each other and work together toward one goal."

The results of visits with three out five Hanuis, who were contacted through informants and newspaper advertisements will be presented. Mrs. Sunu, Mrs. Kang, and Mrs. Choi have seen Mrs. Kook, a Hanui. This Hanui is popular among these informants particularly because she has shown a competent professional and empathic attitude toward her clients and the three informants have had a favorable outcome from her Hanbang clinic. Mrs. Kim and Mrs. Yun were examined by Mr. Yu and purchased Boyak, restoratives, for their lack of vital energy. Each of these two ladies paid about three hundred dollars for a series of Boyak. Although they felt their medicine was somewhat expensive, they know that Boyak is always expensive, and besides they have begun to feel improvement. Thus, on the whole, they are satisfied with Mr. Yu's service. The Hanui, Mr. Kae practices acupuncture. He is popular among elderly Koreans. He renders service without charge and he has shown genuine interest in his friends and their health problems.

Mrs. Kook, the Hanui, is a woman in her forties who was trained as a pharmacist with Western biomedical orientation at a well known university in Korea as shown in Chart 2. A woman Hanui is rare in Korea. Mrs. Kook saw many "blind spots in the Western approach to healing so that she learned traditional Korean medicine as continuing education in a university, although she states that Hanbang also has some disadvantages such as a lack of surgery. She recommended biomedical treatment for such illnesses as appendicitis, fractures, and thyroid problems.

A visit was made to her clinic. She has a neat and attractive nut and tea shop. It is filled with herb fragrance. For most Americans, Mrs. Kook's place is a health food store for medicinal teas and nuts, but to Korean clients, this place is more meaningful than a health food store because it is a Hanbang. Mrs. Kook comments in terms of the symbolic effects of this Hanbang: "Aroma, appearance, and other touches of the healing process of Hanbang give a sense of familiarity to people and it may help them to become well. Mrs. Kook has a room behind her counter. The counter is between the store and treatment room.

CHART 2

CHARACTERISTICS OF THREE HANUIS' DEMOGRAPHIC AND PROFESSIONAL BACKGROUNDS AND TYPES OF CLINICAL PRACTICE

Name	Sex	Age	Type of Training	Type of Practice	Type of Patient	Type of Problem
Mrs. Kook	F	40	Professional bio-medical pharmacist; Some training in Hanbang in a university	Acupuncture; Hanyak	Patients who believe in Hanbang; Patients who are not satisfied with bio-medical care; People who take Boyak; Koreans only	Cardiovascular; Gastrointestinal; Genitourinary; Gynecological; Respiratory; Musculoskeletal; Neurological; Lack of vital energy; Chronic diseases
Mr. Kae	M	72	Professional bio-medical pharmacist; Apprenticeship in Hanbang	Acupuncture; Moxa burn; Cupping	Friends; Patients who believe in Hanbang; Patients who are not satisfied with bio-medical care; Mainly Koreans	Gastrointestinal; Musculoskeletal; Respiratory; Neurological; Psychiatric; Chronic diseases
Mr. Yu	M	45	Observed his father's Hanbang practice	Acupuncture; Hanyak; Moxa burn; Cupping	Same as Mr. Kae's types of patients	Same as Mrs. Kook's types of problems

Mrs. Kook compared Hanbang treatment with the biomedical tradition. There is no scientifically developed diagnostic
method, because East-Asian medicine is established with experience. A long-term therapeutic regimen is often necessary . One
needs to take medicine for a long time for its efficacy except
in acute cases which require immediate efficacy. Side effects
during the treatment process occur rarely. The ultimate purpose
of Hanbang treatment is to restore a total balance of the body.
Mrs. Kook believes that there are two stages in the therapeutic
process: cure and restorative stages. As soon as the curing stage
is over, usually Boyak or other Hanyak is given to make certain
that the cured stage is maintained or to restore the weakened
body. The goal of treatment is "complete cure without recurrence."

Mrs. Kook has a definite idea of types of her clients.
She comments on characteristics of her clients as follow: (1)
People have gone to the Western oriented clinic with medical
symptoms and who have been told that they were not sick, or
that all laboratory tests are normal; and (2) Women who are
between forty to fifty of age. Mrs. Kook believes that this
age group tends to have sickness and they are in a period of
hard work so that heart disease is common. They can afford to
pay medical fees because they earn money and they believe in
Hanbang. The majority of her patients is in this age group.
There are more female patients than male patients because they
have "one more organ, the womb." She states, furthermore, that
the women who have had abortions are usually not healthy.

Mrs. Kook believes that abortion is not a natural process.
When a seemingly localized natural process such pregnancy is
interfered by artificial means such as abortion, systemic bodily weakness or diseases develop, because the whole body system
is synthetically and functionally interrelated.

The proportion of older patients is rather low. Sickness, pain, and discomfort are believed to be natural symptoms
and signs of old age, so that the elderly person herself or her
children tend not to seek treatment. Elderly people also try to
avoid having their children spend what their children earn for
their treatments. Medicare does not cover Hanbang treatment in
this particular area of the United States. Thus, her clientele
consists mostly of people who are not satisfied with other
kinds of treatment , particularly biomedical care, and patients
in middle age many of whom are female patients.

Mrs. Kook did not allow me to observe her practice because she says that if someone else was present, she could not
concentrate on her treatment. When one of her clients telephoned her, she responded as a professional, but with tones of
kindness and sincerity. A Bible verse was seen on the side of
the counter. On her business card there is a Bible verse: "The
preparation of the heart in man, and the answer of the tongue,
is from the Lord" Proverbs 16:1). Her father is a Christian
minister. She added that her practice is her service to human-
kind to glorify God. When she practiced in Korea, she gave free
acupuncture treatment to the poor because she could afford it,
but she could not treat them with herbs or other medicines be-

cause they were expensive.

The principles of Five Elements (Fire, Water, Wood, Metal, and Earth) and Ŭm and Yang are applied to her practice. She reads East-Asian medical books. Some of them are from Japan. She also utilizes biomedical methods such as monitoring blood pressure and body temperature. She has a printed chart for each patient. It includes listed questions about health status by reviewing systems and spaces for other specific questions about history and present illnesses.

Mrs. Kook permitted me to interview her patients. An informant, Mrs. Sunu, who was treated by Mrs. Kook was interviewed. Mrs. Sunu complained of a shooting pain in her back and thighs, an uncomfortable weight gain, and insomnia. She sought biomedical treatment. Her condition was diagnosed as "sacral nerve neuralgia and gastric intestinal trouble" by her biomedical physician and she was given pills for pain. The function of this medicine was "to relieve pain temporarily." She was told by the modern physician that there was no permanent cure for her medical problems.

Mrs. Sunu then went to see Mrs. Kook. Her comment about her treatment experience is as follow:

"The lady Hanui reassured me that there was a cure for me. 'First medicine exists and then disease exists.' That's why a cure is possible. She told me that my kidney function has decreased. That's why I have gained weight. Urine output is decreased. The waste product of the body including salt and water of the body goes to the bone and then accumulates there. When body parts are cold, they get painful like frostbite. The pain can be felt in different parts of body and it moves around.
She checked my blood pressure and took my pulse. Acupuncture was done on my fingers and blood was drawn from

the same fingers.[27] Hanyak was given to me. I stewed and
drank it. The treatment was effective. Urine output has
increased and the pain has been relieved. Weight loss has
been considerable and I can sleep better also. The efficacy of Hanyak has characteristics of a permanent cure
and it takes a long time to be effective. Hanyak is
agreeable to Koreans because they are mainly vegetarians.
I go there again on Friday. She wants to see my progress
and make changes in my treatment plan if necessary."

Mrs. Sunu adds that Mrs. Kook is an understanding and competent

professional who is familiar with both modern and traditional

Korean medical knowledge and skills.

Mrs. Kook seems take obvious pride in her practice.

She comments about her way of publicizing her practice in order

to reach her clients: "I advertized for a month only at the be-

ginning of this Hanbang practice. I get new patients through

my former patients. My old patients tell their friends about

me. Although I have practiced less than one year, I have three

hundred patients now. If I cure well, the news will spread all

over."

Mr. Kae, the second Hanui, is seventy-two years old

and a faithful Christian. He was trained as a Western-oriented

pharmacist many years ago as shown in Chart 2. When he was sick

himself, he was eventually treated by Hanui and then he started

to study Hanbang by himself with some apprenticeship.

In his apartment clinic, his clients are treated as

friends. Usually, his client and family members or friends are

allowed in the treatment session. They start to talk about the

weather, family, and other daily life matters. Sliced oranges

or beverages are served. Then they gradually move into the sub-

---

[27] According to Mrs. Kook, the meridians which influence the kidneys are on the fingers. Blood was drawn from the
fingers to prevent possible infection from acupuncture needles.

ject of health and illness concerns. According to an informant,
Mr. Kae does not charge a client after treatment. As clients
experience efficacy from treatment, they bring a box of oranges,
a bag of rice or other goods as a gift. Mr. Kae and his wife
receive these gifts after first declining them many times.

Mr. Kae expresses his opinion about the present and
future of Hanbang, East-Asian traditional medicine:

> "It would be ideal if one could understand both Han-
> bang and Western medicine because both have merits. Most
> of the modern practitioners in America do not have time.
> However, American medical schools are interested in East-
> Asian medicine. When President Nixon went to China, one
> of his aides was cured by acupuncture. Thus, he recommend-
> ed Chinese medicine to the American people. In the future,
> more people will be interested in East-Asian medicine
> than they are now."

He specializes in acupuncture, although he has knowledge
of Hanyak as well. He limits his service to acupuncture. His
understanding of the acupuncture healing process is that
meridians in the body are stimulated by an acupuncture needle
and then white cells gather to fight germs and defend the
body so that healing takes place. Since Mr. Kae has been familiar with both Western medicine and Hanbang, he combines biomedical explanations and those of traditional Korean medicine
as Mrs. Kook did.

Mr. Kae talks about his clinical experience in terms of
patient selection, characteristics of patients, and efficacy:

> "I ask patients who already have a Western physician,
> to get permission to receive acupuncture from their
> physician. I have treated different ethnic groups:
> Koreans, Jewish people, and other Americans. People
> from far away like California call me and ask me about
> treatment. They heard about me somehow.
> I have treated backaches, respiratory diseases, psycho-

sis, gastrointestinal problems, etc. Here are some examples: A person who was recommended for back surgery by
a neurosurgeon or an orthopedic surgeon was very worried
about his back. He was completely cured by acupuncture.
He was confined to bed but with one needle of acupuncture,
he was able to get up right away. A lady has been taking
medicine for a respiratory disease, asthma, for a long
time, but that was not effective. She feels much better
after acupuncture treatment."

Mr. Kae treats his patients and friends in his living
room. An acupuncture map and one for the Five Elements hang on
the wall. In one corner of his apartment, old traditional
Korean medical books are found. He has a machine to detect
diseased parts of body which break the harmony of the human
physical system. This machine substitutes for pulse checking
which is the most important diagnostic method in Korean traditional medicine. Humans could be inaccurate and subjective.
This electrical machine is connected to the client. Two ends
ends with adult fifth finger-size metal bars are attached to
two equal parts of body, e.g., both palms to compare the two
readings on the meter of the machine and the balance between
the two readings. The figures are also compared with standard
health status scores. He also has a printed record for each
patient.

He examines the patient first with the _Hanbang_ diagnostic method. He observes the color of the face, eyes, vitality,
behavior, mood or emotional affect, and hears the patient in
terms of the strengh or weakness of her voice. He inquires
about family background and history of illness, present illness, and demographic data. Inquiries are also made about
other social data.

Instead of observation of Mr. Kae's clinical session with his client, he demonstrated on me. During the hour long demonstration session, a formal and professional relationship was maintained with considerable mutual respect. Relevant questions were asked in relation to history and present illness. Family and social information was also gathered. He shared his impression of health status with me and explained possible causes and mechanisms of a hypothetical disease state including the treatment plan after examination. His wife takes a few roles in his acupuncture practice as hostess, nurse, and consultant.

In the case of the third Hanui, the following is the experience in Mr. Yu's Hanbang. Mr. Yu is a 45 year old Hanui. His father was also a Hanui. He observed his father practicing Hanbang treatment "over his shoulder." He says that he has been to China seven times to import medicinal material.

His Hanbang is very successful. He has a big truck with his traditional Korean medicine company name on it in front of his residence as well as his clinic and store for herb material. He has a branch clinic in another state also. An advertisement about his clinical practice, herbal, and animal Chinese medicinal material is seen daily and weekly in several Korean newspapers.

His Hanbang clinic is located in a middle class residential area. There was no sign of Hanbang on his house. The first floor was remodeled as a clinic. There was a telephone. His examination room has a table with three chairs around it.

But, there was no examination table, because <u>Hanbang</u> diagnostic methods do not require it. Different medicines are kept in plastic containers with names in Korean or Chinese and they were arranged on shelves. There is a locked cabinet in which Mr. Yu keeps precious medicines such as ginseng, sliced deer horn, and bear gall bladder. Medicines are piled up in every available space from the floor to the ceiling. The family room was converted to a waiting room on one side and on the other side there are two treatment tables against each wall for treatments such as acupuncture, moxa, and cupping. Acupuncture charts are put up on walls. The room is decorated with Chinese style porcelain vases and dried and stuffed yet alive looking animals. A black bear skin with a fierce and live looking face is laid on the floor. In the basement, there are different naturally dried and refined herb medicines.

Mr. Yu's relatives helps him in the treatment and preparation of medicines. This assistant is said to be a university graduate in the area of traditional Korean medicine. appointments are not necessary. The <u>Hanbang</u> is open all year around everyday from 9 in the morning to 9 in the evening including weekends. There is no charge for a physical examination.

According to Mr. Yu's assistant, there are two groups of clients in their <u>Hanbang</u>. One group is composed of patients who have tried other kinds of treatment already, such as biomedical treatment, but their conditions have not been satisfactorily managed. The other group of people go to them for

Boyak, restorative medicines. Their treatment methods are acupuncture, medicaments, moxa burn, and cupping as shown in Chart 2.

The following clinical scene took place in Hanui Yu's Hanbang. Mrs. Kim's daughter brought her mother to this clinic. Part of the time her daughter and her three children stayed in another room. Mrs. Kim believed that she needed Boyak for restoration of vital energy. She said she felt weak and she had lost weight. She complained of other symptoms also such as frequent cramps, cold feet and hands, and frequent indigestion. When her daughter was not present, she expressed concern about her Hwabyung which she believes, has developed due to her daughter's harsh attitude toward her. Mrs. Kim explained:

> "I do not have energy at all. I am very tired and my appetite is poor. The food I take is not digested well. I have lost much weight. My hands and feet are icy cold. The cramps, pins and needles on the tips of toes and fingers bother me."

Mr. Yu asked her whether she had been at his Hanbang before. He took her demographic data, history and present illness. He wrote down this information on a ruled writing pad and took radial pulses on both of her wrists with his second, third, and fourth fingers. He took the patient's left hand pulses with his right hand fingers and vice versa. Then he asked her when and what kind of medicine she had taken. He continued with his examination. He tried to bend her two fifth fingers toward the dorsal direction of her hands and he asked:

Mr. Yu: "Which finger is more painful?"

Mrs. Kim: "My left finger."

Mr. Yu: "That means your brain nerves are involved due to troubles in life such as strenuous interpersonal relationships with children and grandchildren. You have Hwabyung. All these cause frontal headache."

Mrs. Kim: "I am not suprised. I have Hwabyung. That's right I have headaches."

Mr. Yu: "Your liver functions and kidney functions are decreased due to Hwa, old age, and indigestion. These conditions cause anemia and poor circulation which cause cramps, coldness of body, and pins and needles."

Mr. Yu explained her condition to her in lay terms and prescribed and prepared herb medicine with deer horn and other different kinds of herbs. One ingredient called Bucha, a warming agent, was included to warm up her body. Mr. Yu assured her by explaining that poison was extracted from this agent and a small dose was used. Many small packages in a transparent cellophane bags were given to her. This Hanui explained to Mrs. Kim:

"You will be busy preparing stew and drink for about a month. If you have diarrhea or a febrile sickness, you should stop taking this medicine until those symptoms are all cleared up because the medicine will be wasted. You will feel the efficacy about three months later after you have completed the medicine."

As she was leaving, Mrs. Kim saw some children's medicine and bought it for her grandchildren. She asked the Hanui to examine her daughter. After he examined her daughter and told them that her diagnosis was also Hwabyung. Her daughter said, "I do not know why I have Hwabyung. I can't think of any reason!" The Hanui asked, "Your heart was not broken? Nobody bothered You?"

Mr. Yu recommended royal jelly, which is made from honey,for Mrs. Kim's daughter. This medicine is known to cure

all diseases and it is supposed to be good for middle aged
women, but she did not buy it saying, "I may buy that next
time." Her daughter seemed to resent the illness label, Hwabyung.

Mrs. Kim paid three hundred dollars for her medicine
and a little more for her grandson's medicine. The Hanui came
to the door to say "Good-bye." After we all got in the car,
Mrs. Kim's daughter said to her mother, "You caused me Hwabyung!" Mrs. Kim kept silent and appeared embarrassed in the
presence of a non-family member.

Even during the period of taking the herb medicine,
Mrs. Kim happily comments about the favorable outcome of the
Hanyak therapy: "It is a little bit early to talk about efficacy, but I think my appetite is better, and my hands and
feet are not so cold." She was seen in Baek Il Zan Ch'ee, a one
hundred day old birth celebration party. When she was asked
whether her empty plate could be refilled she accepted and
had all of it. Some older Korean women do not attempt to help
themselves to food for fear of showing indulgence.

In summary, these encounters with the traditional
Korean professional medical experience will be summarized
according to Kleinman's categories of the therapeutic relation
between between client and practitioner.

1. Institutional setting. Hanbang is the term given to Korean
traditional medicine. It is the indigenuous professional sector of the Korean health care system.

2. Characteristics of the interpersonal interaction. Patient

usually visits Hanui with family members or friends. They interact rather freely among themselves in the clinical process. The client and practitioner relationship can be episodic or continuous. For example, Mrs. Choi had a single visit while Mrs. Sunu planned a follow up visit. A Hanui, Mrs. Kook saw her patents on a regular basis if possible. The amount of time spent in the clinical process was usually about an hour, at least for the first visit. The relationship between practitioner and patient was essentially formal.

3. The language of communication. Satisfactory explanations about treatment to clients were given by practitioners. Both the practitioner and the patient appreciate the same medical terms. Some of the highly professional terms are purposely avoided. Pathophysiology is usually illustrated in functional and holistic terms.

4. Clinical reality. The therapeutic approach is disease and illness oriented. It is secular and instrumental. It is not related to the sacred or symbolic realm. Acupuncture, Hanyak, moxa burn, and cupping are the main therapeutic methods.

5. Therapeutic stages and mechanisms. Bodily symptoms are always the complaints to express altered health status. The Hanui occasionally interprets these in terms of a psychosocial base. A cure or efficacy is expected in the final therapeutic stage. The cure seems to be determined by the permanent disappearance of symptoms of illness and the return of good appetite, a healthy look, and ability to work. One of the Hanui's criterion is improvement in rate and quality of pulses.

The elderly Korean women believe that efficacy depends
on the Hanui's wisdom, knowledge, experience, and ability to
heal the sick. When sickness is cured, there should be a mutual
understanding between patient and physician. Also, the explanation of the clinical process by a Hanui is important in addition to the Hanui's qualifications. Traditional Korean diagnostic methods, which require knowledge, skill, and experiences
are appreciated. The follwoing comments by Mrs. Hwang reflect
a harmonious therapeutic relationship between patient and
practitioner:

> "Of course I am more comfortable to talk with a Hanui
> than with Western physician because he and I understand
> the same medical tradition and he gives me explanations
> about my illness. If you use Hanyak properly, it is effec-
> tive without side reactions. Hanui tells you what is
> wrong with you by checking pulses and by observations of
> patient. A Western physician asks you many questions
> about your health problems, but he could not tell you
> until he reads scientific laboratory test results, but
> a Hanui knows what is wrong with you right away."

When no efficacy results the responsibility is placed
on the Hanui and the therapeutic relationship is usually dis-
continued. The patient then resorts to different kinds of
therapy. The following comments point to sources of displea-
sure with the Hanui's treatment:

> "When a good Hanui prescribes medicine or treats with
> acupuncture, it is very effective. However, some Hanuis
> do damage. Poorly experienced physicians make people
> deformed by hurting nerves during acupuncture. Also, side-
> effects can happen from herb medicine. For example, in the
> olden days a herb called Bucha was also used as a poison
> to kill people. That's why it can be dangerous when it is
> not used wisely" (Mrs. Kim).

> "My daughter suffered because a Hanui misdiagnosed
> her. I took her to a Western physician, but it was too
> late. The appendix was ruptured; the Western doctor

could not do anything; my daughter died. Since that time,
I do not trust a Hanui" (Mrs. Baik).

Patient and Biomedical Physician

in a Modern Professional Clinic

In the present section, therapeutic interaction between the Korean elderly patients and a biomedical physician
will be compared and contrasted in relation to the diagnostic process, understanding of pathophysiology, treatment approaches, and evaluation of treatment outcomes.

Frequently there were different explanatory medical
models between the Korean patient and the biomedical physician
due to their cultural differences. Often these differences
affected their treatment plans and therapeutic outcomes. Their
differences in understanding illness and curing behaviors
appear to be related to their different medical orientations
the traditional Korean medical and popular beliefs versus
those of biomedical orientation. Generally, the elderly Korean
informants appear to have a holistic and pluralistic understanding of illness practices. These informants have their own
medical language which is related to popular or traditional
Korean medicine.

Their common health care behavior pattern is self and/
or family oriented so they tend to regulate and manage illness
by themselves. They consider subjective illness symptoms as
very important in the diagnostic prodess and these are directly related to decisions such as whether or not treatment is
needed, and if so, what treatment is appropriate. These elderly

Korean women expect to be "cured" of their illness when they receive a treatment, but they are frequently told that their conditions might be recurrent because their symptoms are temporarily controlled. The elderly Korean informants in this study expect their biomedical practitioner to respond within their framework. However, that is mostly not the case. This discussion is mainly based on the observations and interviews conducted in a Korean church clinic. The clinic is located in a building in the church yard. There is an examination room and a waiting room. In the examination room there is an examination table, one desk, and three chairs. No other medical supplies are found. When a patient needs a thorough examination, she is advised to visit the physician's office.

The physician in charge is an elder of the church and an internist. He is a Korean who was trained in Korea as a physician and in the United States he also obtained a license to practice. During the medical examination there are usually several clients with the physician in a small examination room. The physician speaks to the majority of the clients in a moderate tone and uses a respectful pattern of speech. He adds honorific endings when addressing persons, such as a minister's mother or other high ranked clients. The relationship between the middle aged male physician and the elderly female clients is formal.

In this clinic, chronic medical problems are the major problems managed. When a patient comes, she is asked about her chief complaint and her illness history. The physician routinely examines the new patient by checking blood pressure, auscultation of lungs and heart, and taking the pulse. For old patients, blood pressure and pulse are taken, and medicines are prescribed or renewed. It takes about 2 minutes to write out a new prescription, 3 minutes to check blood pressure and write a prescription, and about 5 minutes to examine new patient. This physician commented about health and illness behavior of his elderly patients as follows: "These old people have very little understanding of health and medical knowledge. They have shown a very low degree of compliance. They cling to traditional Korean medicine which is based on experience, but it does not have a scientific foundation."

The informants' conditions which are frequently managed in a biomedical outpatient clinic were arthritis, heart ailment, hypertension, indigestion, neuralgia, dental problems, poor eye sight, diabetes, dizziness, anemia, constipation, and insomnia as shown Table 12.

These informants and biomedical practitioners perceive differently the significance of patients' complaints. There are times when although a patient presents subjective complaints, according to a biomedical pratitioner's view there exists no medical problem. For example, when Mrs. Hwang complained of a tightening and a pressing feeling in her chest, her physician examined her and told her that she did not have any medical problem. She remained in the examination room and talked with her friends about what the physician told her. A while later, as soon as another patient's visit was over, she went back to the physician and asked, "What shall I do? I have a pain here." This time the physician palpated her abdomen. He had already checked her blood pressure and listened to her heart. He prescribed a medication for her finally and said, "You are rather sensitive." A month later Mrs. Hwang announced that the medicine was not effective.

TABLE 12

INFORMANTS' CONDITIONS TREATED

IN A BIOMEDICAL OUTPATIENT CLINIC

Conditions*	Number of Informants
Arthritis	3
Heart ailment	3
Hypertension	3
Indigestion	3
Neuralgia	3
Eye problem	3
Dental problem	2
Diabetes	2
Dizziness	2
Anemia	1
Constipation	1
Insomnia	1

*Conditions are those described by informants.

Mrs. Suh also experienced a similar situation. When she had a severe headache, nausea, and vomiting, she was very concerned and went to the internist. The physician concentrated

on her heart condition because she was taking a cardiotonic,
but the physician did not particularly show interest in her
complaints. He prescribed a new dosage of the medication she
had been taking. Mrs. Suh also did not do much about the symptoms which led her to see the physician. She sat passively and
came home. Often Korean women expect a physician to figure out
what problems they have probably because they are used to the
Hanbang diagnostic method which is mainly established by the
Hanui. They also believe that asking questions and demanding
medical intervention might cause the physician embarrassment.
The patients generally feel shame about playing aggressive
roles in seeking cures for their health problems. After she
returned home she drank water to wash out the disagreeable
effects from the medicine which she had taken. Then her symptoms were relieved.

There is a communication problem between the biomedical
physician and elderly Korean clients due to unfamiliar terminology used. The biomedical physician has his technical professional medical language and he is not familiar with his
client's lay medical language. Mrs. Kang complained of pain
in a certain physical position. She said, "Mach'ida" for the
pain as she was pointing to the right side of her back during
auscultation. I was not sure exactly what that meant either
so I asked the physician if he knew about that after the patient's treatment. He answered that he was not sure about it
but it was not important, while the patient appeared to consider it very serious. The term which the patient used was not

biomedical jargon so that the physician did not understand what the patient attempted to communicate with her practitioner. Although they spoke the same Korean, they could not understand each other due to different subcultural background. Similarly, at a dental clinic, Mrs. Lee complained of a "sour" tooth to her dentist, but she was convinced that the dentist did not understand what she meant. She was helpless because she could not think of alternatives for the equivalent meaning in another expression. Until they understand each other, how can a real therapeutic relationship be established?

Differences in understanding human anatomy exist between the informants and the biomedical physician. For example, when Mrs. Lee came to see her physician, she thought her swollen and aching legs are from nerves or tendons, but the practitioner told her that it was due to bad blood vessels. Their understanding of the anatomical parts of an illness is differently perceived.

Frequently, patient and physician label an illness differently. While some of the informants in this study call neuralgia the pains on shoulders, back and thighs, the biomedical physician labels these symptoms arthritis. The biomedical physician tends to be dependent upon objective highly scientific technological diagnostic methods and he can be insensitive to his patients' subjective functional symptoms. Sometimes scientific medical diagnostic tests find only advanced limited pathological changes but not a slightly altered systemic and functional status which patients are aware of subjectively.

Some of the elderly Korean women do not readily respond
to the biomedical physician's recommendation for different diagnostic tests. They tend to enter the therapeutic stage and
by-pass the modern diagnostic stage. Some of the reasons are:
(1) they greatly rely on their subjective symptoms for diagnosis and treatment; (2) they are used to the examination by
a Hanui of eyes, ears, mouth, nose, and hands only; (3) they
feel that biomedical laboratory tests detect advanced pathological changes rather than early signs of illness. Although,
they feel uncomfortable, they are frequently told that all
their test results are within normal limits; (4) they believe
that the drawing of their blood, which is considered a vital
essence of physical health, is a waste; (5) they feel that
laboratory procedures are not necessary because they are too
old to be cured if something is detected in their old age;
(6) they consider their illness symptoms as signs of old age;
(7) their children are too busy to take them to clinic or
hospital for tests; and (8) they are reluctant to go to clinics
or hospitals with the sick and strangers, and where they do
not understand many different things which are happening.
They greatly depend on their own judgment in naming their
symptoms and managing their problems.

Mrs. Chin strongly believes that she should not depend
on her physician only for her or her family health problems.
Sometimes she follows medical treatment according to her judgment. She comments about her practice: "I usually do not take

medicine as directed by my physician, but I regulate it myself.
When I feel I need it, I take it and if I feel fine, I do not
take medicine. Sometimes I reduce the dosage of the medicine
or I do not take it as many times a physician recommends. Any-
way I do not like to take medicine that much because it might
have side-effects."

This seventy-nine year old woman believes that she has
a good basis for her attitude toward self-regulation of medication. When a modern physician indicated the need of urgent surgery for her son, she refused the surgery and the son is still
alive and well. That made her confident in her medical assessment and judgment. Further evidence of ways in which she exercises her judgment are seen in her management of hypertension.

A biomedical physician has prescribed medicine for her
hypertension. However, she does not take it because she does
not feel "dizzy." According to her if blood pressure is high
enough to require medication, she should be dizzy. To her that
is the cardinal sign of hypertension which needs to be medica-
ted. She does not go by blood pressure readings, which were
taken by a scientific objective medical instrument, for her
treatment. One of her recent blood pressure readings was 190/
105. It should be noted that Mrs. Chin is considered a bright,
sensible, and respected person among her friends. She has also
a high respect for modern professional medicine. She is interested in modern clinica; education. When a modern physician
gives explanations, she enjoys it very much, responds to him,
and lets him know her understanding of what was taught. She

comes to the clinic to check her blood pressure every week. She
asks the physician whether it is all right for her to take
aspirin. However, she also relies on her own medical beliefs.

Mrs. Hahn's blood pressure is even higher than that
of Mrs. Chin. Her systolic blood pressure is 220. Mrs. Hahn
has neither the opportunity to check her blood pressure regularly nor is she on anti-hypertensive medication. She and her husband were not accepted for coverage by the life insurance company when their children had arranged for them to apply for
the insurance. The company physician was very concerned about
her hypertension. Once she said she was not taking it because
she did not have the medication. She regretted that her son
bought his wife a heavy gold necklace, but he did not get her
the important medication. When I insisted that she go to a
clinic which is run by a church, and she di not have to pay
for the examination fee, she declined with this comment:
"When I was on medication for high blood pressure, I was having
severe pain and pressure on the back of my head and neck so that
sometimes I could not even move. Now I do not have it. My husband practices ancestor worship so that I would rather not go
to the church with you. One day I might call you to go there
with you. Thank you very much for your concern about me." She
did not call me.

According to one of her neighbors, she is not taking
medicine for her high blood pressure. She does not take medication because she believes that her symptoms related to hypertension have disappeared although her blood pressure reading

is abnormal. The physician in the church clinic emphasizes
that the blood pressure reading is the only important criterion for diagnosis and treatment. He recognizes objective
data measured by a scientific tool. The following example
supports this view:

> Patient: "I am healthy. My appetite is good. I eat
> meat well and drink beer also."
>
> Physician: "Your blood pressure is high 150/100. Does
> your heart tell you that you are sick? No, it does not.
> You have to check your blood pressure."
>
> Another patient: "I do not seem to pay much attention
> to hypertension, but to painful legs and back. Hyperten-
> sion is not painful."

Some informants utilize more than one different medical
tradition to solve their health problems by the best possible
available resources in a pluralistic medical system. Mrs. Koh
combines biomedical treatment and Hanbang for her coldness of
stomach and indigestion. She takes Hanyak, the traditional
Korean medicament, for her cold stomach and pills prescribed
by a biomedical physician for indigestion. Mrs. Rhim made a
clear statement about her medication: "I do not take any medicine without prescription." However, she took Boyak, traditional Korean restorative medicine, for a month. Boyak is not
viewed as a "medicine" but as a category of food which nourishes
and patches the body without side-effects. It is a natural
smooth process.

Informants who have had negative experience with Hanbang, mainly consult with cosmopolitan medical professionals
unless they are convinced that Hanbang is safe and effective.
For example, Mrs. Baik said that she had "neuralgia," she was

given tablets and she is very satisfied with the biomedical treatment. As stated earlier she believes her daughter died because a Hanui, who treated her daughter, was not competent. She limits herself only to Boyak and Uhwangch'ungsimhwan, "nerve tranquilizer."

The elderly Korean immigrant women tend to believe in permanent cures of illnesses even chronic illnesses such as hypertension and diabetes, while biomedical treatment often aims at maintenance with life time therapeutic requirement. When they have no symptoms, it seems to be considered a cure. Thus, they discontinue medication and diet. Mrs. Hahn, whose symptoms were referred to above, did not take antihypertensive medicine after the pain and pressure in the back of her head and neck diappeared although her blood pressure was 220 systolic. Mrs. Kal, who is a diabetic, commented about her course of illness in terms of cure:

> "I received insulin for diabetes for two years. The condition was cured. I do not take insulin now but take diabetic pills every two or three days. I was told by the doctor, I should take this everyday but my way works fine. Anyway my vulva area was very itchy but it is all gone now."

She added that she was taking the oral hypoglycemic agent "in order to prevent diabetes from recurring." She regulates medication by herself. She said that she was planning to take one pill per week. She evaluates her her diabetic condition by the degree of itching sensation of particular part of her body and not by the conventional method in the professional medical system such as urine sugar or blood sugar.

Two Korean women with heart ailments, who are both

on cardiotonics prescribed by a cosmopolitan internist indicate

their expectation of their heart condition by saying:

> "I asked my son-in-law to tell the doctor to cure
> my disease completely. But I do not know whether he
> told the doctor that or not. I feel much better already.
> They told me to take one pill a day but I take one every
> three days. It is much improved. I do not need medicine
> that much now" (Mrs. Suh).

Mrs. Ahn commented: "They gave these pills 'to cure' my heart

ailment. I take one of these everyday." She remarked that her

condition is checked by an internist monthly to see whether

or not her sickness is "cured."

Mrs. Sunu had excruciating pain in her back and thighs

and sleepless nights with diffused edema. An internist told

her that she has sacral nerve neuralgia and gastrointestinal

trouble, and gave her pills to relieve her pain "temporarily."

She was told that there was no permanent cure. So she resorted

to a Hanui and the Hanui reassured her that there was a cure

because medicine exists first and then disease exists. Mrs.

Sunu is very motivated to comply with all instructions given

to her by a Hanui who convinced her that there is a cure.

Mrs. Yun had severe constipation. Sometimes she did

not have a bowel movement for eight days. She was seen by an

internist in a Korean church clinic. She was given a prescrip-

tion for the problem which she took twice a day morning and

evening. She had bowel movements at the beginning, but as she

took the medicine continuously, she began to have diarrhea.

When I advised her to stop the medication after I had heard

her experience with the medication to cure the constipation

permanently. Whenever she sees me, she says, "What would have

happened if you did not tell me that." Similar situations are
often seen in the service clinic:

> Physician: "How is your constipation?"

> Patient: "It is all healed up."

> Physician:"It does not heal up completely forever. It
> might come up again."

Through the brief encounter with the biomedical professional clinical experience, the following will be summarized
according to Kleinman's categories of therapeutic transactions
between patient and practitioner.

1. Institutional setting. An informal partially equipped volunteer church clinic. There is one waiting room and one examination room.

2. Characteristics of the interpersonal interaction. When the
elderly Koreans arrive in the clinic, they present themselves
in the examination room so that they are able to attend in
open treatment sessions. Every patient is able to listen and
to observe the physician-patient interaction of her friends
and other patients. This group of patients see the physician
episodically unless they see the need for visiting the physician regularly such as hypertensive patients. The physician
and the patient relationship is essentially formal. The physician takes a superior role due to his professional, economic,
and educational background.

3. The language of communication. Communication is mainly disease-oriented. Although the biomedical physician tries to use
lay medical terms, analytical professional jargons are examples
which are not understandable to the people who are oriented to

a holistic and systemic illness principles. There is a communication problem between the biomedical practitioner and patient due to unfamiliar terminologies from different medical traditions. Differences in understanding human anatomy exist between patient and physician, and they have different labels for the same condition. In the diagnostic process, the patient' subjective symptoms are not sufficiently accounted for but the data from the physician's objective examination, are often based on scientific instruments and laboratory results.

4. Clinical reality. This reality is secular and instrumental. No spiritual or symbolic dimensions are involved in the therapeutic procedures. The person who plays a key role i treating patients is the biomedical practitioner. The area of concern in this biomedical setting is limited to diseases, but not illnesses, which are considered separately from other aspects of daily life experience.

5. Therapeutic stages and mechanisms. A conflict relationship is in evidence in the therapeutic relation between the biomedical practitioner and patient due to different understandings of illness. A patient may not express her medical beliefs during a professional medical session. Self-regulation or modification of the treatment plan according to a patient's beliefs are strongly discouraged. Consequently, non-compliance, a combination of biomedical treatment and traditional Korean medical treatment, or selection of alternative treatments entirely such as traditional Korean cures are in practice among these elderly Korean women.

Explanations about an illness between patient and physician are often different so that this fact leads to different
expectations of treatment and efficacy from each other. Physiological data gathered by medical instruments or laboratory
test results take a central role in evaluating therapeutic
outcomes. The biomedical discipline tends to focus on removal
of abnormal scientific data gathered by diagnostic tests and/
or physical examination while the elderly Korean informants
expect that the cure of illness based on improvement in subjective symptoms and functions of the body system is the best
indicator to evaluate efficacy. Termination of the therapeutic relationship is often episodic.

PRACTICES OF POPULAR MEDICINE

Elderly Korean women say "recognizing the presence of
disease becomes sickness" and "not recognizing the existence
of disease becomes medicine." From the time a woman is told
that she is sick or when she realizes her own sickness, she
becomes ill. She has to start to worry about her illness.
What they mean also is that secretly they are reluctant to
know about the presence of ilness because a miserable and
troubled life usually starts. One of the reasons that they
tend to keep their distance from hospitals or clinics is that
they do not want to hear that they are no longer an intact
and whole person, and are threatened about their unknown future.
These elderly Korean women wish to end their life as peace-

fully as possible without painful symptoms or physical disability to make their life miserable. Even when some of them are advised to have examinations, they often decline. They are not customarily told about the nature of their serious diseases by their children or physician, but they are treated.

The concept of natural healing without intervention is found among the elderly Korean women: "There is natural healing without treatment." They tend to avoid taking medicine as much as possible. When they feel they have to take synthetic medicine--because a biomedically oriented physician or family members insist that they do--they reduce the dosage and shorten the length of time they have to be on medication. Instead they believe in nourishing themselves with natural foods, not indulging, keeping clean, sleeping well, and avoiding a reckless life style in order to be healed. These concepts originated from the Chinese concepts of Taoism which teach the importance of natural healing power, and living with natural things as an autonomous being instead of overcoming life artificially. Thus, they value natural physical exercise, mountain herbs, fresh air, clean water, and bright sunshine. Koreans are basically nature-oriented (Adams 1969 and Kluckhohn and Strodtbeck 1961).

In the practices of popular medicine, nourishment and sweating methods are central. First, the nourishment principle and its methods will be discussed and then the sweating method will be presented.

Restoration by Nourishment

There is a saying about the high value of eating quality food with regulation. It says, "Eating well is the same as
taking Boyak, restorative medicine" (Lee 1982:70-71). Restoration of the body is needed when circulation of blood with vital
energy or functions of human organs cause disharmony of the
Ŭm and Yang balance (Kang 1981:111). The harmony in the body
is interfered with when the body organs and/or parts are
weakened or positive or negative energy is wasted. For example,
the bitter plant Yikmoch'o (Leonurus Sibiricus or mother wort)
is a special remedy for a person whose body has become "cold
and hollow" after the positive energy has been taken away in
the summer due to summer heat (Sunu 1982:467). It is ground
and prepared in liquid form. This remedy helps people to have
a better appetite.

Often ginseng and young chicken are boiled together
and taken as nourishment. Bosintang, dog meat soup is known
as a special remedy for lack of Yang. However, Mrs. Kim's
rationale for recommending dog meat soup in the summer is that
one's body heat is neutralized by Bosintang which means body
nourishing soup, because it is a cold food. Thus, there is a
discrepancy between Hanui Sunu's explanation for dog meat soup
as a remedy for summer heat and that of Mrs. Kim, a lay person.
However, one thing that is certain is that Koreans consider
the hot-cold food dichotomy important. Usually, Bosintang is
consumed by men because it is viewed as too crude or inappro-
priate for women.

Mrs. Ahn often states: "Soy bean paste is equivalent to the efficacy of ginseng for nourishing the body." She did not only teach me this health maxim, but she also gave me a bowl of her home-made bean paste which she herself preserved. She wanted me to share this paste with my "pale and thin husband" whom she felt was going to become sick. She also was concerned enough to instruct me on how to cook oxtail soup for my husband. She believes that most of the today's Korean women are not familiar with cooking traditional dishes for their families. She has practiced her beliefs about promoting health and curing illness community-wide.

In order to nourish a weakened liver, beef liver is recommended. Chopped raw beef liver is seasoned with salt, sesame oil, pepper, green onions, finely chopped garlic, and honey or sugar. It is considered more effective to eat raw liver than cooked. Mrs. Rhim had a hard time eating liver. She believes that she is a very "picky and sensitive" person. So she almost has given up having liver. Instead she puts a raw egg in her hot coffee and drinks it.

Beef stomach, tongue, and beef pancreas are valued highly as nourishing foods. These dishes are recommended for people who have "lost vital energy" or who lack this energy.

Human umbilical cord is said to be good for a woman who is "hollow" in the postpartum stage. They believe that this cord is a source of blood. Vital energy can be generated and circulated in the body system only when a proper amount of source of blood, nutrients is available. They try to secure

a good appetite with a good digestive system and the best quality of food to maintain the harmony of vital energy in the
body which is viewed as the essence of health.

Recovery by Sweating

In traditional Korean medicine, a sweating method is
used to remove different influences of causes of illness such
as coldness, dampness, wind, and heat (Kang 1981:109). For
example, Lyu (1975:2) states that sickness develops when cold
"poison" is transferred from the outside to the inside of the
body through the pores of the skin. When the "cold evil" goes
inwards it becomes a fever. If the cold disease has not been
cured, different organs in the body such as the liver, the
spleen, the kidneys, and viscera with bowels may be affected.

High body temperature is recognized as an important
sign of a cold and its manifestation with fatigue. The treatment characteristic for this problem is a hot liquid diet,
warm clothing, and a warm environment without drafts or wind.
The elderly Korean women in this study believe that certain
kinds of conditions with high fever and chills should be controlled by increasing the body warmth. This treatment concept
is called Yiyulch'iyul among Koreans.

There is a condition called Momsalgamgi. The important
objective sign of this condition is a high fever and an acutely
felt subjective symptom is chills combined with aches all over
the body. The cause of this illness is believed to be mental
and physical overwork and the invasion of cold evil. According

to Koreans, when a person is in a weakened and tired state, causes of illness such as cold poisons, dampness, and winds invade the body easily because resistance of the body decreases.

In order to cure Momsalgamgi, Korean women try to keep away from exposure to cold and to provide an atmosphere for the sick person to perspire. When Mrs. Hahn had this condition she tried to avoid cold water and not to eat any cold food. She wore warm clothes. All the windows and doors were closed at all times. Mrs. Hahn ate hot bean sprout soup with ground hot pepper, garlic, and green onion in a well heated room. Then she covered herself with blankets and an electric blanket in order to "sweat." Frequently, she was offered hot honey ginger tea. Providing easily digestible hot food and fluids, a warm atmosphere stimulating the perspiration process are all necessary to recover from Momsalgamgi.

In connection with the sweating curing method, there is a sweating cave called Hanjeungmak in rural as well as in urban Korea. Koreans believe that the sweating process in this Hanjeung cure all diseases. Mrs. Park described a Hanjeung:

> "A big fire is made with wood in a round cave, which is made of rocks and clay. After all the wood burnt, a large amount of water is sprayed in the cave and the inside of the cave becomes very hot and full of steam. People take off their ordinary clothes and cover themselves with hemp cloth and they go into the cave. The temperature of the cave is the lowest at the bottom and the highest on the top. In order to breathe, people put their noses at the bottom especially the beginners."

She continues to explain how Hanjeung lowers her high blood pressure:

"In Hanjeung, the heat comes down from above, so that the high blood pressure comes down. Some people say that heat causes blood pressure to go up, but Hanjeung affects it differently. A university medical research team came and took the blood pressure before and after Hanjeung, they found that blood pressure goes down after Hanjeung treatments. During the Hanjeung, I can hear my blood dropping down from the upper body to my lower body. I could feel my heart and blood vessels fluttering and palpitating also."

Her own physiological conceptualization of changes in blood pressure by Hanjeung is dramatic and unique. This Korean indigenous therapy by perspiration is familiar to the elderly Korean women in this study. Mrs. Hyun, a lady at the church clinic, also complained of pain in her joints which, she thinks, can be relieved by Hanjeung. In the United States, as a substitute she uses a hot tub bath but she says, "It is not nearly like the Hanjeung in Korea." Mrs. Park used Hanjeung for all diseases including her hypertension and Mom-salgamgi.

FOLK AND SACRED HEALING

The conceptualization of indigenous Korean illness and healing in relation to animism or shamanism is familiar to the elderly Korean immigrant women in the Greater Washington Metropolitan Area. As in a study of folk healing in Honolulu, Hawaii, Korean-Americans do not appear to practice shamanistic healing (Snyder 1979:81). It appears as if Christian healing practice substitute for indigenous healing. An informant, who is highly educated and taking leadership roles in the elderly Korean community equated the principles of shamanistic healing with Christian healing. In her words: "Healing by Mudang, a female shaman, and the healing described in the Bible are the same. It is based on the patient's faith." Another informant interprets Mudang healing as a result of hypnosis. Most of the elderly Korean women in the present research believe in Christian faith healing.

Korean Folk Healing

In Korea, indigenous shamanistic and animistic healing belong to the folk sector of the health care system. The healing process itself takes place in the client's home or in the healer's sacred therapeutic shrine. Family, healer, and neighbors or community members often participate in healing rituals. The shaman and patient relationship is established periodically when illness is recognized and evaluated as serious enough to consult the shaman. The shaman and client relationship is informal. All share in a similar explanation of illness which is related to the animistic power which has been interfered with by human behavior. Usually sacred symbolic rituals are performed. A spirit medium is not always needed, but could be replaced by respected benevolent people in the community. Responsibility for sickness and for healing is imposed mainly on an individual or family members' fulfillment of filial piety. There is emphasis on not breaking certain norms and rules. When a person becomes ill, in order to be healed, he or she should follow a shaman or geomancer's instructions with utmost care. Usually healing is permanent.

Although it appears as if the elderly Korean informants
in Washington do not use this traditional folk healing, those
from rural areas had memories of having used it in Korea. Ceremonial and symbolic healing rituals were characteristically
therapeutic. Mrs. Hahn experienced the following practices
associated with the healing arts of the Mudang:

> "When I was about ten years old, I had a bad blood lump
> in my chest, so that it was painful and difficult to
> breathe. A Hanui diagnosed it as an abscess in my chest
> cavity. The doctor recommended an incision and it should
> be drained the next day. Although, my mother was a Cath-
> olic, she took me to a Mudang. She told my mother that
> something was wrong with the pole which was changed for
> repair in storage. She asked my mother to prepare food
> and invite three knowledgeable people to pray. My mother
> invited a Buddhist monk, my scholar uncle, and someone
> else respected in our village and the ceremony started,
> During the ritual, my mother could hear something from
> where I was lying down and she came to the room, she
> found that I was singing. I recovered that fast and I did
> not need the incision and drainage. I could not ignore
> the shamanistic power."

Animism is involved here. The spirit of the pole in their
storage room must have been angered by mistreatment of household members and as a result, the child became sick. In this
case, the Mudang did not perform the ritual by herself, but
consulted the informant's mother in terms of cause and treatment methods according to their cultural context. The Mudang
advised the mother to select wise and respected people and prepare food for the ritual. In order to appease the spirit, wise
human resources and sacrifices prepared with utmost care are
required. The prayer part includes apology for wrong doing
and the request for forgiveness. The spirit, as part of nature,
responds quickly to human wishes by healing the informant

when all the prescribed rituals are performed. This healing process is sacred, miraculous, mystical, and symbolic. Cure takes place dramatically through involvement of the whole family and community.

Mrs. Yun witnessed a situation in her farming neighborhood in which an infant was very sick with breathing difficulty. In spite of different treatments with popular remedies, the infant did not improve. Several neighborhood women gathered to pray for the recovery of this child. An old woman among them prayed to the gods to heal this child. Some prayed and some young women did not do much out embarrassment. Still they did not observe any sign of improvement. Mrs. Yun went around the child's house to see if anything was wrong. In the backyard, she saw a furnace covered with a heavy iron plate. She removed the plate immediately. Charcoals in the furnace looked black with little white ashes on them, but they were warm. She could see bright charcoal flame come up. The child cried and his color returned to normal with easy breathing. Mrs. Yun interpreted the fire as a symbol of life. Mrs. Yun stated that this represented the view that three gods govern childbirth. After a baby is born, fires should be kept burning for three days. In the sick new born baby's case, the broken rule was corrected and healing took place. By the way, Mrs. Yun called a Mudang to perform a shamanistic healing ritual when her husband was ill.

Mrs. Hahn recollected an event which had happened to one of her neighbors. In her neighbor's household, family mem-

bers were affected by grave sicknesses. When they consulted
with a shaman, she was told that the ancestor's spirits were
not at rest and that this was the cause of family illnesses.
This woman's husband saw a geomancer to select an auspicious
grave site for his ancestor's final resting place. He followed
the geomancer's instruction and the family illnesses subsided.
To be free from illnesses, filial obligation must be fulfilled.

Faith Healing

Among Christian informants, various faith healing
experiences are shared. The healing process is sacred and symbolic. A spirit medium such as a minister does not seem to be
always necessary in Christian faith healing. The outcome
could be miraculous healing or no cure at all is believed and
experienced. Sometimes an unexpected adverse outcome can result.

Mrs. Yun, a Catholic informant, said, "Although I have
been going to the Korean Catholic Church for thirty years now,
still I do not know anything about the religion. However, I feel
if I am sincere enough, God will help me to sleep better." She
believes and hopes to be healed by her Christian faith.

Mrs. Choi could not see. So she avoided gossip and prayed constantly. Although a few different ophthalmologists had
said that she needed an eye operation, on the morning of her
operation an ophthalmologist examined her eyes and told her
that she did not need that operation. She said, "God helped me!"
These elderly Korean women prayed hard with the hope of healing

or God's judgment on their health.

In certain cases, faith healing has not been granted.
Mrs. Koh said, "I tried faith healing but it did not work."
I did not pursue it further. Mrs. Yik, a professed Christian,
criticized as "fanatics" a group of young ill women in Korea
who fasted for many days and tried to cross a flood in order
to be healed by God, but they failed and died from drowning.
Thus, there are examples of the healed and the non-healed.

SUMMARY

The health care system, which is utilized by the elderly Korean informants in this study, has been discussed in terms
of their health and illness practices in the professional sector, the popular sector, and the folk sector which make a pluralistic medical care system. The patient and physician therapeutic interaction has been examined also by using A. Kleinman's
explanatory model.

Traditional Korean medicine which is part of the professional sector has been influenced by traditional Chinese
medical principles which are oriented by cosmological concepts.
The ultimate therapeutic goal is to maintain a harmonious flow
of Ki, vital energy, in the body system so that systemic function can be restored. Traditional Korean medicine is practiced
holistically and synthetically contrary to the analytically
oriented biomedical practice. Common therapeutic methods of
traditional Korean medical sector are Hanyak, traditional
Korean medicaments; Ch'im, acupuncture; D'um, moxa burn; and

Buhwang, cupping.

The therapeutic interaction between informants and the Hanui, the traditional Korean physician, is congruent while the therapeutic transaction between informants and the biomedical practitioner is rather incongruent because the majority of informants share a similar explanatory model which is related to cosmological concepts.

The health beliefs which are part of the popular sector among these informants are influenced by traditional Korean medical concepts which have been popularized. Commonly applied popular medical practices are nourishment and "sweating," which are utilized to secure a balanced circulation of vital energy through the body system.

The informants had memories of having used folk shamanistic healing in Korea, although it appears as if the informants in this study do not use this traditional folk healing. The majority of the informants seem to have substituted Christian faith healing instead of the traditional healing of the Mudang, the female shaman.

CHAPTER VII

SUMMARY AND CONCLUSION

This study was conceived because there were gaps in
the knowledge about the influence of social cultural factors
on the perception and management of health problems among elderly Korean immigrants. The main purpose of this study was
to examine the health beliefs, values, and practices of elderly Korean immigrant women. My specific research aims were:
(1) to describe and interpret the sociocultural aspects of the
changing lives of elderly Korean immigrant women, (2) to study
the health and illness beliefs and practices of the elderly
Korean immigrant women, (3) to discuss a pattern of cultural
construction of a Korean popular illness called Hwabyung
among elderly Korean immigrant women, and (4) to describe and
analyze transactions between clients and practitioners in traditional Korean professional medical practice and in biomedical
practice.

As the number of Korean immigrants to the United States
increased, there was a need for information on the pattern of
elderly Koreans' daily life, their health and illness beliefs
and practices in their sociocultural context. I was told by
health practitioners and researchers that the unavailability

of research evidence about the health behavior among Korean
immigrants made it difficult to do health planning and give
proper health care to this population. An area of specific concern was the interplay between Korean medical traditions and
those in the United States.

Health and illness beliefs and practices differ among
different cultures. A health care system is a cultural system
which encompasses patterns of belief about causes of illness;
norms influencing direction of treatment and evaluation of
treatment results; recognized statuses, roles, power relationships, and interractional clinical settings. The conceptual
framework for this study followed Kleinman's model of health
care systems as social and cultural constructions. An individual's health and illness behavior in a health care system is
influenced by a systems of symbolic meanings, the norms of
society, his perception of the world, his communication with
others, and his understanding of his own world view as it is
shaped in an interpersonal environment.

According to Kleinman, a health care system is divided
into external and internal structures. In this research, I
emphasized the internal structure of health care system which
consists of three over lapping segments: the popular, professional, and folk sectors.

In the professional sector, classical indigenous
medical tradition such as traditional Chinese and Korean medicine are viewed as professional medicine as well as the biomedical discipline. Traditional Korean medicine is professional

medicine because it has been influenced by traditional Chinese medicine. Historically, through the processes of indigenization, Chinese medicine was transformed and it became part of the medical care pattern which is proper to a Korean culture.

The traditional Korean medical principles are related to cosmology which is explained in terms of the Five Elements (Fire, Water, Wood, Metal, and Earth), Ŭm and Yang, and Ki (vital energy). The ultimate aim of treatment is to establish bodily harmony by maintaining delicate interrelationships among these cosmological factors. The main treatment modalities are medicaments, acupuncture, moxa burn, and cupping.

The popular sector is "lay, non-professional, non-specialist." A. Kleinman states that in the popular sector the majority of people understand their illnesses and initiate treatment. The popular sector is managed by an individual herself, family, friends, or another social networks. Certain aspects in professional medical practice are transformed into a pattern of care which is appropriate to the popular sector of a health care system. This process is called popularization. Most of the principles of Korean popular medicine originated from those of the traditional Korean professional medicine. Popular treatment approaches are similar to those of the traditional Korean medicine, while some popular medical practices are related to folk medical practices in Korea which mainly related to the spiritual realm.

The folk sector is closely related to the popular sector and the professional sector. The characteristics of folk

medical practice can be secular, sacred, or a mixture of these
two aspects. Koreans believe in spiritual causes of illness
such as gods in the animistic world and spirits of ancestors.
Thus, when it comes to healing, usually a sacred symbolic
ceremonial ritual is performed.

Kleinman emphasizes that illness is always a cultural
construction. Specific concepts of illness are based on particular historical circumstances, as well as physiological,
psychological, behavioral, and cultural factors. These aspects
are interpreted in terms of moral, cosmological, and religious
orientations. These orientations give meaning to symbols.
Kleinman disusses how somatization, as a culturally constructed
response, can be understood in relation to the links between
sociocultural influences on emotional and phsysiological processes. Kleinman developed an explanatory model framework in
order to examine the communication interaction required to manage particular illness episodes cross-culturally. This model
helps to study the dynamics of communicative transactions in
health care. In the present research, the explanatory framework was used as a guide to understand health and illness beliefs and practices, cultural construction of illness and to
analyze transactions between Korean elderly women and healers
from traditional and biomedical settings. It was hoped that
this model would make it possible to understand different or
similar explanations of illness beliefs and practices between
individual patients and practitioners.

Furthermore, according to Kleinman, the study of therapeutic interaction between patients and practitioners reveals the cognitive basis of illness experiences and the cognitive operations of clinical practice. Kleinman states that cognitive structures reveal the dynamic relationships between patients and healers. The aim of categories for comparing therapeutic relationships is to understand different healing systems in order to determine their universal and culture specific aspects. A comparison of transactions between patients and practitioners in terms of explanatory models and clinical realities is important because it is directly related to the sociocultural understanding of therapeutic processes. Kleinman employs the following major categories for comparing therapeutic relationships to determine similarities and differences: institutional setting, characteristics of the interpersonal interaction, idiom of communication, clinical reality, and therapeutic stages and mechanisms.

THE STUDY POPULATION

There were three reasons why I decided to choose elderly Korean women as my informants: (1) elderly women in Korea households are considered consultants as well as practitioners in treating family health problems; (2) as older persons they are believed to be conservative enough to retain traditional health and illness beliefs and practices while they come in contact with the host society, and (3) as a woman researcher, it was   cultually acceptable for me to interview and observe other women.

The population chosen was a convenience sample of
twenty elderly Korean immigrant women residents in the Greater
Washington Metropolitan area who were sixty years old or older.
These informants were contacted through personal and community
networks. All of the informants had been invited by their children to come to the United States except for one person who came
with her husband. The length of residence in the United States
ranged from 6 months to 20 years with the ages of the informants
spanning from 62 to 79. Seventy-five percent of the informants
were widows and twenty-five percent of them were married. Sixty-
five percent of these informants lived with their son's or
daughter's. The rest lived in senior citizen's housing apart
from their children. Most of the informants said that they were
Christians except for two who practiced ancestor worship and
one Buddhist. Fifteen percent of the informants were university
graduates, twenty percent were high school graduates, while
fifty percent had primary school education and the remaining
fifteen percent had no formal education. Only five women or
twenty-five percent spoke a little "survival" English while the
rest did not speak English at all.

Key informants from the study population and from the
Korean community offered detailed insights. In addition, during
the months of July to December 1982, I observed 35 other Korean
older men and women patents during clinical consultation
in a Korean church clinic. The actual 10 month period of fieldwork extended from April 1982 to January 1983, but the previous
initial contacts had been made during a pilot study from May to
August in 1981.

METHODOLOGY

The methods used for data collection were participant
observation, semi-structured interviews, key informant information, and examination of documentary sources.

Participant observation focused on sociocultural influences on aging particularly in relation to sociocultural
change, adaptation patterns in family and society, health and
illness beliefs and practices, and alternative health practices
of elderly Korean immigrant women. The activities of elderly
Korean immigrant groups were observed in settings of private
homes, senior citizen's apartments, church, the Elderly Korean
Association meetings, elderly picnics and parties, small social
groups, and the elderly university. Other activities included
attendance at a clinic run by a biomedical physician in a Korean
church, and visits to the offices of Korean traditional physicians.

The semi-structured interview guide had six parts:
(1) demographic and background information, (2) concepts related to meaning of old age, (3) significance of children,
(4) daily life patterns, (5) health beliefs and practices, and
(6) illness beliefs and practices. All interviews were conducted in Korean.

The following documentary materials were mainly used:
East Asian and Korean traditional medical documents, reports,
newsletters, newspapers, and journals about elderly Korean
immigrant life, and Korean ethnographic materials. The data

in this study were analyzed according to content analysis and inferential interpretation. Demographic data and material on health and illness beliefs and practices were also analyzed quantitatively to show frequency and distribution of certain factors and possible relationships among them.

CHANGING LIVES OF ELDERLY KOREAN IMMIGRANT WOMEN

The everyday lives of the informants in this study have been influenced by the impact of changes due to old age, immigration, and social and cultural changes.

To the informants in this study old age means a series of changes. Changes occur in appearance, in behavior, and in social, physical, emotional, and intellectual factors. Spiritual and personality changes also take place. Generally, the informants have a negative recognition of changes of old age particularly psychosocial aspects of changes. Their negative perception of old age has become accentuated in changing culture and society. The informants' role and status in the Korean immigrant family are markedly deteriorated due to their lack of knowledge, skill, and economic power necessary in the host society. They are no longer able to assume the traditional elder's role as an influential person who advises and guides particularly in family matters. In American society old age requires a series of changes in their life style such as relocation to a senior citizen's housing away from children. The elderly Korean women are no longer able to communicate with their children and participate in activities with their children. The individualistically and independently oriented American society encourages individuals to create a nuclear family or live alone. The informants in this study strongly feel that they interfere or burden their children with their deteriorating signs and symptoms of old age. The Korean immigrant family has lost the ability to respect and support their elderly parents as was done in the extended family in traditional Korea. The informants have   come to view old age unfavorably because of discontinuity of traditional family and social values of elders' status.

Although thirteen informants lived with their children out of the total twenty informants, four of them lived with their unmarried or separated children for their children's health or for security reasons instead of being dependent on their children. Five of the informants lived with their married daughters. Only three of them lived with their married sons which is considered the classical traditional Korean family structure.

The traditional role and status of the informants, who lived with their children, have changed significantly. Respect and deference are not as evident for older Koreans. The positions of adult children and grandchildren have become increasingly important while those of elderly parents have become peripheral. The elderly women's advice is seldom accepted by their children. Their traditional privilege of leisure has been threatened due to the responsibility they have acquired for child care and housework because their daughter or daughter-in-law with whom these informants reside is employed outside.

Particularly for some traditionally oriented informants, it is difficult to accept changes taking place in the Korean immigrant family as relations shift from the traditional hierarchical structure to a more individually oriented pattern. The elderly Korean immigrant women's heightened concerns about burdening their children's daily lives might be related to the adjustment to the immigrant life and the awareness of the importance of individualism in family and society. In Korea, the extended family was able to provide any necessary care for the elderly. In America, the care of the elderly places an added burden on the children who are struggling to adjust to the pressures of a new way of life. In the transitional period, the elderly Korean informants were trying very hard not to depend on and interfere with their children's lives, but to meet the changing society's demand for an independent individual life.

American society encourages older persons to live independently by providing pension benefits. Thirty-five percent of the women in this study have moved from a traditional extended household to an independent one. These informants lived in government supported housings and were economically independent from their children. They depended mainly on a Social Security pension or some kind of financial aid from the county, state, or federal government. Their interaction level with their family has decreased while ties with friends and members

in the community have increased. Their economic dependence has
also shifted from their children to government pension sources.
Those informants living independently are relatively Western-
ized and do not usually have family responsibilities such as
the care of grandchildren. They have been living in the United
States longer than five years.

Living independently serves to meet the psychosocial
needs of the informants in this study. They are able to maintain their dignity as individuals in their old age in a changing society while continuing a harmonious relationship with
their children through mutual respect. The informants who
lived apart from their children enjoyed more leisure than the
informants who lived with their children. However, the informants who live with their children maintain more continuity of
traditional family values than the informants who live independently from their children. On the whole, the elderly Korean
immigrant women view this diminishing traditional relationship
with their children as inevitable and try to continue the parent-children bond as much as possible.

Regardless of these informants' residential patterns,
they all put their highest priority on their children's welfare
and happiness. Even, the informants' social activities were to
do some beneficial things for their children such as obtaining
information about business opportunities, sharing foods, bar-
tering goods, and exchanging labor. Their last wish at the time
of death reflects concerns about their children. The elderly
Korean women wish to die as quickly as possible when the time

of death comes so that they do not have to burden their children in taking care of them. This attitude is intense enough to
lead to modifications in some of the health practices followed
by informants. Some of the informants refrain from taking restorative tonics which are believed to be very effective, because they do not want to prolong their lives and thus burden
their children.

HEALTH AND ILLNESS BELIEFS AND PRACTICES

The women in this research associate definitions of
good health with concepts of invincible strength, physical and
functional maintenance, genetic inheritance, physical activities and participation, freedom, independence, happiness,
good appetite, and fate. Since Ki, vital energy, is generated
in the abdomen, they consider the ability to eat and digest
well as very important. A good appetite is a positive sign of
good health. In addition, harmony in interpersonal and social
relationships is essential in order to preserve happiness and
health. A few of the informants suggested that a good harmonious relationship extends to their ancestors and other spirits.
Ultimately, they believe that their health depends on their
fate which is related to their cosmological world view. If a
person is born with good luck, he will enjoy good health and
a long life. Fate, however, is used as an explanation for incurable or fatal diseases.

Health is understood as an interrelated state of the

human body with the environment, and society. It includes biological, psychological, social, spiritual, cosmological, and
philosophical dimensions. In other words, an understanding of
health among Koreans is based on a comprehensive view which
includes well being and an optimum level of participation in
daily life, and proper social, ethical, and moral conduct.
Health and ill-health do not only influence the individual's
life but also significant people particularly   elderly women's children. Among the elderly Korean immigrant women, the
earnest desire for health is not primarily for their own well-
being but for their children's. They believe that if they are
healthy, they will not burden their children.

Two sets of health problems are the major types of
complaints of the elderly Korean women: symptoms of old age
and those of illness. Symptoms of old age include poor appetite,
general physical weakness, dizziness, senility, poor eye-sight,
hearing difficulty, memory loss, and missing teeth. These symptoms tend to be accepted rather casually and a part of a natural
process. Illness is defined as inevitable dependency. Elderly
Korean women tend to delay reporting their illnesses until they
feel it is absolutely necessary. Before reporting health problems
to   family   members, these women usually take care of themselves with popular remedies, traditional Korean medicaments,
or over-the-counter medicines as much as they can. Sometimes
they are cared for by their friends if they live apart from
their children.

The elderly Korean immigrant women's understanding of

the causes of illness is related to popularized traditional
Korean professional medical principles. To them, the illness
state is equated with the disharmonious state of vital energy
in the body system. They believe that physical exertion, poor
control of food intake, lack of blood, and external factors
such as cold, dampness, wind, and heat cause illness by interfering with the vital energy in the body. Physical exertion is
believed to interrupt the free flow of vital energy resulting
in an imbalance of the Ŭm and Yang. This imbalance is believed
to cause some illnesses such as neuralgia, arthritis, hepatitis, high blood pressure, tired and red eyes, and sore throats.

Elderly Korean women believe that a good digestive system has a central role in securing general health because Ki,
vital energy, source is generated in the abdomen. Poor control
of food intake in relation to kinds of food, amount, and frequency disturbs or weakens the adequate supply of vital energy
to the general body system. Among these women, blood is identified as the source of vital energy. They also believe that blood
dries in old age and can also become bad. It lingers in sickness, and it hardens during anesthesia. All these altered states
of blood interfere with the proper circulation of vital energy
and ultimately cause different diseases.

Coldness, dampness, heat, and wind, which are considered
external factors, usually invade the body through the pores and
interfere with the harmony of Ki by weakening of the Yang energy. The informants believe that neuralgia, arthritis, cold
stomach, indigestion, and asthma are also caused by these exter-

nal factors. Some of the informants predict that the prevalence of neuralgia among elderly Korean immigrant women will increase because they wear short sleeves and short skirts in America, and not long dresses as they did in Korea. Air conditioning system is indicated as a contributing factor to the prevalence of neuralgia and arthritis. The elderly Korean women are familiar with a sickness called wind disease, which is explained as a pathogenic force which can develop with the acute onset of disease such as stroke, erysipelas, and falling teeth. Another condition which occurred with frequency was exhaustion from summer heat. They believe that summer heat causes lack of vital energy.

The general conceptualizations of illnesses among Korean elderly women are synthesis oriented as Porkert (1976) pointed out about Chinese medicine. The traditional Korean medical principles are based on interrelated cosmological energy and physical function: Ŭm and Yang, the Five Evolutive Elements (Fire, Water, Wood, Metal, and Earth), and Ki (vital energy). Diseases are understood in terms of deficiencies or redundancies of energy and diagnosis and treatment of diseases are mainly based on symptoms and functional disorders. In contrast, the biomedical practice emphasizes scientific and technological diagnostic methods.

With regard to forms of treatment, pluralistic illness practices are found among the elderly Korean immigrant women. Modes of treatment are not mutually exclusive of the other and the people are able to select one or combine two or more which

are relevant to them in relation to beliefs about causation of
illness and specific symptoms. Thus, they may combine biomedical practices with Korean traditional professional medicine or
specific folk treatments. It is evident that biomedical principles are being popularized among these informants in this
study.

Traditional Korean professional medicine called Hanbang
is an indispensable source of care for the elderly Korean immigrant women. Most of the informants are familiar with the traditional Korean medicaments, acupuncture, moxa burn, and cupping which are practiced by traditional Korean medical practioners or by the informants by themselves. Ninety percent of
the informants have used one or several kinds of Hanyak, traditional Korean medicaments, and fifty percent of them have
been treated by acupuncture. Herb medicines are used exten-
sively for restorative purposes. The central purpose of these
forms of treatment is to restore or strengthen general systemic bodily functions by rechannelling vital energy through the
whole body system.

Hanbang is valued by the informants for the following reasons:
(1) the elderly Korean women are more familiar with the theory and practice of Hanbang than those of biomedical medicine;
(2) the informants are at ease with Hanui who practice Hanbang
because they share a similar understanding of the social and
cultural factors which influence illness beliefs and practices;
(3) patient's subjective symptoms and complaints of functional
disorders are respected in Hanbang; (4) Hanbang examination

methods provides a rapid diagnosis with simple methods and they can detect early signs of disease; (5) side-effects from treatment are rare; (6) Hanbang is believed to remove the root of the disease so that a permanent cure is expected; (7) Hanbang is believed to be effective in certain "incurable diseases" which have already been treated by other types of treatment; (8) treatment procedures are explained by Hanui to clients and understood by clients; (9) the hours for consultation are conveniently arranged. For example, a Hanbang is opened until late hours and on weekends, and an appointment is not necessary.

Hanbang occupies a subsector of the traditional professional sector which provides instrumental secular treatments such as medicaments, acupuncture, moxa burn, and cupping. Illness is sometimes recognized and treated but the major focus of treatment is on diseases. The relationship between the patient and the traditional Korean physician is essentially a formal one. However, they share a more similar sociocultural background than between patient and biomedical physician. As pointed out earlier in relation to Porkert's model of Chinese medicine (1976:63-81), the synthesis-oriented medical explanatory model is reflected in the traditional Korean professional clinical practice and the informants in this study did find themselves comfortable with it. The informants and the Hanui used a mutually understandable medical language and the Hanui provided physically oriented treatments which are mostly expected by the informants in Hanbang.

Ninety percent of the informants in this study have received treatment in biomedical settings in America. In this sector the relationship between client and physician is formal. Findings in this study showed that sometimes they do not communicate adequately in the therapeutic relationship because the client is oriented to the traditional Korean medical model while the physician is oriented to that of the biomedical discipline. Korean patients and the biomedical physicians often hold concepts of illness cause which are in conflict such as indigestion.

Sometimes, diagnostic methods and outcomes from these methods disappoint the patients. One area of concern was the biomedical physician's dependence on laboratory tests for diagnosis and treatment. Patients who felt sick were often told that "nothing is wrong" if diagnostic tests did not show abnormalities. A related area was the opposite one in which a woman was given a diagnosis that she was sick based on medical reports, although she did not feel sick. With regard to expectations about outcome of treatment, a problem commonly found was that the Koreans expected a permanent cure from the physician while the biomedical professionals offer treatment for "temporary relief" of symptoms, or "maintenance" therapy.

The biomedical physician practices his medicine based on highly analytical and objective medical technological principles such as histological pathology, biochemistry, and bacteriology (Porkert 1976:64). Biomedical practice is mainly concerned with specific biological aspects usually without considering the interrelated functions among organs or between the body and mind. Biomedical practice does not relate itself with sociocultural and environmental factors in order to understand an illness in a holistic term. Biomedicine is frequently practiced as though it were culture free. Biomedical practices were disease oriented so that sociocultural implications were seldom dealt with. In terms of treatment patterns, the informants in this study utilize alternative medical care resources while the professional physician views the biomedical professional sector as the only effective available medical care system.

In the popular sector, it is evident that traditional Korean professional medicine has been popularized. Hanyak, traditional Korean medicaments, acupuncture, moxa burn, and cupping, which originally belonged to the traditional Korean medical domain, are practiced among the informants in this study. The primary aim for popular medical practices is to restore vital energy and obtain functional bodily harmony as it is in traditional Korean professional medicine. This harmony is maintained by taking nourishments such as bean paste soup and by practicing Hanjeung (sweating) among the elderly Korean immigrants.

In the folk sector, some women associated illness with ancestral spirits, animistic gods, and Christianity. They believe that when ancestral spirits are not at rest, it is because they are ignored or mistreated by their offsprings, or misfortunes such as sickness occur in the family. They believe that there are gods everywhere in the world and if the gods are offended or their territory is trespassed, the people in quesion will become ill. Some of the informants believe that

illnesses occur as a form of warning or punishment from God,
or a trial of evil when they do not follow the will of God
in Christian faith. Although the informants did not have any
Mudangs available for consultation in Washington, they described their past experiences with animistic and cosmological
medical practices. Symbolic and sacred therapeutic rituals were
known as major interventions for different kinds of illnesses
in the folk cultural frame of reference. Folk therapy has a
sacred nature and it requires a spiritual medium most of the
time. The participants in therapeutic sessions or rituals are
patients, a specialist, and family and community members.

Christian faith healing was practiced among the elderly
Korean immigrants. They practiced it by themselves or with the
assistance of a minister. Findings in this research suggest that
Christian faith healing is a substitute for the traditional shamanistic healing. Thus, for the elderly Korean immigrant women
Christian faith healing has the function of syncretism. They co
that both the Christian minister and the Mudang have
the role of the spiritual medium to heal illness.

HWABYUNG: A CULTURAL CONSTRUCTION OF ILLNESS

Hwabyung is the most popular mode through which Korean
elderly women construct illness. It is a basic syndrome which
informants use to interpret illness. According to traditional
Korean medical principles, when the seven emotions (joy, sadness, depression, worry, anger, fright, and fear) are overly

stimulated or when they are in distress, these injured emotions
accumulate in the body and become fire. Consequently, this fire
or Yang energy, destroys the harmony in the Ki by weakening the
Ŭm, negative energy. This disturbed vital energy can cause illness in different parts of the body. For example, anger injures
the liver, excessive joy injures the heart, worry injures the
spleen, depression injures the lungs, and fear injures the kidney. Hwabyung is a culturally influenced syndrome which helps
to resolve the emotional stresses associated with different
life problems. The concept of Hwabyung helps individuals to explain symptoms of illness which are experienced at the onset of
intolerable life problems and particularly when the individual,
family members or friends perceive the problem as most strenuous.

Hwabyung is present among the informants of all socioeconomic and educational levels. Sixteen informants (80 %) ad-
mitted directly or indirectly that at one time or another
they have experienced Hwabyung. The life problems associated
with Hwabyung symptoms were death of spouse or children, sickness of spouse or children, disloyalty of spouse, a strained
interpersonal relationship with daughter-in-law, friend, and
daughter, insecurity about children's welfare and health, lack
of support from children, separation from children, contempt
for others, incompatibility in married life, unfair treatment
by others, and physically and psychologically demanding work.

The specific somatic complaints associated with Hwabyung were gastrointestinal symptoms such as poor appetite;

chronic indigestion; abdominal discomfort or pain; constipation; diarrhea; heart problems; shortness of breath; neuralgia; kidney disease with decreased urine output, weight gain, and pains on thighs and legs; dizziness; high blood pressure; hyperthyroidism; chest pain or discomfort; blindness or poor eyesight; hearing impairment; neurlogical symptoms; vomiting blood; liver disease; sensory changes; and cold hands and feet.

The treatment aim for various symptoms of Hwabyung is a physical cure because patients complain of physical symptoms and they expect to have bodily treatments. The common treatment choices were traditional Korean medical treatment and biomedical treatment according to the explanations of the illnesses. When the informants with Hwabyung symptoms go to a biomedical physician, the physician diagnoses their Hwabyung conditions in biomedical principles, since Hwabyung is not recognized in the biomedical discipline.

Traditional Korean professional physicians diagnosed some of the informants' conditions as Hwabyung and treated them mainly with traditional Korean medicaments and acupuncture. Symptomatic treatments for different conditions of Hwabyung were with popular remedies, popularized traditional Korean medicines, or over-the-counter drugs. Christian faith healing through individual prayers is also practiced.

Suppression of emotions is taught in Korean society and this contributes to the construction of Hwabyung. Mental illness is stigmatized and psychotherapy is associated with shame. Emotional distresses associated with troubling life problems are manifested as somatic symptoms rather than verbal expressions. Hwabyung as a culturally constructed illness among elderly Korean women is an explanatory model of a sickness based on Korean medical thought, values and beliefs, and historical and socioeconomical circumstances.

The findings in the present study show that Hwabyung, as a culture specific model of illness among Koreans is associated with disturbances in the seven emotions of happiness, sadness, depression, worry, anger, fright, and fear. As noted earlier, when emotions are overly stimulated or when they are in distress, the injured emotions accumulate in the body and become fire. Consequently, this fire, Yang energy, destroy the harmony in Ki, vital energy, by weakening Ŭm energy. This disturbed vital energy can cause illness in different parts of the body. These finding are of interest in light of the work of Lee (1977) who studied Hwabyung as an anger-syndrome in Korea, and Lin's work (1983) about Hwabyung as a possible culture-bound syndrome among Koreans in the United States. Lee states that Hwabyung is associated specifically with the emotion of anger while in the present research, informants identify Hwabyung in relation to the range of emotions sadness, depression, worry, anger, fright, and fear. Lin's research shows that Hwabyung focuses on physical complaints and particularly gastric problems with mass. This present study shows that a wide range of physical complaints are associated with Hwabyung. Probably because the typical physical complaint of Hwabyung, bodily suffering with indigestion and chest discomfort affected

by a mass in digestive and/or respiratory system, has been
broadened by popularization of biomedical knowledge in interpretation of Hwabyung symptoms among the informants.

Hwabyung can be viewed as a culture-bound syndrome.
Hwabyung is a Korean culture specific illness which is embedded
with Korean historical, sociocultural values and beliefs, and
traditional Korean medical principles based on the interrelationship between cosmological energy and human body. Hwabyung
is a sociocultural and psychobiological adaptive response to
troubling life problems in Korean culture.

This study offers findings about patterns of daily life,
health, and illness beliefs and practices of elderly Korean women in the Washington Metopolitan Area. It points to ways
through which Kleinman's concepts of explanatory models and
cultural construction of illness are helpful in research on
health care systems.

Three recommendations for further study are:

1 To examine differences and similarities in explanatory models of common illnesses of elderly Korean immigrants,
between elderly Korean immigrants and their children, and the
impact on health and illness management of the elderly Korean
immigrants in relation to compliance and level of satisfac-
tion in treatment results.

2 To determine how a biomedical practitioner, who works
with elderly Korean immigrants, negotiates with his elderly
Korean immigrant patients in "the reconceptualization and re-
formation of medical beliefs ... and particularly linkages be-

tween popular medical beliefs and practices and the scientific

biomedical tradition" as suggested by L. Cohen (1979:38).

3 To compare and contrast <u>Hwabyung</u> among different

time waves of Korean immigrant groups in terms of changes in

interpretation of this popular Korean illness and repatterning

of the illness behavior in order to better understand its mani-

festation and its prevalence.

GLOSSARY OF SELECTED TERMS

Note: Terms are romanized according to the McCune-Reischauer
      System

Romanization	Definition	Character	
		Korean	Chinese
Bosintang	Dog meat soup as restorative	보신탕	補身湯
Boyak	Restorative medicine or tonic	보 약	補藥
Buhwang	Cupping therapeutic method	부 항	
Bucha	Herb providing warmth medically (Radix Aconiti carmichaelii)	부 자	荷子
Ch'im	Acupuncture	침	鍼
Chôm	Divination	검	占
Danchôn	Lower abdominal breath-ing exercise	단 전	丹田
D'ŭm	Moxa burn	뜸	
Gut	Ceremonial rituals per-formed by Mudang. Healing rite is one of them	굿	
Hanbang	The traditional Korean professional medical system or clinic	한 방	漢方
Hanjŭng	Indigenous Korean sweating method	한 증	汗蒸
Hanui	Traditional Korean professional medical physician	한 의	漢醫
Hanyak	Traditional Korean professional medicaments	한 약	漢藥
Hwa	Abnormal inner bodily fire or heat. Emotional distress or anger. A "mass or lump" related to overly disturbed emotions	화	火

334

Glossary Continued

Hwabyung	A popular illness caused by Hwa among Koreans	화 병 火病
Insam	Ginseng	인 삼 人蔘
Ikmoch'o	Motherwort(Leonurus Sibiricus)	익모초 益母草
Ki	Vital energy or cosmological energy	기 氣
Koryochang	A legendary custom in Korea: parents over 70 years old were buried alive with some food	고려장 高麗葬
Mach'ida	Pain is felt in certain bodily movement or position	마치다
Momsalgam-ki	Cold symptoms with aches, chills, and fever	몸살감기
Mudang	A female shaman	우 당 巫堂
Nokyong	Medicinal deer horn	늑 용 鹿茸
Ochang	Five storage body organs: lungs, spleen, heart, kidneys, and liver	오 장 五臓
Palcha	Fate, luck, destiny	팔 짜
Pung	Wind. Rapidly progressing disease	풍 風
Sakwan	A kind of acupuncture treatment method which is commonly applied for indigestion	사 관
Siepchon dabotang	Traditional Korean restorative medicinal formulary	십전대보탕
Sida	Twinging aches	시 다
Simhwa	Inner abnormal bodily heat or fire related to emotional distress. Overly stimulated emotions	심 화 心火
Sinbyung	An illness caused by possession of spirits	신 병
Uhwang-ch'ungsim-hwan	Bezoar antifebrile pills to facilitate vital energy quickly. A popular home remedy	우황청심환 牛黄清心丸

Ŭm and Yang	Negative energy and positive energy in cosmology	음양	陰陽
Yiyul ch'iyul	Control high fever with warm therapeutic methods	이열치닐	以熱治熱
Yukbu	Six working body organs: stomach, small intestine, gall bladder, triple warmer, large intestine, urinary bladder	육부	六腑

APPENDIX

SEMI-STRUCTURED INTERVIEW GUIDE *

I. Demographic and Background Information

1.	Name	2.	Telephone Number
3.	Address	4.	Age
5.	Religion	6.	Education
7.	Household Member	8.	Marital Status
9.	Living Arrangement	10.	Source of Income
11.	Length of Residence in the U.S.		

II. Old Age

1. How do you know that you have become an old person?

2. How do you feel and think about being an old person?

3. Have you seen any changes in what you think and what you do as you get old?

4. What are some of your wishes in old age?

III. Children

1. What meaning do children have for you?

2. What thoughts do you have toward your children?

3. What do you expect from yourself and your children?

4. What are the main sources of conflict in your relationship with your children?

IV. Daily Life

1. How do you usually spend the day?

2. What changes have taken place in your life since you came to the United States?

* Translation from Korean original

3. Would you tell me about your social life?

4. What are your concerns about your daily life?

V. Health Beliefs and Practices

1. What is health?

2. What brings good health?

3. What do you do to maintain or promote health?

4. Has your health status been changed since you came to the United States

VI. Illness Beliefs and Practices

1. What is illness?

2 What illnesses have you had?

3. What do you call them?

4. What signs and symptoms did the illness show?

5. Why do you think it started when it did?

6. Usually when did the illness get worse and when did it get better?

7. What did you fear most about illness?

8. What are the chief problems your illness has caused for you?

9. What kinds of illnesses do you take care of at home? Why? How?

10. What was done for the illness before you went to a clinic or a hospital?

11. To whom do you first consult about your illness?

12. What was the choice of treatment? Why?

13. What were the most important results you hoped to receive from the treatment?

14. Did you receive the efficacy that you expected? If not, why?

15. What kind of treatment did you receive next? Why?

16. How do you know whether your illness is cured or controlled?

17. Have you had side-effects during a treatment? If so, would you please explain?

18. What other healing methods are you familiar with?

19. Do you use different treatment methods in America from those used in Korea for the same illness? Why?

20. Has the number of your illness episodes decreased or increased since you came to the United States? Why?

BIBLIOGRAPHY

Adams, Don
    1969   "The Monkey and the Fish: Cultural Pitfalls of
                an Educational Advisor." The Cross-cultural
                Approach to Health. L.R. Lynch (ed.). Madison:
                Fairleigh Dickinson. Pp. 436-444.

Adams, Edward B.
    1980   Korea Guide. Seoul: Seoul International Tourist
                Publishing Co.

Agren, H.
    1971   Handbook of Acupuncture and Moxibustion Therapy.
                Hong Kong: Commercial Press.

Anomymous
    n.d.   Materially d lia Opisaniia Korei. (Data for a
                Description of Korea).

Becker, Howard, and Harry E. Barnes
    1961   Social Thought from Lore to Science. New York:
                Dover Publications, Inc.

Bennet, S.J.
    1978   "Chinese Medicine Theory and Practice." Philosophy
                East and West. 28: 439-453.

Bonica, John J.
    1974   "Therapeutic Acupuncture in the People's Republic
                of China." JAMA (Journal of the American Medical
                Association). 228: 1544-1551.

Borman, N.H.
    1966   "The History of Ancient Korean Medicine." Yonsei
                Medical Journal. 7: 103-118.

Brandt, Vincent S.R.
    1969   "Some Ways of Looking at Village Value." Studies
                in the Developmental Aspects of Korea. Andrew
                Nahm (ed.). Kalamazoo Michigan: Western Michigan
                University. Pp. 84-89.
    1971   A Korean Village: Between Farm and Sea. Cambridge:
                Harvard University Press.

Caudill, William
    1976   "The Cultural and Interpersonal Context of Every-
            day Health and Illness in Japan and America."
            <u>Asian Medical Systems: A Comparative Study.</u> C.
            Leslie (ed.). Berkeley: University of California
            Press. Pp. 157-177.

Cha, Sungman
    1978   "Korean Heritage in Medicine. A Glimpse of History."
            <u>Yonsei Medical Journal.</u> 19: 75-84.

Chang, Suk C. et al.
    1973   "Psychiatry in South Korea." <u>American Journal of</u>
            <u>Psychiatry.</u> 130: 667-669.

Cheong, Chae-Hyok
    1977   <u>Tongsŏ Uihak Wonron.</u>   東西醫學原論
            Seoul: Hangrim Press.

Choy, Bong-Youn
    1979   <u>Koreans in America.</u> Chicago: Nelson Hall.

Choi, Jai Seuk
    1964   "Traditional Values in Korean Family." <u>Journal of</u>
            <u>Asiatic Studies.</u> 7: 43-47.

Chung, Chin-Yong and Byong-Ho Lee
    1981   Personal Conversation about Role and Status of
            Elderly in Traditional Korea. July 27, 1981.

Chung, Joon Young
    1982   Personal Interview about Korean Immigrant popula-
            tion in the Greater Washington Metropolitan Area.
            May 7, 1982.

Cohen, Lucy M.
    1979   <u>Culture, Disease, and Stress among Latino Immi-</u>
            <u>rants.</u> Washington, D.C.: Smithsonian Institu-
            tion, Research Institute on Immigration and Ethnic
            Studies.

Confucius?
            <u>Hyo Kyung.</u> 孝經
            (Classic of Filial Piety) Chapter 1.

Covell, Jon Carter
    1982   <u>Koreans's Cultural Roots.</u> Seoul: Moth House.

Creel, Herrlee Glessner
    1953   <u>Chinese Thought from Confucius to Mao Tse-Tung.</u>
            Chicago: Mentor Book, The New American Library.

Croizier, Ralph C.
    1968   <u>Traditional Medicine in Modern China.</u> Cambridge:
            Harvard University Press.

1976   "The Ideology of Medical Revivalism in Modern
             Asia." Asian Medical System: A Comparative
             Study. C. Leslie (ed.). Berkeley: University
             of California Press. Pp. 341-355.

Dallet, Charles
    1874   Histoire de L'eglise de Coree, Precedee d'une
                 L'histoire, Les Institutions, la Langue, les
                 Moeurs et Coutumes Coreennes. Paris: Victor
                 Palme.
    1954   Traditional Korea. New Haven: Human Relations
                 Area Files. (English Translation). Originally
                 published as Choson Kyohoesa. Lee, Nung-Jik and
                 J. Yoon (trans.). (Korean Translation). 1947.

Decker, David L.
    1980   Social Gerontology. Boston: Little, Brown and Co.

Dix, Griffin
    1979   "How To Do Things with Ritual: The Logic of
                 Ancestor Worship and Other Offerings in Rural
                 Korea." Studies on Korea in Transition. D.R.
                 McCune et al. (eds.). Honolulu: University of
                 Hawaii Press. Pp. 57-88.

Dong-A Ilbo.(Korean Newspaper). 東亞日報
    1981   June 30; July 2, 13; September 3; December 15, 30,
                 1981.

Dredge, Paul C.
    1976   "Social Rules of Speech in Korean: The Views of
                 Comic Strip Character." Korea Journal. 16: 4-14.

Dunn, Fred L.
    1976   "Traditional Asian Medicine and Cosmopolitan
                 Medicine as Adaptive Systems." Asian Medical
                 Systems. C. Leslie (ed.). Berkeley: University
                 of California Press. Pp. 133-158.

Ebrey, Patricia Buckley (ed.).
    1981   Chinese Civilization and Society. A Sourcebook.
                 New York: The Free Press.

Foster, George M.
    1978   "Medical Anthropology and International Health
                 Planning." Health and the Human Condition:
                 Perspectives in Medical Anthropology. M. Logan
                 and E. Hunt (ed.). Belmont: Duxbury Press. Pp.
                 301-313.

Gallin, Bernard
    1978   "Comments on Contemporary Sociocultural Studies of
                 Medicine in Chinese Societies." Culture and Healing
                 in Asian Societies. A. Kleinman et al. (eds.).
                 Boston: G.K. Hall and Co. Pp. 173-181.

Gernet, Jacques
    1962   Daily Life in China on the Eve of the Mongol
            Invasion 1250-1276. Stanford: Stanford University
            Press (Translated from the French by H.M. Wright).

Glick, Leonard B.
    1977   "Medicine as an Ethnographic Category: The Gimi
            of the New Guinea Highlanders." Culture, Disease,
            and Healing. D. Landy (ed.). New York: Macmillan
            Publishing Co. Pp. 58-70.

Good, Byron J.
    1981   "The Meaning of Symptoms: A Cultural Hermeneutic
            Model for Clinical Practice." The Relevance of
            Social Science for Medicine. L. Eisenberg and A.
            Kleinman (eds.). Boston: D. Reidel Publishing
            Co. Pp. 165-196.

Griffis, William Elliot
    1883   "Corean Medical Science." The Overland Monthly.
            1: 44-46.

Hahn, Dongse
    1964   "A Clinical and Anthropological Study of Hysteria
            in Korean Urban Society." Neuropsychiatry. 3: 327.

Hall, Rosetta Sherwood
    1897   The Life of Rev. William James Hall, M.D. Medical
            Missionary to the Slums of New York, Pioneer Mission-
            ary to Pyong Yang, Korea. New York: Press of Eaton
            and Mains.

Hall, Sherwood
    1978   With Stethoscope in Asia: Korea. McLean, Virginia:
            Press.

Han, Woo-Keun
    1974   The History of Korea. (Translated by K. Lee). The
            University of Hawaii Press.

Harris, Diana and William E. Cole
    1981   Sociology of Aging. Boston: Houghton Mifflin Co.

Harvey, Youngsook Kim
    1976   "The Korean Mudang as a Household Therapist."
            Culture-Bound Syndromes, Ethnopsychiatry and
            Alternative Therapies. Vol. IV. of Mental Health
            Research in Asia and Pacific. W. P. Lebra (ed.).
            Honolulu: University of Hawaii Press.

    1979   Six Korean Women: The Socialization of Shamans.
            St. Paul: West Publishing Co.

Hess, Beth and Elizabeth W. Markson
    1980   Aging and Old Age. New York: Macmillan Publishing
            Co.

Hessler, Richard M. et al.
    1978   "Intra Ethnic Diversity: Health Care of the
              Chinese Americans." <u>Health and the Human Condi-
              tion. Perspectives on Medical Anthropology.</u> M.
              H. Logan and E.E. Hunt Jr. (eds.). North Scituate:
              Duxbury Press. Pp. 348-362.

Ho, Chun   許浚
    1966   <u>Dong Eui Bo Gam.</u> 東醫宝鑑

              (Treasure Book of Eastern Medicine). Seoul: Pung-
              nyun-sa.

Hong, Wonshik
    1972   <u>Hwangje Naegyŏng Somun Haesŏk.</u> 黃帝內經素問 解釋
              Seoul: Komun-sa.
    1975   <u>Hwangje Naegyŏng Ryŏngch'u Haesŏk.</u>黃帝內經靈樞 解釋
              Seoul: Komun-sa.

Hou, Joseph P.
    1978   <u>The Myth and Truth about Ginseng.</u> South Brunswick:
              A.S. Barnes and Co.

Huang-ti
    1975   <u>Huang-ti Nei-ching Ling-shu.</u> 黃帝內經靈樞
              (The Yellow Emperor's Classic of Internal Medicine-
              Mystical Gate). Shanghai: New First Edition.
              Chapter 20.
    1959   <u>Huang-ti Nei-Ching Su-Wen.</u> 黃帝內經素問
              (The Yellow Emperor's Classic of Internal Medicine-
              Plain Question). Shanghai. Chapter 42.

Hulbert, Homer B. (ed.)
    1902   "Burial Customs." <u>The Korean Review.</u> 2: 241-246,
              294-300.

Hume, Edward Hicks
    1940   <u>The Chinese Way in Medicine.</u> Baltimore: The Johns
              Hopkins Press.

Janelli, Roger L. and Dawnhee Yim Janelli
    1982   <u>Ancestor Worship and Korean Society.</u> Stanford:
              Stanford University Press.

Kang, Hyo Shin 姜孝信
    1981   <u>Dongyang Euihak Gaeron.</u> 東洋醫學 概論
              (Introduction to East Asian Medicine). Seoul:
              Komun-sa.

Kark, Sidney et al.
    1962   "A Practice of Social Medicine." <u>A Practice of
              Social Medicine: A South African Team's Experiences
              in Different African Communities.</u> S. Kark and
              G. Steuart (eds). Edinburgh: E. and S. Livingstone
              Pp. 3-39.

Kart, Cary S.
    1981   The Realities of Aging. Boston: Allyn and Bacon
                Inc.

Keith, Jennie
    1980   "'The Best is Yet To Be'" Annual Review of Anthro-
                pology. 9: 339-364.

Kiefer, Christie W.
    1971   "Notes on Anthropology and the Minority Elderly."
                Gerontologist. 11: 94-98.

    1974   Chaning Culture, Chaning Lives: An Ethnographic
                Study of Three Generations of Japanese Americans.
                San Francisco: Jossey-Bass Publishers.

Kim, Bok-Lim C.
    1976   "An Appraisal of Korean Immigrant Service Needs."
                Social Casework. 57: 139-148.

Kim, Byung-Suh
    1980   "Epilogue: The Functions of Conflict in the Con-
                struction of Korean-American Communities." The
                Korean Immigrants in America. B. Kim and S.H. Lee
                (eds.). Montclaire: The Association of Korean
                Christian Scholar in North America, Inc. Pp. 147-162.

Kim, Doo Jong
    n.d.   "History of Medicine of Ancient and Medieval Korea."
                (An Abstract in English). Seoul: Seoul National
                University. Pp. 1-38.

Kim, Gih Seol   金起卨
    1981   Minsok ye nat'anan Kŏngang Kwannyŏm.民俗에 나타난 健康觀念,
                (Health in Folk Customs). The Korean Folklore.
                14: 41-58.

Kim, Hyun Soon and Sonia Strawn
    1979   "The Women's Rights Movement in Korea." Human
                Right in Minority Perspectives. D.S. Kim and
                B. Kim (eds.). Montclair: The Association of
                Korean Christian Scholars in North America Inc.
                Pp. 91-110.

Kim, Il Soon   金馹孫
    1983   "Changsu pigyŏl un ŏpta."   Dong-A Ilbo. July
                1983. 長壽秘訣은 없다

Kim, Kwang-Iei et al.
    1976   "A Review of Korean Cultural Psychiatry." Trans-
                cultural Psychiatric Research. 13: 101-114.

Kim, Wonsik
    1967   "Korean Shamanism and Hypnosis." The American
                Journal of Clinical Hypnosis. 9: 193-199.

1969   "A Further Study of Korean Shamanism and Hypnosis."
American Journal of Clinical Hypnosis. 11: 183-190

Kim, Young-Key and Dorothea Sich
1977   "A Study on Traditional Healing Techniques and
Illness Behavior in a Rural Korean Township."
Anthropological Study. 3: 75-111.

Kleinman, Arthur
1977   "Depression, Somatization, and the 'New Cross-
Cultural Psychiatry." Social Science and Medicine.
2: 3-10.
1978   "Problems and Prospects in Comparative Cross-
Cultural Medical and Psychiatric Studies." Culture
and Healing in Asian Societies. A. Kleinman et al.
(eds.). Boston: G.K. Hall E. Co. Pp. 407-439.
1980   Patients and Healers in the Context of Culture.
Berkeley: University of California Press.

Kleinman, Arthur and Tsung-Yi Lin
1980   "Introduction." Normal and Abnormal Behavior in
Chinese Culture. A. Kleinman and T.Y. Lin (eds.).
Boston: Reidal Publishing Co. Pp. xiii-xxiii.

Kluckhohn, Florence R. and Fred L. Strodtbeck
1961   Variations in Value Orientations. Evanston: Row,
Peterson.

Kunstadter, Peter
1975   "Do Cultural Differences Make Any Difference?
Choice Points in Medical Systems Available in
Northwestern Thailand." Medicine in Chinese
Cultures: Comparative Studies of Health Care in
Chinese and Other Societies. A. Kleinman et al.
(eds.). Washington, D.C.: U.S. Government Print-
ing Office for Fogarty International Center, NIH,
DHEW Publication No. 75-653. Pp. 351-384.
1978   "The Comparative Anthropological Study of Medical
Systems in Society." Culture and Healing in Asian
Societies. A. Kleinman et al. (ed.). Boston:
G.K. Hall E. Co. Pp. 393-405.

Kwon, Ju Won 權周遠
1965   Kajŏng Saenghwal Ch'ongram. 가정 생활 총람
(Reference for Family Life). Seoul: Mungu-sa.

Lee, Chae Kon 李在崑
1974   "Kyŏngbuk Donghae'an ui Mingan Ryobob." 慶北東海岸 의
民間療法 (Popular Medical Practice in
East Coast of Kyongbuk Province). Korean Folklore.
7: 111-121.

Lee, Hyo-Jae
1971   Life in Urban Korea. Seoul: Taewon Publishing Co.

347

Lee, Ki Baik 李基白
1973   Hanguksa Shinron. 韓国史新論
        (Outline of Korean History). Seoul: Ilchogak.

Lee, O Young
1967   In this Earth and in That Wind: This is Korea.
        Seoul: Hollym Corp. D.I. Steinberg (trans.).

Lee, Si Hyung
1977   "A Study on the Hwa-Byung(Anger Syndrome."
        Journal of Korean General Hospital. 1: 63-69.

Lee, Sil Kyong 李實敬
1982   "Hŭpyŏn Noin ŭl wihan Sikp'um." 吸煙老人言 위한 食品
        (Diet for the Elderly People Who Smoke). Noin
        Saenghwal. 老人生活   (The Elderly Life).
        25: 70-72.

Lee, Tai Young
1979   "Asian Christian Women for Human Liberation."
        Human Rights in Minority Perspectives. D. S. Kim
        and B. Kim (eds.). Montclair: Association of
        Korean Christian Scholars in North America, Inc.
        Pp. 65-89.

Leslie, Charles
1976a   "Introduction." Asian Medical Systems: A Compara-
        tive Study. C. Leslie (ed.). Berkeley: University
        of California Press. Pp. 1-12.
1976b   "The Ambiguities of Medical Revivalism in Modern
        India." Asian Medical Systems: A Comparative
        Study. C. Leslie (ed.). Berkeley: University of
        California Press. Pp. 356-367.

Liebow, Eliot
1967   Tally's Corner. Boston: Little Brown and Co.

Lin, Keh-Ming
1980   "Traditional Chinese Medical Beliefs and Their
        Relevance for Mental Illness and Psychiatry."
        Normal and Abnormal Behavior in Chinese Culture.
        A. Kleinman and T.Y. Lin (ed.). Boston: D. Reidel
        Publishing Co. Pp. 95-111.
1983   "Hwa-Byung: A Korean Culture-Bound Syndrome?"
        American Journal of Psychiatry. 140: 105-107.

Lock, Margaret M.
1980   East Asian Medicine in Urban Japan. Comparative
        Studies of Health Systems and Medical Care.
        Berkeley: University of California Press.

Lyu, Heui-Young (ed.) 柳熙英
1975   Tongyang Jŏngsin Kwahak. 東洋精神科學
        (A Textbook of Psychiatry in Oriental Medicine).
        Seoul: Research Institute of Community Medicine.

MacMahon, Hugh
     1977   "Confucianism." The Korean Way. The Christian
              Literature Society of Korea. Seoul: Samsung Co.
              Pp. 62-69.

Maloney, William
     1956   "The Healing Arts in Korea." The Journal Lancet.
              76: 381-384.

Materi, Irma Tennant
     1949   My Life in Korea. New York: W.W. Furton and Co.

McCune, George M. and E. O. Reischauer
     1939   "The Romanization of the Korean Language, based
              upon Its Phonetic Structure." Transaction of the
              Korean Branch of the Royal Asiatic Society. 29:
              1-55.

Metzger, Thomas A.
     1980   "Selfhood and Authority in Neo-Confucian Political
              Cultural." Normal and Abnormal Behavior in Chinese
              Culture. A. Kleinman and T.Y. Lin (eds.). Boston:
              D. Reidel Publishing Co. Pp. 7-27.

Miju Dong-A. (Korean Newspaper). December 15, 1981. 미주동아

Miju Hanguk. (Washington D.C. Korean Newspaper). 미주한국
              Feb. 12, 1983.

Monteiro, Lois
     1980   "Immigrants and the Medical Care System: The
              Example of the Portuguese." Sourcebook on the
              New Immigration Implications for the United States
              and The International Community. R.S. Bryce Laporte
              (ed.). New Brunswick: Transaction Books. Pp. 185-
              194.

Myerhoff, Barbara
     1978   Number Our Days. New York: Dutton.

Osgood, Cornelius
     1962   The Koreans and Their Culture. Tokyo: Charles
              Tuttle Co.

Palos, Stephen
     1971   The Chinese Art of Healing. New York: Herder and
              Herder.

Parish, Lawrence and Sheila Gail Parish
     1971   "Ancient Korean Medicine." Transactions and Studies
              of the College of Physician of Philadelphia. 38:
              161-167 (Issue No. 3).

Park, Jae Kan
     1981   "A Survey of Life Patterns and Attitudes of the
              Aged and Young Adults in Korea." The Dong-A Ilbo
              Series. Pp. 1-21.

349

Pelto, Pertti J. and Gretel H. Pelto
    1979   Anthropological Research. The Structure of In-
            quiry. Cambridge: Cambridge University Press.

Porkert, Manfred
    1976   "The Intellectual and Social Impulses Behind the
            Evolution of Traditional Chinese Medicine." Asian
            Medical Systems: A Comparative Study. C. Leslie
            (ed.). Berkeley: University of California Press.
            Pp. 63-81.

Quinn, Joseph R.
    1973   Medicine and Public Health in the People's Republic
            of China. Publication No. 73-69. Fogarty Inter-
            national Center, NIH.

Rader, Edith
    1977   "Shamanism." The Korean Way. Christian Literature
            Society of Korea (ed.). Seoul: Samsung Co.

Reischauer, Edwin O. and John K. Fairbank
    1960   East Asia, The Great Tradition. Boston: Houghton
            Mifflin Co.

Republic of Korea
    1963   Korea, Its Land, People and Culture of All Ages.
            Seoul: Rakwon-sa.
    1976   Yearbook of Public Health and Social Statistics.
            Ministry of Health and Social Affairs.
    1979   Korea Statistical Yearbook. Economic Planning
            Board. 26: 26-66.
    1981   The Government Announcement Paper. No. 8857, Old
            Age Welfare Law." (Law N. 3. 453). Passed June
            5. 89-92.

Rhi, Bou Yong
    1970   "The Folk Psychiatry of Korea." Neuropsychiatry.
            9: 35-46.

Rhim, Soon Man
    1978   "The Status of Women in Traditional Korean Society."
            Korean Women: In a Struggle for Humanization. H.H.
            Sunoo and D.S. Kim (eds.). Memphis: Association of
            Korean Christian Scholars in North America. Pp. 11-
            37.

Rockhill, William Woodville
    1891   "Notes on Some of the Laws, Customs, and Supersti-
            tions of Korea." American Anthropologist. 4: 177-
            187.

Rogers, Fred B.
    1962   A Syllabus of Medical History. Boston: Little
            Brown and Co. (translated into Korean by J.H.
            Choi in 1966).

Rosow, Irving
1973   "The Social Context of the Aging Self."
          Gerontologist. 13: 82-87.

Rutt, Richard
1964   Korean Works and Days: Notes from the Diary of
          a Country Priest. Tokyo: Charles E. Tuttle Co.

Rutt, Richard and Chang Un Kim (eds)
1974   Virtuous Women: Three Masterpieces of Traditional
          Korean Fiction. Seoul: Korean National Commission
          for UNESCO.

Schafer, Edward H.
1967   Ancient China, Great Ages of Man. New York: Time
          Life Books.

Schutz, Alfred
1968   On Phenomenology and Social Relations. Chicago:
          University of Chicago Press.

Schwartz, Lola R.
1969   "The Hierarchy of Resort in Curative Practices:
          The Admiralty Islands, Melanesia." Journal of
          Health and Social Behavior. 10: 201-209.

Sherley-Price, Lionel Digby
1951   Confucius and Christ: A Christian Estimate of
          Confucius. Westminster, England: Dacre Press.

Son, Dugsoo
1978   "The Status of Korean Women from the Perspective
          of the Women's Emancipation Movement." Korean
          Women: In a Struggle for Humanization. H.H.
          Sunoo and D.S. Kim (eds.). Memphis: Association
          of Korean Christian Scholar in North America, Inc.
          Pp. 257-282.

Song, Yo-in
1976   "The Meaning of Hwan-gap." Korea Journal. 16:37.

Soothill, William Edward
1923   The Three Religions of China. London: Oxford
          University Press.

Spector, Rachel E.
1979   "Health and Illness in the Asian-American Community."
          Cultural Diversity in Health and Illness. R.E.
          Spector (ed.). New York: Appleton-Century-Crofts.
          Pp. 211-227.

Spradley, James P.
1979   The Ethnographic Interview. New York: Holt, Rine-
          hart and Winston.

1980   Participant Observation. New York: Holt, Rinehart
            and Winston.

Spradley, James
   1975   The Cultural Perspective. New York: John Wiley
            and Sons.

Sunu, Ki   鮮于基
   1982a   "Hyôndae Byông un Hanbang urodo natnunda."
            現代病는 漢方으로도 낫는다.
            (Modern Diseases are Cured also by the Hanbang.).
            Shin-Dong-A. 212: 452-461.
   1982b   "Yôrumch'ôl ui Yangsaenghak." 여름철의 養生学
            (Health Care in Summer.). Shin-Dong-A. 215: 464-
            471.
   1982c   "Hanbang urodo hyohyôm itnun Nanch'ibyông."
            漢方으로도 効驗있는 難治病
            (Hanbang is also effective for Incurable Diseases.).
            Shin-Dong-A. 223: 496-503.
   1983   "Ch'im uro chal natnun Byôngdûl." 針으로 잘 낫는 病들
            (Diseases which are treated well by acupuncture.).
            Shin-Dong-A. 226: 434-441.

Topley, Marjorie
   1976   "Chinese Traditional Etiology and Methods of Cure
            in Hong Kong." Asian Medical Systems: A Compara-
            tive Study. C. Leslie (ed.). Berkeley: University
            of California Press. Pp. 246-253.

Toupin, Elizabeth Sook Wha Ahn
   1981   "Counseling Asians: Psychotherapy in the Context
            of Racism and Asian-American History." American
            Journal of Orthopsychiatry. 16: 237-245.

U.S. Constitution. Public Law 89-236, October 3.
   1965

U.S. Department of Justice. Immigration and Naturalization
   1962 and Annual Report. Washington, D.C.: Government
   1974   Printing Office.

Tseng, Wen-Shing
   1975   "The Nature of Somatic Complaints among Psychiatric
            Patients: The Chinese Case." Comprehensive Psy-
            chiatry. 16: 237-245.

Veith, Ilza (trans.)
   1949   Huang Ti Nei Ching Su Wen: The Yellow Emperor's
            Internal Medicine. Baltimore: Williams and Wil-
            kins.
   1963   "The Supernatural in Far Eastern Concepts of Men-
            tal Disease." Bulletin of the History of Medicine.
            37: 139-158.

1973   The Yellow Emperor's Classic of Internal Medicine, A Translation of Huang Ti Nei Ching Su Wen. Berkeley: University of California Press. Pp. 97-99.

Vreeland, Nena et al.
1975   Area Handbook for South Korea. Second Edition. Washington, D.C.: Foreign Area Studies, American University.

Williamson, John B. et al.
1980   Aging and Society. New York: Holt, Rinehart, and Winston.

Yoo, Seung Bum (ed.)
1979   Korea Annal: A Comprehensive Handbook on Korea. Seoul: The Hapdong News Agency.

Yu, Eui-Young
1980   "Koreans in America: Social and Economic Adjustments." Korean Immigrants in America. B. Kim and S.H. Lee (eds.). Montclair: The Association of Korean Christian Scholars in North America, Inc. Pp. 75-98.

Yŏn, Ha Ch'ŏng and H.Y. Kim 延 河淸　金學永
1980   Bogŏn Uiryo Chawŏn kwa Chinryo Saenghwalkwŏn. 保建医療 資源 과 診療生活圈 (Health and Medical Resources and Treatment Activity Area.). Seoul: Korean Developmental Research Institute.

UNPUBLISHED MATERIAL

Choi, Doe Hyun
n.d.   "Lecture to Hong Kong Association of University Women about Sugi, Finger Pressure." Unpublished Typescript. Pp. 1-10.

Clark, Margaret
1980   "Beyond Diagnosis: The Influence of Culture on Health." Faculty Research Lecture. University of California, San Francisco. May 29, 1980.

Janelli, Roger L.
1975   Korean Rituals of Ancestor Worship: An Ethnography Folklore Performance. Unpublished Doctoral Dissertation. University of Pennsylvania.

Kendis, Randall
    1980   The Elderly Japanese in America: An Analysis
                of Their Adaptation to Aging. Ph.D. Dissertation.
                University of Pittsburgh.

Luhmann, Hee-Chung
    1978   The Correlation of the Frequency of Social Inter-
                action and the Level of Life Satisfaction among
                Older Korean Immigrants Residents in the Metro-
                politan Washington, D.C. and New York City Who
                Came to the United States at Age 55 or Over.
                Unpublished M.S.W. thesis. National Catholic
                School of Social Service, Catholic University of
                America.

Roh, Chang Shub and Thomas H. Kang
    1981   "Newly Emerging Problems of the Aging in Korea."
                A Paper Presented for the 10th Annual Meeting
                of the Mid-Atlantic Region of the Association
                for Asian Studies. Oct. 16-18, at the Univer-
                sity of Maryland.

Snyder, Patricia Jean
    1979   Folk Healing in Honolulu, Hawaii. Ph.D. Disser-
                tation. University of Hawaii.

Yang, Eun Sik
    1983   "Korean Women in America: From Subordinate to
                Partnership, 1903-1930." Presented at the Sym-
                posium on Korean Women. California State Univer-
                sity, Los Angeles, June 24-25, 1983. Pp. 1-31.

INDEX